Greg Jenner is the Historical Consultant to CBBC's multi-award-winning *Horrible Histories* and its various spin-offs. As well as contributing sketches and song lyrics, and co-writing Stephen Fry's links, Greg has been solely responsible for the factual accuracy of nearly 1,200 comedy sketches that span the entirety of human history. He studied at the University of York and, after dropping plans for a PhD, has spent the past decade making historical documentaries and dramas for television.

www.gregjenner.com
@greg_jenner

A MILLION YEARS IN A DAY

A Curious History of Daily Life

GREG JENNER

WEIDENFELD & NICOLSON

First published in Great Britain in 2015
by Weidenfeld & Nicolson
This paperback edition published in 2016
by Weidenfeld & Nicolson,
an imprint of the Orion Publishing Group Ltd,
Carmelite House, 50 Victoria Embankment,
London EC4Y 0DZ

An Hachette UK Company

5 7 9 10 8 6

A CIP catalogue record for this book
is available from the British Library.

ISBN 978 1 780 22565 4

Typeset at The Spartan Press Ltd,
Lymington, Hants

Printed and bound by the CPI Group (UK) Ltd,
Croydon, CR0 4YY

MIX
Paper from
responsible sources
FSC® C104740

www.orionbooks.co.uk

CONTENTS

INTRODUCTION

If I had to guess, I'd say you're probably sitting down right now. Perhaps you're in that bountifully upholstered armchair, the bastion of upright comfort, cradling this book with open palms and half-cocked arm? Or perhaps you're the archetypal sofa slumper, sprawled inelegantly across a couch designed for three? Of course, if you're anything like me, you're reading this standing up on an overcrowded and overpriced commuter train, your face hovering barely inches from a stranger's sweat-dampened armpit, while you shuttle between your home and your workplace. But, I bet I can guess where you're not reading this.

I bet you're not in a cave...

Though it boggles the mind to truly contemplate it, you and I are no different anatomically from people who lived 30,000 years ago. While we delight in cartoonish portrayals of people we might dub Ug and Nug, smashing each other over the heads with clubs and dragging women around like wheelie bins, the truth is rather more nuanced. For starters, they weren't grunting numpties. In fact, they had the full faculty of language, the intellect to solve problems and the urge to protect their loved ones and bury their mourned-for dead. They were, in every regard, modern humans like you or me. Yet our lives are hugely different from theirs. So, how did we end up living as we do now?

Well, just look around you. Every single aspect of your life is the by-product of history, thousands of years in the making. Have a wander around your home and a lot will appear unquestionably recent at first glance, but there's an extraordinary legacy to everything. Look at the clock on the wall. Have you ever stopped to consider who first attempted to measure time and how they may have done it, or why some countries change the clocks in the summer?

Consider the book in your hand – it was invented two thousand years ago, and would be recognisable to St Paul or Emperor Nero. These words are written in an alphabet that evolved over millennia from the prototype created by the ancient Phoenicians, following in a communication tradition that extended back through hieroglyphs and cuneiform-impressed wax tablets all the way to the earliest prehistoric doodles on the walls of caves. The food in your cupboards comes from all over the world, and might once have been recognisable only to the Aztecs. The clothes in your wardrobe might be woven from fabrics first planted five thousand years ago in ancient India, and your bed sheets could have a lot in common with the linen underpants worn by King Tutankhamun, in the distant Bronze Age.

Every day of our lives, most of us rotate through the same ritual habits that humans have been repeating for millennia – getting out of bed, going to the toilet, grabbing some breakfast, washing our bodies, choosing our clothes, telling the time, communicating with others, eating together, having a drink, cleaning our teeth, getting into bed and setting the alarm clock… All of these daily events bring with them a story written over countless generations by our predecessors.

I've scribbled this book as if it were describing the routine events of a modern Saturday, with each chapter focusing on a distinct activity that you might find familiar, but I've used that to spring backwards into the past to explore where these routines came from. Though it's surprising to imagine that we have anything in common with Stone Age cave-loiterers, the things we do every day are the things we've pretty much always done. We tend to think of 'cavemen' as shuffling idiots when we compare them with us. But could they have worked an iPhone or driven a car? Surprisingly, yes, if someone had shown them how. Alas, they were doomed by circumstance never to enjoy a joyride in a finely engineered Mercedes, or secretly listen to Bon Jovi's *Greatest Hits* on a train while pretending to read *Madame Bovary*, because while we reside in the latest chapter of the epic human story they were scrabbling around in the boring bit at the beginning where the author thanks their colleagues, family members and the person who does the type-setting.

So, this book, in some small way, partly aims to rehabilitate the reputation of our ancestors, while answering long-held questions about why your life is the way it is. That's not to say there won't be moments when we roll our eyes in wonderment at the weirdness of the past, and I've tried to find humour in our differences. But I hope – above all – that you'll be astonished at how much we have in common with those who lived and died centuries, or even millennia, ago.

Ultimately, this is a book about you and me. But it just happens to be set mostly in the past.

RISE AND SHINE

The shrill klaxon of the alarm clock startles us from a deep snooze. We lift our head from the warm pillow, our moistened drool pooling in its folds, and prise apart our gunk-glued eyes to squint at the time, desperately hoping the clock has malfunctioned and there are at least two more hours of slumber available. Sadly, a corroborating glance at our mobile phone proves it's definitely time to get up.

Why does the clock's testimony matter so much? Why don't we just go back to sleep until we're fully rested? Well, because time is the architecture that governs the rhythms of our existence, and to ignore it is to invite chaos into our lives. Yet, though time is a stable entity that has reliably flowed for millions of years, its measurement has always been a tricky conundrum. Our strict division of standardised units – seconds, minutes, hours, days, weeks, months, years – is not a universal law echoed through eternity, but an agreed-upon rubric adopted over the course of many centuries in a desperate attempt to avoid mind-scrambling confusion. In fact, to delve into the history of timekeeping is similar to watching a Belgian soap opera without the subtitles; at first it's baffling, but slowly it becomes strangely compelling.

GOOD DAY!

Today is Saturday, and we know that because yesterday was Friday. But what do we mean when we talk about 'a day'? The English language is often dubbed the most bountiful of all, with an ever-swelling vocabulary, so it's faintly ridiculous that in English-speaking countries we deploy one word, 'day', to mean two different things: i) a 24-hour rotation of the Earth on its axis, and ii) the opposite of night. Despite it clearly being a communication trip hazard, we persist with this clumsy inelegance because we're proudly stubborn and, clearly, a little bit thick. Many other languages don't go in for such silliness. The Dutch, for example, sidestep confusion with two words instead, *Dag* (the daylight hours) and *Etmaal* (24 hours), while Bulgarians, Danes, Italians, Finns, Russians and Poles all do something similar. But the closest English-speakers get to *Etmaal* is with the ludicrously thrilling *Nychthemeron* ('night and day' in Greek), a name more befitting a Finnish heavy metal band. I've never actually heard it used in conversation, and even scientists ignore it, so it's become the under-nourished pet of etymologists who take it out of the box at special occasions to coo at its grandiose absurdity.

But Anglophones muddle through regardless, or occasionally move the goalposts by measuring time's duration in nights instead, as when we book hotel rooms, by cunningly deploying the Anglo-Saxon word 'fortnight' to indicate a block of 14 nights in a row. But even this doesn't entirely work, because the travel agent will inevitably ask: 'is that fourteen days, thirteen nights?' and we have to start counting it out on our fingers, like kids learning their times tables. But let's not judge too harshly, as it's partially an inherited failing; terminology for what constitutes a day has always been an awkward problem. In the third century, the Roman philosopher Censorinus argued that the 24-hour cycle should be named a 'civil day' while daylight hours should instead constitute a 'natural day'. While this was seemingly sensible, a gaggle of meddling seventh-century pedants sowed confusion by switching 'natural day' to instead mean the 24-hour rotation cycle, and introducing 'artificial day' to cover the daylight period.

But don't bother committing these definitions to memory in the hope of wowing your friends because modern astronomy has once again reverted to using a 'civil day' to describe a full rotation of the Earth. Consequently, 'natural day' has gone from meaning two separate things to now meaning nothing at all, while 'artificial day' is now what comes out of a light bulb. Got that? No, me neither... but I'm afraid almost nothing in this chapter is simple, not even the definition of when a day begins and ends.

IN THE MIDNIGHT HOUR

Opening our tired eyes wider, we see that the sunlight is streaming through a chink in the curtains, so it's definitely the morning; except, daylight is not a prerequisite for morning, is it? In both the modern West and East, a new day begins in the dark at 00:00, which is why British revellers at New Year's Eve parties drunkenly garble the first two lines of 'Auld Lang Syne' as the clock strikes midnight. But imagine the chaos if these intoxicated partygoers were forced to wait until dawn, getting drunker and drunker – it would sound less like a communal singsong and more like a herd of cattle being drowned at sea. Midnight, though, is a confusing word. Its syllables say 'this is the middle of the night', and yet it actually signals the start of the morning, leading us to wrongly label 1 a.m. TV broadcasts as 'late night telly', or boast about being 'up all night partying' when we get home at 4 a.m. This blurring of the lines, letting a day stay up past its official bedtime, shows that the way we live our life has a surprising thing in common with a civilisation that reached its peak around 3,500 years ago: ancient Egypt.

In their hyper-religious culture it was dawn that commenced a new day, not midnight. Consequently, the sunrise was heralded as a sacred event, the beginning of the daily commute undertaken by the sun god Ra in which he charged across the sky in his chariot and then had to fight an epic battle with the serpentine chaos god, Apophis. But, to validate this eternal routine, and make the sun rise, a dawn ceremony required the semi-divine pharaoh to perform cleansing rituals in the sacred temples of Karnak or Heliopolis. In practice, a proxy likely stood in for the king, who may often have been elsewhere in the empire, though it's very tempting to enjoy the mental image of a priest hastily having to mumble the half-remembered words while anxious servants desperately try to haul a grumpy Tutankhamun out of bed.

But beginning a day at dawn wasn't a universal ancient custom. Four thousand years ago, the Babylonians – the occupants of majestic cities in what's now Iraq – shared much in common with their Bronze Age Egyptian neighbours, but their new day commenced at dusk, moments before they went to bed. This was later mimicked by the ancient Greeks, Celts, Germanic tribes and even medieval Italians, who knew this timekeeping system as Florentine Reckoning, which sounds like a great title for a murder mystery novel. Neither is this a relic from the long-dead past, as an Orthodox Jew will still observe the Shabbat between Friday sundown and Saturday dusk. So, how did the modern world end up with the midnight cut-off point? The answer is probably from the Romans who divided the day and night into two blocks of 12 hours.

Of course, the big question is who invented timekeeping in the first place? Did a Sumerian just wake up one morning, decide that it was 7 a.m., and everyone else just shrugged in nonplussed agreement? That seems unlikely. I think we might have to go further back to find an answer.

THE CLOCK IN THE SKY

The Makapan Valley in the Limpopo province of South Africa is one of those gorgeous landscapes that looks like it's been digitally rendered by a Hollywood FX artist. It's a lush V-shaped valley – sprouting with green trees that turn russet in the autumn – and you wouldn't be entirely surprised to see pterodactyls swooping overhead. Jutting out of the forests are imposing limestone hills, in which a network of caves was slowly carved by ancient water erosion, and it's in these secluded shelters that archaeologists have discovered some extraordinary prehistoric remains, including the bones of one of our earliest ancestors – *Homo Australopithecus*.

Here, three million years ago, one of these diminutive upright creatures must have noticed the lengthening shadows in the evening gloom and waddled off to the safety of the caves. Though the stone walls may have offered temporary shelter, they couldn't prevent the inevitable, and the sheltering *hominin* breathed its last breath within the limestone cavern, only to be rediscovered by palaeontologists in the twentieth century. *Australopithecus* possessed virtually none of our intellectual powers, and would have been really inept at crosswords, yet even this primitive creature might have noticed the natural world's cyclical rhythms: the waxing and waning of the moon, the lapping of the tides, and the parade of quarterly seasons. The Earth ceaselessly revolves on its axis, flooding our lives with light and darkness like an incessant heartbeat, and *Australopithecus* could have relied upon the sun's arced journey through the sky each day, knowing it would return after dark. In short, he or she probably had a basic comprehension of time.

This, however, is just guesswork. Where's the actual evidence

5

for Stone Age timekeeping? If we fast-forward to 30,000 years ago – a time when modern humans shared the planet with Neanderthals – then we encounter an enticingly ambiguous object found at Le Placard in the Dordogne region of France. It's an eagle bone, and scratched across its surface are a series of notches, carved horizontally at different times, which appear to chart the waxing of the moon through 14 days, from new to full. It's sorely tempting, therefore, to refer to this bone as the world's oldest known calendar.

Though it's not impossible that this was made by a Neanderthal, many archaeologists suspect that this rival clan of *Homo* was ill-matched against our superior cognitive adaptability – they were the Judge Dredd to our Sherlock Holmes: stronger, more robust, better at punching a bear right in its stupid, ursine face… but more likely to scream in frustration if you'd asked them to adjust the clock on a microwave. Instead, it was probably a human like us – an inventive *Homo sapiens* brimming with natural curiosity – who conceivably peered at the moon in wonder and decided to chart its phases on a bit of a bone salvaged from last night's dinner, taxing its refined brain in the pursuit of elemental understanding about how the cosmos functioned. But, then again, maybe it was just someone doodling while having a poo.

After all, just because we are using our clock to measure time in a uniform way doesn't mean our ancestors did. Even just a couple of centuries ago, there was a major temporal shift that dramatically chucked out the 24-hour clock we hold so dear…

VIVE LA RÉVOLUTION!

The year was 1793 and France was in the grip of a violent revolution. King Louis XVI was already minus his head, having fallen victim to the guillotine that would soon stain the Parisian cobbles with a scarlet treacle of noble and peasant blood, and European politicians were gawping in horror at the tumult which might infect their own populace at any moment. The world was aflame with big ideas and French society was being redrawn on a blank sheet of paper by a cadre of radical intellectuals fired up by Enlightenment philosophy. Nothing would escape their gaze, and even time itself was about to get a top-down redesign ...

For over 4,000 years the duodecimal mathematics of the Babylonians had stubbornly prevailed, but why had it been based on the number 12 and not 10? Well, 10 is only divisible by integers of 2 and 5, whereas 12 is divisible by 2, 3, 4 and 6, making it much more versatile in mathematical calculations. What's more, the use of a lunisolar calendar, based on observations of both the sun and the moon, relied on there being 12 lunar phases per year (with a 13th 'leap' month chucked in every two or three years), so 12 was the numerical cornerstone of the universe. Logically, therefore, time should operate in a duodecimal rubric, with 60 seconds in a minute and 24 hours in a day.

But that was ancient thought and this was 1793! The French Revolution wasn't just about bewigged aristos getting their come-uppance from a hungry mob, its leaders also sought to break with the traditions of the corrupted past, in favour of scientific rationalism. For more than two centuries, European philosophers had been muttering among themselves about a possible metric system, but now a window in which to test it had arrived. So, on 5 October, a proposal lodged a year earlier by Jean-Charles de Borda was voted into law by the new National Assembly. The 24-hour day was suddenly chopped up into ten distinct hours, with each hour comprising 100 minutes, and each minute lasting 100 seconds.

As you might have guessed, the rest of the calendar was also carefully redrafted, so weeks became ten-day *décades* – thereby unintentionally mirroring the ancient Egyptian week – and the year shrank to ten newly christened months with splendidly prosaic names like *Ventôse* (the windy month), which referred to blustery February rather than the Christmas period when we often find ourselves embarrassingly gaseous from overindulgence. This decimalised timekeeping was proudly pronounced as evidence of French innovation, but in fact the ancient Chinese had already dabbled with it for centuries until, somewhat ironically, they'd been convinced to ditch it by European merchants. Clearly, the French authorities had not received the memo. Soon, they would regret their ignorance.

Yes, metric time was woefully unpopular and, despite attempts at appeasement by building hybrid clocks showing both 24 hours and ten hours on their faces, this endeavour was widely considered a literal waste of time. Mass guillotining the French could just about stomach, but ten-hour clocks? Madness! Embarrassingly for all involved, the much-vaunted decimal revolution endured barely 18 months (or was it 14 decimal months . . . ?) before being hastily replaced by good old duodecimal time.

'But hang on a second,' I hear you exclaim in unison, 'what was that bit about the Egyptians having a ten-day week? That's not duodecimal!' Yeah, about that . . . Now's probably a good moment to get to grips with the 'how' of horological history. You might need to concentrate for this bit, so make yourself comfy. It's about to get fairly technical.

SEASONS IN THE SUN

If we were to look at a calendar on our wall, we would see that our system allots seven days to each week, imitating that of the Babylonians, but Egyptians fused that custom with their own innovations to produce a separate timekeeping system. Unlike the Mesopotamians, they chose to cram their annual calendar with 36 weeks of ten days, leaving a spare five bonus days to be arbitrarily tacked on at the end. What's more, having ten-day weeks also meant they preferred to recognise only three seasons of four months, instead of our four seasons of three months. This was mostly due to the River Nile's capricious mood-swings that brought annual flooding during a large part of the year, and resulted in a calendar carved up into agricultural cycles of flooding, crop-sowing and harvesting, rather than our spring, summer, autumn and winter.

But how was a day parcelled up? Well, an Egyptian 24-hour *Nychthemeron* (sorry, it's just such fun to type...) was not defined like our two daily halves of 12 hours, but as four phases: one hour of half-light, followed by ten hours of daylight, chased by another hour of half-light, and then 12 hours of darkness. The big questions, then, are whether Egyptians could measure hours and, if so, how? When it came to daylight hours, sundials were the preferred technology, and we'll get to those shortly, but it's the night hours that were much harder to track, which is what makes the Egyptian solution so ingenious.

WRITTEN IN THE STARS

Have you ever gazed at the stars just before the dawn? As romantic 18-year-olds, my friends and I thought we'd do it on the first morning of the new Millennium. We'd quite literally partied like it was 1999 and then we drunkenly clambered up a hill to watch the sun rise on this glorious new epoch. Sadly for us, the sky was cloudy and the glorious sunrise was ruined by the orange glow of Sevenoaks' streetlights, so we trudged back to the house and ate doughnuts instead. So much for romance... But if we'd chosen a less light-polluted promontory, and a country with better weather, we might have glimpsed something known to astronomers as heliacal rising.

Just before the dawn, certain stars called Decans briefly peek over the eastern horizon. These groups of 36 constellations drift westerly each day by a single degree, appearing each morning slightly further across, until they pass out of view for a whole year. A new star peeps, like a curious meerkat, over the eastern horizon every ten days (hence the name, *Dekanoi* means 'tenths' in Greek), and this possibly influenced the Egyptians to choose a ten-day week. But what does this have to do with telling the time? Well, scribbled on sarcophagi, and inscribed on tomb walls, ancient Egyptian scholars left behind their star charts and calendars which have allowed modern archaeo-astronomers to decipher their cunning system for turning heliacal rising into a nocturnal clock. The Diagonal Star Table, at first glance – and several increasingly confused glances after that – resembled what might happen if an unfortunate software glitch converted a bus timetable into hieroglyphs. Running horizontally along the top of the chart were the 36 weeks of the year, each of which contain ten days, and below each of these 36 columns were symbols representing when each Decan was visible in which week of the year. In the simplest terms possible, if you knew what the exact date was, the Diagonal Star Table allowed you to match the position of a specific Decan star in the sky to the data in the chart, thereby revealing the approximate hour.

In around 1500 BCE, this system was replaced with an even more complex alternative called the Ramesside Star Clock. Its most notable novelty, besides sounding like the name of a 1970s prog rock album, was that it required the year to be divided into 24 months of 15 days, and focused on a new gaggle of 47 'hour stars'. Also, to look at this design – again, depicted on tombs and sarcophagi – is to wonder if we're staring at the instructions for a complex board game. At the bottom of the image is a kneeling male priest in a nifty linen kilt and above his head is a chequered grid comprising seven vertical transecting lines, resembling a sort of archaic chessboard, in which star movements could be charted.

As far as scholars can tell, a budding astronomer was supposed to mimic the position of this priest, holding perhaps a plumb-bob in his outstretched hand, and using his own body parts as comparative references for the positions of these stars, lined up to the vertical lines. Perhaps he was also meant to squat over a pool of water, to reflect the stars above him, as he did so? The debate rages on.

THE WONKY HOURS

Tracking the transit of stars was a cunning response to the thorny problem of nocturnal timekeeping, but an Egyptian hour was not a standardised unit like our 60 minutes. Instead it stretched and shrank to match the seasons – a daylight hour could be just 45 modern minutes in winter, and closer to 75 minutes in the sun-drenched summer. The ancients explained this by theorising that the sun orbited the Earth, not around the equator, but following an ecliptic plane which started below the equator in the winter and then sloped upwards so that it rose above it in the summer, before descending again. If that doesn't quite make sense, imagine a ringed Frisbee placed at a diagonal slant over the middle of a beach ball so it's lower on the left and higher on the right. This, at least in Egyptian eyes, explained why the sun was higher in the summer sky.

Consequently, there were always ten hours of full daylight (plus two of half-light), but each of those hours was longer in July than in December, a phenomenon we might call seasonal hours. But even a seasonal hour was impossible to measure by stars alone in the middle of the day, so ancient timekeepers had to find another way of keeping track...

GIVE ME SUNSHINE

When the stars vanished and the sun came out, the methods changed again. Herodotus – the ancient Greek writer often dubbed the 'Father of History' – claimed it was those cunning Babylonians who first conjured up the sundial, but it probably sprang up independently in various cultures, as the basic technological requirements are little more than an upright stick poking out of the ground.

Anyway, if I asked you to name a famous ancient sundial, you wouldn't plump for anything Babylonian; but if you live in Paris, London or New York then you might suggest an Egyptian example that you've often walked past; and not one secreted behind glass cases in museums, but proudly erected in the open air. What am I referring to? Well, they're popularly nicknamed Cleopatra's Needles, despite having nothing to do with the famous queen. In fact, they're nearly 3,500 years old, and by the time she was bumping uglies with Julius Caesar these obelisks had already been standing guard in the sun-worshipping city of Heliopolis for 1,400 years.

To be honest, archaeologists don't know if their purpose was deliberately temporal or if they were just massive ornaments that accidentally happened to cast a shadow. And, even if they were designed to tell the time, their size made them impractical for day-to-day usage, so smaller alternatives were sought. The simplest of these were shadow clocks which were essentially just a long plank with an upright T-shape stuck on one end, similar to the rear spoiler on a racing dragster, thereby elevating the crossbar off the ground so as to cast a diagonal shadow onto the long plank. When the sun was low in the sky, the shadow was elongated and reached the very end of the plank, like a black cat stretching out to bask in the midday heat, but by late morning the sun would be at its zenith, almost directly over the crossbar, so the shadow would shorten.

At noon, the shadow clock would suddenly become useless. Even by mobile phone standards, this is a lightning-quick rate of obsolescence, but no expensive upgrade was required – all you had to do was turn the clock around to face the west instead of the east, so it could measure the sun's descent, rather than its rise. Or at least, that's the current theory. The problem is that no Egyptian examples – whether written, archaeological or illustrated – actually show any evidence of a crossbar ever existing. Basically, we don't actually know how shadow clocks worked, or if they even had crossbars at all.

We can be a bit more authoritative about sundials, though. By the eighth century BCE, the Egyptians had developed elegantly sloping stone blocks to better capture the sun's position in the sky, and translate that into detailed measures by tracking the drifting shadow along its exposed face. From Egypt, these sundials were introduced into Greece by the philosopher Anaximander of Miletus, somewhere around the year 546 BCE, and they soon joined philosophy, olive oil and sex with pre-pubescent boys as integral parts of ancient Aegean culture. By the beginning of the third century BCE, Berosus of Chaldea had redesigned the sundial as the hemi-cycle which, though it may sound like a weird kind of ancient bike, was actually a block of stone scalloped into a curved, concave basin – a bit like an unfinished bathroom sink – and key to its functionality was the gnomon, the pointy shadow-casting indicator positioned at the centre.

Greek clever-clogs with lustrous beards were known as the creative geniuses of their day, but the ancient technology market was about to become a lot more brutal with the emergence of some Italian upstarts looking to muscle their way in. In 264 BCE, these aggressive Romans invaded the Greek island colony of Sicily and, after accidentally-on-purpose slaughtering its most famous resident – the brilliantly eccentric, Eureka-bellowing Archimedes – they added insult to fatal injury by making off with the city's official sundial. In a charming example of karmic comeuppance, these Roman pilferers had failed to understand that the sundial was calibrated to local latitude and when they got back to Rome the alignment was found to be four degrees out, making it completely inaccurate. Still, the stubborn looters hadn't carried it all that way for nothing, so they installed it anyway and then presumably spent a century muttering to visitors: 'No, it's meant to be like that, honest' until it was finally upgraded in 164 BCE.

As Roman power expanded across Europe and into the Middle East, and it transitioned from Republic to Empire, communication between disparate cities saw sundials began to pop up all over the ancient world, and by the time the brilliant Roman architect Vitruvius was scribbling his treatises on how to build complex stuff like aqueducts, he could list 13 different designs for the timekeeping gadget. Even the great Emperor Caesar Augustus erected a huge Egyptian obelisk as a gnomon in the Campus Martius, while his closest lieutenant, Marcus Agrippa, built Rome's original Pantheon temple. After being destroyed twice (by fire and then by lightning), this glorious building was reconstructed by Emperor Hadrian. It famously features a large hole (*oculus*) in the roof: an intriguing recent history suggests this allowed the sun to stream through at a specific hour.

Given all the sundials on display, we might assume that the Roman world was governed by the reliable rhythm of solar hours. Indeed, there's an oft-quoted line from a play by Plautus in which a character angrily laments that the sundial's arrival has enforced rigidity on his day and stopped him eating lunch whenever he fancies it. It's feasible, then, that the average Roman could have found out the time if they so wished but, because sundials are silent, many might not have noticed the hours slipping away. Our modern obsession with the ceaseless drumbeat of time might have struck them as oddly perverse. Where, then, does our relentless clock-checking come from? Well, you can probably blame God for that, or at least his mortal representatives...

THE GODLY HOURS

Imagine the scene: it's dawn and the bell is chiming again. You've already been up for a while, so the sound comes as no cruel surprise. In fact, this happens every day, come rain or shine, and will continue to do so until you snuff it. What you're hearing is the call to prayer, the first of the day (Lauds), and it will be followed by a series of others, beginning with Prime, then spooling through Terce, Sext, Nones, Vespers, Compline at dusk, and then the three offices of the night watch (Matins) which will rouse you from your bed at 9 p.m., at midnight and at 3 a.m. Then you'll start all over again, at dawn, with Lauds. Sounds taxing? No one said being a monk was meant to be a giggle-fest...

If you were a monk or nun in the Middle Ages, then your life had a metronomic tempo dictated by the daily rituals of prayer – the Divine Offices, otherwise known as the canonical hours. Following an enormously influential edict by the seventh-century Pope Sabinian, each of these prayers was proclaimed with the tolling of a bell and, while the endless bonging was only meant to apply to the servants of God, it didn't go unnoticed by others – how could it? Bonging sure ain't subtle. In the heightened world of medieval godliness, Europeans were never too far from a church, monastery or cathedral, and so were rarely out of earshot from God's deafening alarm clock. So, inadvertently, the canonical hours came to provide the pulsing beat of daily life for millions of ordinary people, in much the same way that I can reliably set my watch by the sound of noisy kids running amok at lunchtime in the school playground opposite my house.

A religious division of the day wasn't solely a Western Christian innovation, either. In the Islamic world, the five periods of daily prayer, Salah, applied to everyone – not just those who'd taken holy vows – so a mass notification system was put in place, with public sundials mounted on walls and rooftop callers beckoning people to prayer. But, while the Islamic world was comfortably adapted to seasonal hours of varying lengths, it was also a hotbed of scientific genius, and one man in particular had a fascination with the link between time and the heavens. Ibn al-Shāṭir was probably the greatest astronomer of the fourteenth century, which was pretty handy seeing as he was also the official timekeeper of the Umayyad Mosque in Damascus, and his great contribution to world history was to pioneer the equal-hours solar clock.

His construction, a 2 x 1 metre horizontal sundial, which he placed on the minaret of the mosque in 1371, featured three dials designed to measure the hours since sunset, until sunset and the exact time itself. But crucially he aligned the latitude of his solar timepiece to make it parallel to the Earth's polar axis, so, with some detailed charts to help him, he vanquished the old adversary of seasonal time and produced hours of equal 60-minute length, no matter what the season. This signalled the beginning of temporal modernity. In fact, never mind the temporal bit. The world was on the brink of enormous change, and timekeeping would play a crucial role.

TIME IS MONEY

As we drowsily sit up in bed, the warm covers pulled up over our chest, we look again at the clock on our bedside table. It's a relaxing Saturday morning, and there's nothing we must do for several hours, and yet we can't help obsessing over the time. We may even feel as if our days are a constant race against the clock, and I use that phrase deliberately.

It's no coincidence that the thirteenth century, which birthed the mercantilism that supercharged many Europeans cities into economic powerhouses, also witnessed the debut of the mechanical clock. These massive devices were perched high in civic belltowers, so that instead of silent sundials – possibly ignored by most Romans – they acted as a constant noisy reminder of the here and now; of the slippery, fleeting resource of useful business hours during which you could be out on the streets raking in the cash, like a medieval Donald Trump but with less ridiculous hair. Under the watchful eye of the clock tower, feudalism capitulated to capitalism. Suddenly, time was money.

So, better timekeeping had seemingly spawned a new obsession with profit and efficiency. Yet, within a few centuries, profit and efficiency would spawn a new obsession with better timekeeping...

CANNONS AT DAWN

One morning in 1784, America's diplomatic emissary to France got a rude awakening. Benjamin Franklin had forgotten to close the shutters on his window and found himself bathed in warm Parisian sunlight. Staring at his pocket watch in baffled horror, the eminent scientist noted something rather strange – it was 6 a.m. What on Earth was the sun doing up so early? Was he dreaming? Was he drunk? He hurriedly leafed through the solar almanac for the day, and corroborated that his watch hadn't stopped. Then, he repeated the experiment thrice more that week until his suspicions were scientifically confirmed. Yes, it was unquestionable – the sun rises at dawn!

This, I hope you'll have realised, was Franklin wearing his metaphorical satirist's hat, as opposed to his very real beaver-fur hat which started a weird European fashion craze. Though a man of towering political responsibility, he had not lost any of the youthful glee with which he had, in his adolescence, hoaxed gullible newspaper readers into thinking he was a cantankerous old woman named Silence Dogood. Now elderly, Franklin was cooped up in his Parisian house, occasionally setting his world-class mind to solving cute little problems set by his fabulously monikered pal, Antoine-Alexis-François Cadet de Vaux. Grateful for the distraction, Franklin had crafted this spoof letter of discovery to amuse his patron, who just happened to be the editor of *Le Journal de Paris*.

Your readers, who with me have never seen any signs of sunshine before noon, and seldom regard the astronomical part of the almanac, will be as much astonished as I was, when they hear of his rising so early; and especially when I assure them, that he gives light as soon as he rises.

Its comedic origins were clear. Franklin had only recently witnessed the glamorous unveiling of a novel form of oil lamp – the eighteenth-century equivalent of an Apple product launch – but he had concerns about its fuel efficiency. He was also keenly aware that candles were a pricey domestic outgoing, so the famous 'First American' included in his spoof a typically Franklinesque cost analysis. Joking that the average Parisian woke up at noon (the cheek!), he deduced that 128,100,000 candlelit hours were being expended in the evenings between March and September, resulting in the burning of an extra 64 million lb of candle wax. To save money, Franklin had satirically recommended that the French government de-incentivise morning laziness with stiff taxes on window shutters, and a deafening volley of cannons at dawn 'to wake the sluggards'. This scientific hoax was intended as a harmless in-joke with his pals, but it was an intriguing insight into the economics of light.

Franklin had sarcastically suggested waking people up earlier, but why coerce people into changing their habits when you can instead manipulate time itself? In 1895, an English-born New Zealander called George Vernon Hudson submitted a paper to the Wellington Philosophical Society suggesting exactly that. Hudson was one of New Zealand's foremost insect collectors, but more importantly he was also a postman so rose earlier than everyone else. Having noticed the world snooze through dawn, Hudson's paper suggested that by simply shifting the clock forward, a whole extra hour of daylight could be conserved for use when most people were awake. The idea was good, but it wouldn't be Hudson's voice that carried the day. Instead, the world trundled on unchanged for a decade until another chap came to the same conclusion.

William Willett was a resplendently moustachioed English businessman who ran a respectable house-building company noted for its upmarket clientele. Each day he took his horse out for a ride at 7 a.m. and cantered through the woodland near his Kent home, but one morning he noticed nearby houses had their blinds down. The sun was out, the day had started, but no one was up to enjoy it. Willett may have seemed an uptight Edwardian captain of industry, but beneath his starched shirt was a heart brimming with unbridled passion . . . but not the scandalous type favoured by the lusty King Edward VII. No, Willett's obsession was with capturing natural light, and he proudly proclaimed that a 'Willett-built' home maximised nature's illumination like no other.

Eager that the slumbering inhabitants of Chislehurst be alerted to what they were missing, he trotted home and pondered. There would be no need for Franklin's cannon volleys at dawn; he was thinking more conceptually. In 1907, he published a pamphlet entitled *The Waste of Daylight*, in which he argued for a novel concept called Daylight Saving Time (DST), achieved by setting the clocks forward by 20 minutes on each of the four Sundays in April, thereby stealing back a considerable chunk of evening daylight during the summer.

DON'T MISS THE TRAIN!

Though staying up to midnight to faff about with clocks eight times per year sounds rather unnecessary, in fairness to Willett many were used to time being a wandering entity. For centuries people had measured the hours of the day locally by charting the sun's shadows, and this had meant that the further west or east you travelled in longitude the more you had to adjust your watch. Bristol, for example, is about 116 miles due west from London, so the sun rises nine minutes later there, meaning Bristolians were probably still tucked up in bed by the time most cockneys were already shuffling around in their slippers, practising their Dick Van Dyke impressions.

Every city had its own relationship with dawn and dusk until the arrival of passenger trains in the 1840s meant that far-flung places were suddenly linked up by a high-speed transport network. This was obviously excellent news, not least for nerdy train spotters who now had something to do with their Sundays, but it induced an unforeseen episode of temporal chaos. For example, a train between London and Bristol would chug out of the capital, under London local time, at noon but it would arrive four hours later at 3.51 p.m., not 4 p.m. Somewhere along the way, nine minutes had vanished. Understandably, this prompted a whirlwind of puzzlement among commuters who immediately began missing trains en masse.

Recognising the issue, the train companies leapt into action and adopted Greenwich Mean Time on all their routes. This produced train timetables that were logically consistent across the nation, but didn't entirely solve the problem for individual commuters. After all, unless a passenger was standing in the station already, and could see the amended railway clock, then their day was still being governed by the local time of pocket watches and cathedral clocks, leaving them to saunter nonchalantly towards the station only to see their train thunder past in a cloud of super-heated steam.

What was needed was the standardisation of time not just for railways, but for the nation; yet not everyone felt the urge to modernise. Unwilling to sacrifice their own local solar rhythms – regional traditions dating back millennia – places like Exeter and Oxford mirrored the ill-fated compromise of the French metric disaster with curious hybrid clocks featuring an extra minute-hand bolted onto the face to simultaneously display local time and 'Railway Time'. But this clunky half-measure wasn't going to cling on for long, particularly when the arrival of telegraphic communication in the 1860s proved that accurate unilateral timekeeping was crucial in an increasingly globalised culture. Eventually, in 1880, the traditionalists conceded defeat and Greenwich Mean Time finally stamped its authority over the entire British nation. This was great news for everyone except chronic over-sleepers who now had to invent other feeble excuses for missing their train.

SPRING FORWARD, FALL BACK

So, when William Willett suggested that individuals could change their clocks by 20 minutes on specific days, he wasn't espousing some crackpot idea; many people would have recalled adjusting their pocket watches when arriving at a distant location. Backed by a young Winston Churchill and a not-so-young David Lloyd George, Willett confidently appeared before a Parliamentary Select Committee and deployed his trump argument: a child born after the introduction of such a measure would reach his 28th birthday having enjoyed a whole extra year of daylight. Who could disagree with such glorious logic! Alas, Willett hadn't factored in just how strong the opposition would be. After three decades of temporal standardisation across the country, there weren't many wistful nostalgics pining for the days when messing about with a clock was necessary, least of all eight times per year.

Having begun the process as an upstanding gent, Willett ended the battle as a comedy punchline, widely derided as an impractical loony. With his credibility in ruins, Willett's parliamentary application was rejected six years on the trot. Finally – and typically for a man who liked to get things done earlier than everyone else – he dropped dead aged just 58. It was 1915, the First World War was raging, Britain's King George V was desperately trying to shed his alarmingly Germanic surname, and there was no way in hell Britain would ever embrace Daylight Saving Time. And then, out of the blue in April 1916, Germany adopted it instead.

Rather cleverly, the Kaiser's advisors had spotted that increasing the availability of natural daylight would reduce the need for artificial lighting, allowing all the conserved fuel to be redirected towards the war effort. This was a persuasive argument; so persuasive, in fact, that it managed to cross the Channel. Suddenly, many of the naysayers who had so publicly mocked William Willett began staring at their shoes and mumbling that maybe DST wasn't such a stupid idea, after all. Just one month after Germany took the plunge, so too did Britain. The creeping 20-minute plan was wisely replaced by a simpler single-hour leap, but at last Daylight Saving Time was a reality. Just like the rapper MC Hammer, the recently deceased William Willett was popularly allotted his own distinct unit of time, though sadly no

one thought to put on parachute pants and shout: 'Now, stop...
Willett time!' By the close of the First World War, many nations
had embraced the new system – including Australia and much of
Europe – but the controversy was only just beginning.

In particular, America's adoption of the idea backfired spectacularly and, like an excitable kitten tangling itself in a ball of
wool, the country become trapped for half a century in a crisis
of its own making.

THE DISUNITED STATES OF AMERICA

A standardised time across the vast expanses of the USA was not
going to be acceptable, otherwise the Dolly Parton song about
'working 9 to 5' would have had some pretty strange lyrics about
trying to do her job in the dark. Initially, a Canadian railway
engineer named Sandford Fleming pushed for a single standard
time, based on the 24-hour clock, for the entire globe. This so-
called 'cosmic time' was his grand idea, and he hoped that all
nationalities would wear watches with both local and cosmic time
displayed upon them. When this didn't come to pass, Fleming
altered his plan to advocate a new system of 24 regional time
zones; each was delineated neatly at every 15 degrees of longitude
and so each gained an hour. Here was a pragmatic answer to
railway chaos, and in 1883 five separate time zones were created
in North America: Eastern, Central, Mountain, Pacific and the
Intercolonial, named after Fleming's engineering triumph, the
Intercolonial Railway of Canada.

To add further stability, the following year an international
conference recommended Greenwich Mean Time be the prime-
meridian for global measurement of longitude, though the
affronted French lived up to their petulant reputation by refusing
to drop Paris from the centre on their maps. Regardless of the

Gallic sulking, in America the new time zones worked pretty well, though some cities, such as Detroit and Cleveland, switched zones to earn themselves more evening light, but this was a local decision, made by local people with local concerns. In contrast, the nationwide switch to Daylight Saving Time in 1918 – again to conserve electricity in wartime – was a total disaster.

As is now so patently obvious in American elections, there are very few things that unite opinion across all 50 states, but dislike for Daylight Saving Time came damn close. After a mere eight months, it was unceremoniously dumped from national law. Foolishly, however, the government still allowed individual states and cities the freedom to decide whether to opt in or out, as had been the case before the war, but now new technology had changed the face of the nation. After 1945, there were glamorous new nationwide industries, such as passenger airlines and TV broadcasters, that tried to integrate their businesses into American life, but their detailed schedules were impossible to manage on account of all the varying time zones. Even local bus timetables were lucky to survive a fortnight without having to be totally rewritten, as cities and states embraced, and then abandoned, Daylight Saving Time like fickle children instantly bored by their once-desired Christmas presents.

Given that America only had five time zones, it was almost impressive that one bus timetable saw a 35-mile stretch of highway between Moundsville, West Virginia and Steubenville, Ohio, span seven different time zones, meaning particularly assiduous passengers had to adjust their watches every eight minutes. Commuters weren't much better off in their cars, either. There were numerous reports of people crawling through the usual rush hour traffic, and rejoicing as they finally escaped over state lines, only to become trapped in yet more rush-hour snarl-ups because the neighbouring state was an hour behind.

In the 1950s and early Sixties, a trip to the bank, or an official appointment at the courthouse, could sometimes result in an embarrassing apology for tardiness, or a frustrated kick at a locked door. In Idaho, shoppers had to contend with different stores in the same street subscribing to variable opening hours, and it didn't even matter if businesses shared the same building. Every now and again, the eye-rolling nuisance of it all morphed into genuine risk and motorists might drive nonchalantly over level-crossings only for unexpected cargo trains – supposedly not due for an hour – to suddenly thunder towards them, with horn blaring in panicked warning...

For ordinary citizens, life was governed by a temporal system so bewilderingly arcane it could have come straight from the pages of *Gulliver's Travels*, and Dr William Markowitz, from the United States Naval Observatory, wasn't kidding around when he branded America 'the worst timekeeper in the world'.

A TIME FOR CHANGE

While America asynchronously flailed around, into the breach stepped the heroically titled Committee For Time Uniformity – a lobby group of major players in afflicted industries – which finally twisted the governmental arm into action. The 1966 Uniform Time Act standardised a period of six months for DST across America, between the last Sunday in April and the last Sunday in October (though four states immediately withdrew). Despite high hopes, this was not the silver bullet and more turbulence was yet to come when President Nixon was forced to briefly reintroduce emergency War Time in 1973, following the oil shortage resulting from the Yom Kippur War.

In the face of such extraordinary confusion, America was finally forced to admit that it had a problem and went into temporal rehab, eventually emerging clean and sober with a much more workable solution of seven months of Daylight Saving Time – a success story that has yet to lead to an embarrassing relapse.

But that's not the end of the DST controversy...

BRITAIN'S LAST HURRAH (AGAIN)

If you were living in Scotland or Northern Ireland in 1968, you might have found winter particularly depressing. Britain – an island floating defiantly apart from the European mainland – was suddenly overcome by the intoxicating notion of international harmony and flung itself into a three-year experiment called British Standard Time, which brought the UK into clock alignment with most of Europe. This was lovely when you were trying to sell a Belgian a British car, but if you were living in the northern parts of the British Isles it suddenly transformed winter mornings into bleak, post-apocalyptic bouts of protracted darkness during which the sun sometimes refused to rise until 9.45 a.m. The experiment was abandoned in 1971 due to the ferocity of the public response north of the border, even though the lighter evenings were shown to reduce road deaths, but – like a schlocky Hollywood horror villain – British Standard Time occasionally lurches out from the grave to haunt political debate, even now.

What this reveals is how, even in a small country, the natural world and the one-size-fits-all whims of politics won't always snugly interlock. We live in an era when time is an ever-present metronome to our life and we no longer have to adjust our watches when travelling only 100 miles. But when we look at the fine print, it becomes clear that the way we regulate time is born mostly of compromise, practicality and best endeavours. It's surprising that even in a world where atomic clocks can be accurate to within a nanosecond that so much of how we divide up the day is still influenced by sensible pragmatism. Timekeeping is not just an area of scientific enquiry, but also part of our cultural heritage. We define time just as much as it defines us.

But enough of all that! It's time we got up, and, after a long night's sleep, the first thing we must do is answer the call of nature. Whereas the mounting housework can be cheerfully ignored, the same doesn't apply to the bladder. So, let's start this day by scooping our feet into our bedside slippers and shuffling hastily to the bathroom.

ANSWERING THE CALL OF NATURE

Having dragged ourselves out of bed, we suddenly feel the pressing pangs of hunger as we wander past the kitchen. Caffeine and cornflakes would be delicious and stimulating at this juncture, but the demands of the bladder will always outgun those of the stomach, and right now it's holding us to ransom like a piss-filled terrorist.

And so, off we scurry to the... well, what do you call it?

THE 'YOU KNOW WHERE'

In English there are many lovely synonyms for the humble toilet: the john, loo, can, bog, lav, commode, potty, shitter, urinal, latrine, privy, porcelain, head, etc. These are informal terms, even vulgar, and in British public places we're much more likely to see signs for the toilet, gents, ladies or, occasionally, WC (water closet). Americans, on the other hand, tend to visit bathrooms and restrooms, where they neither bathe nor rest, unless they suffer from narcolepsy and accidentally fall asleep in the wash basin.

It seems we're happy to be vulgar among friends, but as a society our labelling is charmingly euphemistic. A large British house might have several commodes, meaning at least one will probably be kept in its own walk-in cupboard, stationed next to a sink. This little room will often be dubbed the loo, toilet or lavatory. There's some debate, but it's plausible that these were all French words originally. 'Loo' is the trickiest to pin down; it's possibly derived from the polite word *lieu,* meaning the 'place' – French eighteenth-century aristocrats called their toilets *les lieux à l'anglaise* (the places of the English) – but 'loo' isn't really recorded in English usage until the 1920s, so there's more likelihood of it being an abbreviation of Waterloo Cisterns, a brand frequently stamped on outdoor toilets in the early twentieth century.

The word 'toilet' derives from *toilette*, which initially meant a medieval cloth, then a washing cloth, then a room with a washing basin, and finally – only by the late 1800s – a room with a commode. On a similar note, 'lavatory' comes from *laver*, the French verb 'to wash'. So, weirdly, the room that hosts our toilet is not labelled accordingly. Indeed, a home with only a single toilet will probably have it plumbed in next to the shower or bathtub, resulting in the room losing the name 'toilet', 'lavatory' or 'loo' and instead becoming the 'bathroom', because the bath somehow trumps the bog in the naming hierarchy. Surely 'lavatory' would be much better suited, as it would be both a washing room *and* it contains a toilet! Strange, isn't it?

I mention all this because language is a portal to our past, even if it's not always clear. In the English-speaking West, people frequently chuck around interchangeable words for everyday things without realising that such terms were once specific in their meanings, and were intimately tied up with associations of class and custom. Today, Western sanitation facilities are standardised, no matter what your earning potential, but not so long ago owning a plumbed-in toilet was a sign of wealth, and what you called it revealed the quality of your upbringing.

In fact, while our sanitation facilities are increasingly homogenised, and our labels for them interchangeable, the past witnessed great variability in how our ancestors dealt with their necessary evacuations. While it's true that the yuk-factor is instinctively biological, and the need to jettison turds is a recurring theme in history, the key question was always 'how far must one fling a poo before it's safely out of harm's way?' The result was that differing eras emerged with their own unique answers, and if we were planning on travelling back in history, and were desperate for the toilet, we might be better off sending our time machine back 4,000 years rather than just 300 years. Those eighteenth-century Georgians may have had very lovely frocks, but they weren't opposed to tossing urine out of a window!

So, as we stumble into the bathroom and perch our buttocks down on the cold loo seat, let's start with the obvious question – how old are toilets?

STONE AGE SANITATION

Çatalhöyük is one of the most important archaeological sites in the world, which is enormously annoying because I can never pronounce it properly. A town in modern Turkey, perhaps as early as 9,500 years ago, it's a remarkable time capsule from an epoch when our ancestors were just beginning to permanently settle down in sizeable numbers. Whereas the earliest human communities were probably no bigger than 150 people, Çatalhöyük may have housed up to 10,000. That may not sound like much to those of us who've been to an international football match in a fully crammed stadium, but try imagining each one of those people emptying their bowels on just a single day... that's quite a turd heap to deal with, isn't it? Okay, now multiply that by 365 days. Et voilà, here is the first great problem of civilisation – where do you put all the crap?

In truth, the Neolithic (meaning New Stone Age) response at Çatalhöyük wasn't particularly sophisticated. As far as archaeological excavations can prove, the sanitation policy seems to have been one of piling any unwanted material, including manure, on landfill sites in designated courtyards near the houses. These so-called middens were seemingly levelled off from time to time, presumably to stop them turning into poo mountains, which can't have been a terribly pleasant job for whichever muggins was handed the rake. Of course, to us, the notion of having a gaggle of closely clustered homes stood next to a putrid mound of sun-baked waste may not sound terribly hygienic and... well, yeah, it wasn't.

For various reasons – diet change, parasite-harbouring live-stock, poor sanitation and close human proximity – the Neolithic Revolution, often heralded as one of the greatest transitions in human history, also paradoxically led to a sizeable decrease in human health. As the nineteenth-century Victorians would later prove, urban life often wielded greater peril than the primitive nomadic wandering that went before it. Yes, there were fewer cave bears threatening to eviscerate your guts, but the bacteria and viruses were actually far more deadly.

Despite this, the Neolithic experiment ploughed on – quite literally – and, after embarking on an enormous European tour that traipsed westwards over several millennia, the farming revolution finally rolled into the Orkney Islands in around 3100 BCE, and it's here that we can see familiar toilet behaviour on a much smaller scale. A magnificently preserved Neolithic village comprising only eight stone houses, Skara Brae, on Mainland, resembles the verdant abode of J.R.R. Tolkien's furry-toed hobbits, but the mounds of grassy earth that shield the buildings from the fierce Scottish winds were not always so postcard pretty.

Originally numbering probably fewer than one hundred people, the early occupants on the island had been typically lax in disposing of their waste, and massive midden piles had accumulated, but rather than getting as far away as possible from the stinking refuse, the villagers recycled their trash by utilising these heaps as organic cocoons to insulate their new homes. Though to visit them today is to be confronted with a sort of prehistoric Tellytubby land, seemingly sunk below ground level, actually the houses were built on flat turf but were deliberately stationed between large mounds of unwanted refuse which towered either side of them.

But let's not decry the primitiveness of Neolithic hygiene too hastily, for Skara Brae does seem to harbour evidence of indoor toilets that emptied into crude sewer systems. Cubicle-like cells in the corner of the homes, built over drainage channels, suggest they were distinct zones for doing one's business, and perhaps this is also an intriguing insight into Stone Age notions of privacy. Maybe they were like us and preferred to answer the call of nature without an audience, or maybe it was simply easier to keep out smells if the toilet could be cordoned off from the living room. What's more clear is that the lack of running water suggests that when it came to cleansing their mucky backsides, the inhabitants were wipers rather than washers, with most archaeologists theorising that moss, seaweed or leaves were the Stone Age equivalent of our loo roll.

So, the Neolithic was the pilot programme for urban living; a flawed early blueprint for future generations to remodel, and, true enough, the Bronze Age delivered on its promise with the vastly superior Version 2.0.

CITY SHITTERS

Imagine the scenario. A person has been busy at work when suddenly their stomach contracts, and their bowels loosen. They must have eaten something dodgy! Desperate, they drop everything and run into the bathroom, pulling down their pants to plonk their cheeks down on the seat. Relaxing, their bowels empty into the toilet below and they exhale in relief as the threat of a messy accident evaporates away. Their business done, they reach for some wiping material, clean up behind and drop it down the hole, before flushing it away with a brief torrent of water. As they wash their hands, they relax in the knowledge that their turd will be carried far from their home by the sewers.

How much of this sounds familiar? A toilet with a seat, wiping material, water to flush away the turd, and sewers? You might confidently assume we're dealing with a twentieth-century arrangement here, but perhaps you'd plump for nineteenth-century to be safe. Well, you'd be out by around 4,500 years. What I was describing was the sanitation system in Bronze Age Pakistan.

Located in the Indus River Valley, and sprawling out through the north-western part of the Indian continent, the cities of the advanced Harappan civilisation were first founded in around 2600 BCE. Subsequently named after the first of these cities to be archaeologically excavated, the Harappans were obsessed with cleanliness and banished their unwanted effluent via a network of pipes that linked homes to purpose-built cesspits. The more affluent houses even had toilets, separate from bathing areas, which were simple but effective in design – a seat was positioned over a chute that led directly to the sewers, and dirty bathwater was sluiced down after each toilet visit as a sort of manual flush. Though not everyone could afford such elaborate bogs, and lower status people probably squatted over a sunken jar that would need regular emptying, at least its contents could be slung unceremoniously into the cesspit, rather than piled in next door's garden like some sort of faecal art installation.

Hopefully you'll have noticed that I've mentioned toilet seats. Yes, it's thanks to the Harappans that people first began to avoid squatting over the toilet like a sumo wrestler, although it's thought that, around the same time, the ancient Egyptian upper classes also parked their bums on U-shaped stone-carved loo seats. Fans of Neolithic middens, however, will be delighted to learn that, despite such inventiveness, the Bronze Age didn't entirely do away with piles of poo, at least not in poorer areas of Egypt where domestic waste was simply dumped outside the house to bake in the burning Saharan heat. Though this sounds wholly unhygienic, it was rather more pragmatic – manure was a useful fertiliser that could occasionally be added into the ingredients of adobe mud bricks, and it was commonly mixed with straw to be turned into winter fuel for heating and cooking. Presumably this gave dinner a certain unwanted tang, but let's try not to think about it too much ...

Of course, on this modern Saturday morning, we enter our own bathroom and have to decide whether to stand or sit while we drain our bladder. Usually, this depends on whether it's a number one or two, but it might also be influenced by our gender – in Britain, at least, blokes tend to pee standing up. Yet, the ancient Greek historian Herodotus, who may have visited Egypt in the fifth century BCE, intriguingly suggested that Egyptian women urinated while upright, and it was men who sat down to piddle. In truth, this is an example lifted from a whole paragraph detailing the weird otherness of Egyptians compared with Greeks, so it might be an illustrative exaggeration, but his observations on privacy are interesting: 'Their homes they use for defecating in, while the streets outside are where they eat – this on the principle that anything which is embarrassing but unavoidable should be done behind closed doors, while anything that is not a cause of shame should be done fully in public.'

If true, such modesty sounds familiar to our sensibilities, and the timidity around public pant-dropping was also shared by the ancient Jews, who placed a tremendous emphasis on spiritual cleanliness through physical hygiene. For example, it's still forbidden for Orthodox Jews to ponder the Torah's teachings, or utter the sacred prayer of Sh'ma, while on a toilet or even facing a toilet. *The Encyclopaedia Talmudica* helpfully suggests thinking of one's finances instead, except on the Sabbath day, when this is also forbidden, in which case one should think of beautiful art.

More crucially, the treatment of faeces and urine is carefully legislated for in Deuteronomy 23:12–14, which declares: 'Designate a place outside the camp where you can go to relieve yourself. As part of your equipment have something to dig with, and when you relieve yourself, dig a hole and cover up your excrement.' Was this a hygienic response to the threat of disease? Actually, it was more a case of religious courtesy: 'For the LORD your God moves about in your camp to protect you and to deliver your enemies to you. Your camp must be holy, so that he will not see among you anything indecent and turn away from you.' God may be all-seeing, but that doesn't mean he wants to see it all.

This fastidious waste management was impressive in theory, but didn't always come good in practice. In the Middle Ages, Old Jerusalem had an entrance/exit point unromantically monikered the Dung Gate, or *Sha'ar Ha'ashpot,* through which waste was hauled out of the city and burned, or piled up into a dunghill. But it wasn't just the Jews who struggled to reach their own exalted standards. When we think of ancient Athens, with its marble temples and robed philosophers, it's easy to fall for the myth of classical sophistication, but that is perhaps a lavender-scented view of the past.

POTTIES, PLAYWRIGHTS AND PHILOSOPHERS

Blepyrus awakes in the night needing to have a poo, but after looking around the room it suddenly dawns on him that his wife is missing, and so are his clothes – the cheeky minx has stolen them in order to pass herself off as a man. Old Blepyrus is forced to throw on her clothes and slippers instead, before stumbling out into the street to do his business. After a quick check to see if the coast is clear, he squats down outside his house and is about to empty his bowels when, unfortunately, a nosy neighbour spots him and demands to know what he's playing at. An embarrassed Blepyrus is forced to explain both his cross-dressing and the public defecation: 'as I urgently needed to crap, I popped my feet into these slippers, so as not to soil my brand new blanket.' Poor fella, it's really not the best start to the day, is it?

Still, there's no need to cringe too much, as Blepyrus was merely a character in *Women in the Assembly*, a comic play by the great Aristophanes, for whom toilets were the joke that kept on giving. But his fictional existence doesn't mean Blepyrus wasn't a mirror to the realities of Athenian society. While the ancient Greeks are often upheld as the glorious champions of civilisation, they weren't a patch on the Harappans when it came to public sanitation infrastructure. The closest mention we get to a designated defecation space is perhaps with the description by the philosopher Theophrastus of his stock idiot, a man who goes for a midnight poo in the garden outhouse, and trips over the neighbour's ferocious dog.

But for most it seems chamber pots were the go-to solution; men peed in an *amis* whereas women got their own bowl-shaped one called a *skaphion*. Oddly enough, *skaphion* was also a Greek word for a style of Beatles-esque bowl haircut, which suggests potties were upturned onto heads by overzealous barbers short of equipment. One really hopes they were scrubbed clean first. Of course, most of us only use potties when we're bawling toddlers, and the Greeks, like us, had a clever bit of kit to handle this dinky demographic – they plonked their babies in highchairs, with specially cut holes for their chunky little legs to slide through, and a hole in the seat for any inevitable waste to drop down into a *skaphion* below. All this domestic mess, from baby and adult, was commonly tipped into the cesspit, or *kopron*, which was emptied by professional waste disposers called *koprologoi* who sold it to farmers for fertiliser.

This arrangement sounds perfectly sensible, but what happened if a Greek was caught short away from the home? You and I could probably duck into a public lavatory, maybe one in a shop or park, but no such things existed in Greece. The seventh-century-BCE poet Hesiod wrote that it was bad form to urinate outdoors, as it disrespected the notoriously tetchy gods. In Hesiod's opinion, weeing on roads, near roads, while facing the sun, or during the night, was tantamount to swaggering assertively up to the all-powerful deities and pissing on their shoes. It seems, then, that many Greeks tried to hold it in. In fact, such stoicism was common enough to become a matter of medical curiosity – a scribbled afterthought on the back of a medical papyrus, written by Anonymus Londinensis, ponders: 'For those who are caught short . . . if they hold it in for some time, either they can no longer poo (when they get somewhere suitable) or else manage only a small and dry one. Why is that?'

But if someone was utterly bursting for an al fresco evacuation, then dawn and dusk were the best times to go – the gods being particularly fond of the night – and care had to be taken not to flash too much flesh. The fact that Hesiod felt compelled to write such advice suggests it was fairly common to publicly behold bare buttocks and tinkling todgers, and the glamorous über-jerk Alcibiades, who was famed for his arrogant ostentation, was even said to have begun a fashion for openly pissing in polite company; the poets Eupolis and Epicrates of Ambracia both mention slave boys scurrying into the midst of drunken aristocratic parties with chamber pot in hand.

But was piddling and pooing separate? Certainly, British men in modern pubs are comfortable urinating side by side, but vanish into secret cubicles for a 'number two'. Were the Greeks the same? We're not sure. But it seems the Romans were much less ashamed of their bodily functions. Indeed, for them a trip to the toilet could be something of a social occasion.

WHEN IN ROME...

Roman public bogs (*foricae*) were open rooms where people, possibly of mixed genders, sat side by side on long benches and gossiped politely while they emptied their bowels into the sewers below. Being a Briton for whom even eye contact on a tube train is unbearably intrusive, this fills me with mortifying dread, but the Romans were clearly not perturbed. Their capital city alone hosted 144 of these public establishments, all of them festooned with a parade of buttocks, and many more sprung up across the Empire too.

At Apamea in Syria, a super-latrine welcomed about 80 people at a time, though elsewhere the norm appears to have been closer to a (dirty) dozen. Wash basins and gently tinkling fountains were likely installed in the corner of the *forica* and an interior channel of water ran around the edge of the floor, to ensure basic hygiene. It's also hard to know just how well lit these rooms were, particularly as some were windowless, so perhaps a shadowy gloom helped keep things more anonymous.

But, conversely, decorative art might also adorn the walls, perhaps as a means to distract the self-conscious pooper from the inevitable sound of straining, or maybe simply to beautify this noble public edifice? In any case, you don't paint a wall if it's too murky to see, so visibility wasn't at zero. At Ostia Antica, one communal bog housed in the Room of the Seven Sages boasted a beautiful mural of Greek philosophers sitting around discussing their bowel movements. Various comedy captions are added, including: 'the cunning Chilon taught how to fart unnoticed.'

Was this a jovial way to acknowledge the echoey orchestra of a dozen trumpeting anuses? Or was it a coded message, subtly demanding modesty and consideration for others? It does seem that squeezing it out, rather than holding it all in, was the usual custom and if things weren't proceeding smoothly then the answer was to grit one's teeth and redouble one's efforts. At Ostia, another caption says: 'Thales recommended that those who defecate with difficulty should strain.' With many probably taking his advice, it seems chitchat and the sound of splashing water would have been necessary distractions from the guttural exertions of the chronically constipated, but there would've been nothing anyone could have done about the stench rising up from open sewers below.

Perhaps the most unsettling aspect of the public toilet tradition was the wiping of the backside – it wasn't just the toilets that were shared, but the bum-fodder too. While archaeological explorations of ancient sewers show up a lot of soiled rags, the written sources from the era speak of a sponge on the end of a stick (*xylospongion*) that was passed between the users. It was probably washed in the water channel running around the floor's perimeter, and was kept in a vase of vinegar wine to reduce the smell, but it can't have been terribly hygienic. In one particularly alarming story, the philosopher Seneca tells of a German gladiator who, rather than be forced to fight in the arena, fled into the toilets and deliberately choked himself to death on this shit-sponge.

He was not the only tragic victim of Roman sanitation. There had also been a high suicide rate among the workers forced to build Rome's massive civic sewer, the Cloaca Maxima, during the reign of the very early Roman King Tarquinius Superbus in around 500 BCE. The job was so horribly arduous that the labourers resorted to fleeing, or even killing themselves, forcing the King to use the threat of crucifixion to get them back on the job, because the only thing worse than a quick death is a slow one. Understandably, the tyrannical Tarquinius was soon overthrown and replaced with the famed Roman Republic, which itself was later replaced by the Empire in the reign of Augustus.

During this largely peaceful reign, Caesar Augustus – or rather his right-hand man, Agrippa – greatly expanded the Cloaca Maxima into seven tributary branches leading off a central conduit, with the whole network being so magnificent in scale that Agrippa was able to row a boat through the sewers during his inspections, like a subterranean gondolier floating on a river of turds. Although the sewers might have been a glorious example of Roman engineering, they weren't freely available to all. Access was only open to fee-payers, which meant that the majority of the poor might only make contributions to this underground tide of effluent from the seat of the public toilets, and not from the comfort of their own homes.

Indeed, like the Greeks, domestic toilet needs were largely catered for by chamber pots. Those minted with cash might have had an individual latrine in the home, but they'd still be the proud owner of a pimped-out potty befitting their status. According to his detractors, Mark Antony's was solid gold, while others were encrusted with jewels, showing that even attending to the body's most basic functions could still be an excuse to show off. For the lowly masses, chamber pots were commonly emptied onto the streets, sometimes even out of windows onto the unfortunate bystanders below, and, like the Greek *koprologoi*, a professional class of manure and urine dealers made good money by collecting the public's potty contents and flogging it to farmers and fullers for fertilising crops and dyeing cloth. In fact, such was the profit in this trade that Emperor Vespasian – a notoriously penny-pinching ruler – gleefully boasted about how he could produce good clean cash from taxing human waste. He was quite literally taking the piss...

BUM-FODDER

And now, for an authentic medieval joke:

Q. What's the cleanest leaf in the forest?
A. Holly, because no one dares wipe his arse on it!

In terms of toilet history, humanity peaked way too soon. It was mostly downhill after the Indus Harappans, although a decent standard of hygiene was still maintained in the orbit of the ancient Mediterranean superpowers. Yet, when the overstretched Western Roman Empire dramatically collapsed in the late fifth century, the quality of plumbing mostly went with it. This early medieval period is often characterised as a brutal, backwards world of murder, rape and gullible idiocy, which isn't a fair assessment, but it's not all that easy to defend its standards of hygiene. There were no more flowing fountains, public loos or sponges on sticks – the Vikings defecated mostly in their back gardens, and were much more likely to wipe their backsides with clumps of wool, leaves, moss and seaweed.

Intriguingly, though Islam took hygiene very seriously indeed – and washing would ensure no filth remained after a trip to the loo – a quotation ascribed to the Prophet Muhammad says that if the anus were to be scraped clean with pebbles, then an odd number had to be used, suggesting that the early Arabs might have used stone scrapers as bum wipers. Given the discomfort this might cause, I would definitely have plumped for one pebble rather than three. Anyway, as we sit on our loo to perform our morning necessities, nearby there is a roll of toilet paper awaiting its big moment. Seeing as the Egyptians wrote on papyrus, and the Romans had scrolls, you might justifiably wonder if medieval people had access to low-quality wiping paper. Well, not in Europe, no. But in China? Quite probably.

Paper was possibly in use as early as the second century BCE, but the classical legend is that in 105 CE – barely 25 years after the Roman Colosseum had opened its doors – a Chinese court eunuch called Ts'ai Lun embarked on a quest to produce a quality writing material. His experiments were pretty odd, as they saw him endlessly pulping whatever random stuff he had happened to wander past. Basically, Ts'ai Lun's ceaseless curiosity was the ancient equivalent of when we buy a new kitchen blender and spend several wide-eyed minutes wondrously slicing up assorted things found on the nearest table: 'I wonder if it does turnips . . . ? It does! What about pineapples? Oh, it's broken.' After some dogged experimentation, Ts'ai Lun finally hit upon a strange-but-reliable combination – paper could be made by mashing up mulberry tree bark, fishing nets and cloth rags.

So, is toilet paper nearly 2,000 years old? Not quite. His goal had been to create writing stationery, not bum-fodder, and the earliest verifiable references to its hygienic uses were only recorded by travellers in the ninth century. Paper was apparently brought from China to nearby Japan in the early seventh century, but it seems the Japanese had no intention of using it on their posteriors – they preferred seaweed, or a wooden scraping stick called a *chugi*, and archaeologists have found plenty of these in medieval castle sites. What's more, while most Japanese squatted over a cesspit, a ninth-century loo found by archaeologists at Akita Castle in Tohoku seems to have comprised two wooden boards, rather than the Bronze Age U-shaped seat, built over a run-off channel that led to the castle moat. While it's not 100 per cent proven, the fact that the old Japanese word for toilet is *kawa-ya*, which may mean 'river house', does suggest toilets could sometimes be stationed near water.

WHATEVER YOU DO, DON'T FALL IN THE CESSPIT

The Japanese were not alone in dumping their ordure into water. In late medieval England, London Bridge famously had public toilets built along its length, so that every time someone took a dump the offending turd would plummet gracefully into the River Thames below or – equally commonly – onto the head of some unsuspecting boatman pootling up the river. This might not sound pleasant, but it kept the bridge smelling relatively fresh, as no sewers or cesspits were required, and the Thames dispatched the excrement away from the city.

Dumping waste into a fast-flowing river was a sensible option, as it didn't pollute the water supply or lead to stinking, stagnant pools, but the practice was not without some drawbacks. Monasteries, for example, commonly built their loos to flow into nearby rivers and streams, but seasonal flooding had the nasty habit of forcing the sewage back up from whence it came. Urban citizens, on the other hand, seem to have been rather fond of a bit of weekend DIY as there are many medieval references to people trying to bodge their own domestic plumbing solutions, such as connecting their privies to rain gutters or cheekily diverting their waste onto other people's land. Civic authorities were often quick to punish them – it's a myth that medieval urban sanitation was unregulated and chaotic – but, even if they dodged a fine, these cheaters often got their comeuppance when the pipe clogged and the malodorous excrement poured back into their houses.

Still, if being up to your ankles in faeces sounds unappealing, spare a thought for the tiny minority who very occasionally found their whole bodies caked in human filth. These might include besieging soldiers, like those who snuck into Chateau Gaillard in 1203 by clambering up the brown-stained toilet chutes, or the *Shawshank Redemption*-style escape by the eleventh-century aristocrat Gerald of Wales, who was forced to flee to safety from Cilgerran Castle by sliding down the toilet chute and crawling out through the cesspit. Still, at least these guys made it out alive.

Those who cleaned the cesspits were known as *gongfermers*, and it was such a disgusting job that these men were only allowed to work while others slept. For obvious reasons, they were handsomely paid for the hardship, but this didn't mean they were respected – *gongfermers* were the hedge-fund managers of the medieval world. Another reason for their decent salary was the risk, as the fumes could be intolerably noxious and might cause a man to collapse into the sewage and drown, but a certain Richard the Raker suffered an even crueller demise: the rotten floorboards of his own cesspit gave way, drowning him in a bubbling quagmire of his own making. For a *gongfermer* to drown at home, in his own shit, on his day off, was pretty much the definition of irony.

PANS, PRIVIES AND PUBLIC POOING

That said, in very rare instances, cleaning up the contents of someone else's potty was a privileged position. Henry VIII titled his royal bum-wiper The Groom of the Stool, and it was this man's responsibility to inspect the king's regal droppings and inhale his majestic farts, seeking any subtle clues of ill health. Yes, the job was quite literally to work with an arsehole, but it paid handsomely and was tremendously prestigious – after all, how many people in England could enjoy the privilege of getting *that* close to the nation's most powerful man?

Of course, these days only infants and the infirm tend to use potties and pans. The toilet that we are currently using is a flushable one, a relatively recent technology, but the prototype is over four centuries old, and has a rather nice story attached to it. King Henry VIII's daughter Elizabeth I had a talented but somewhat controversial godson called Sir John Harington who, having offended his godmother with the translation of a naughty poem, was exiled from her court. But rather than sulking, he dedicated some of his banishment time to inventing a rather cunning device, one which earned him a place back in Lizzie's good books – a flushing toilet. Charmed once more by her 'saucy godson', she had this royal privy installed at Richmond Palace.

But, by the sounds of it, Elizabeth soon after regretted her leniency as, in 1596, the irrepressibly cheeky Harington published *The Metamorphosis of Ajax*, a toilet-themed political satire aimed squarely at her closest advisors (Ajax being a pun on 'a jakes', another word for loo). But, it wasn't just a scatological broadside against his illustrious godmother's reign; Harington was genuinely interested in what caused urban disease and was advocating a higher standard of public sanitation. His libellous satire may have got him exiled again, but he probably deserves to be applauded for his scientific foresight. And that's not all . . . Not only did he invent the flushing loo, but as we sit on our lavvy, flicking through a cheery bog-book, or last month's glossy magazine, we're actually following in Harington's footsteps, as he imagined readable copies of his *Metamorphosis* would be hung from a chain in every privy in the palace.

Reading on the loo is perfectly civilised, but writing about your stools is surely less so? Surprisingly, then, this was exactly what Martin Luther, the German monk whose ideas initiated the rise of Protestantism, chose to do. Suffering from intractable constipation that saw him spend hours trying to squeeze out his infernal stools, Luther had a permanent toilet installed in the corner of his office, upon which much of his religious ideology was pondered. But that wasn't the end of the celebrated monk's bowel-related output. He also began writing astonishingly frank letters to friends, providing intimate details of his Herculean bowel battles, and directed scatological insults at Satan in his theological writings, including the splendid: 'But if that is not enough for you, Devil, I have also shit and pissed; wipe your mouth on that and take a hearty bite.'

But Luther's openness with his trusted confidants was nothing compared with the shamelessness of the French royal court in the seventeenth century, where even basic toilet decency was rarer than an uncooked steak...

LOO-UIS THE FOURTEENTH

Imagine, you're a new courtier arriving at Louis XIV's golden palace of Versailles. As you approach by carriage, you take in the stunning architecture and crane your neck to survey the vast botanical perfection of the manicured lawns and gushing fountains. You disembark from your coach, nervous with excitement, and are led into the palace where you're immediately overwhelmed by the luxury on display. Eyes popping from their sockets, you stagger disbelievingly into the gold-strewn Hall of Mirrors, where you anxiously wait to be beckoned. After what seems like an age, you're finally ushered into the King's own apartment complex – a parade of seven gorgeous rooms. You turn the corner and are greeted by one final door. You do not knock, but follow the custom of scratching gently into the wood with the nail of your left pinkie. A voice beckons you in; you step through the doorway – and there he is, the most powerful man in all of Europe... having a shit.

Until 1684, when he opted to surround himself with a crimson curtain, King Louis XIV could frequently be found chatting with others while sat with his breeches around his ankles and his bum pressed firmly into his close-stool – a wooden box that housed a removable potty. Despite suggestions from his architects, the king found the idea of a specific toilet room to be a waste of money and effort, and so his daily bowel movements were conducted wherever he happened to be at the time. His relaxed attitude to privacy didn't apply to his subjects, however, and those who rode in a carriage with him were forced to hold their bladders for the entire journey, even if they were desperate.

But it wasn't just Louis who cheerfully pooed while sat before his nobles. The Duchesse de Bourgogne claimed she 'was never able to speak more openly' than when sitting on her close-stool, and the Duc de Vendôme horrified the Bishop of Parma by greeting the illustrious prelate while perched on the potty, and then added insult to injury by getting up halfway through the discussion to wipe his arse. Still, those who knew him wouldn't have been shocked by this; Vendôme also ate some of his meals while sat on the lav.

Even more surprising is that the public areas of glorious French palaces, such as Versailles, were so extensively sullied by a foul sheen of excrement. Around the time of Louis XIV's death, an edict declared that faeces would be cleaned from the corridors of Versailles once per week, giving rise to two questions: i) there were actually turds littering the royal palace? and ii) the stools were left to fester for a *whole week*? Incredibly, it wasn't only servants and out-of-town visitors who left unwanted souvenirs behind. King Louis' own mother had once been spotted pissing behind a tapestry, and it was so common for people to use staircases as public lavatories that an earlier king, Henry IV, had been forced to issue fines to anyone caught in the act. Most revolting of all, the Count de Guiche was caught short during a state ball and decided to urinate in his dance partner's hand muff, which would be like us whizzing into a woman's handbag.

Meanwhile, those who travelled with the king to Fontainebleau Palace discovered the only place to defecate was out in the open, meaning lords and ladies were often spotted hunched over in gardens and streets, taking clandestine shits in bushes like velvet-clad foxes. Nor was it just the French, either. When the Great Plague struck London in 1665, King Charles II moved his court to Oxford, where a disgusted local resident reported that the king's entourage 'left their excrements in every corner, in chimneys, studies, coalhouses, cellars.' Cleaning that house must have been like a hugely unpleasant Easter egg hunt.

Those who didn't own a regal close-stool continued the Roman tradition of the bedpan, or jerry, which was the mainstay in middle-class homes throughout the sixteenth to eighteenth centuries and played occasional cameo roles in the diary of Samuel Pepys, the famous English diarist of the 1660s. The jerry was undoubtedly easy to use, but it did have its drawbacks. For starters, you had to actually find it. When we're bursting for the loo, we don't usually have to embark on an unwanted game of hide and seek with our toilet – we just scurry to the bathroom and drop our trousers. By comparison, in 1665 Pepys was staying in an unfamiliar house and awoke in the night with loose bowels. Desperately he searched in the dark for a potty, but the maid had forgotten to put it under his bed, so he had to take drastic action: 'I was forced in this strange house to rise and shit in the chimney twice'. That wasn't even his worst toilet anecdote. In 1663, his wife and his maid managed to drop the jerry between them, spilling turds and urine all over their floor.

The fact that the jerry was portable meant that, even in the refined dining rooms of the eighteenth century, it was still perfectly common for bedpans to be brought in by servants so that a well-bred dinner guest could step away from the table and take a piddle in the corner, while everyone else chatted about house prices, or whatever topic passed for dinner party conversation back then. You didn't go to the toilet, it came to you … but things were slowly changing.

A ROOM WITH A POO

Guests at the Michie Tavern, owned by William Michie, could enjoy food, drink and the exciting knowledge that they were only a few miles from Thomas Jefferson's Monticello House in Virginia. But if they'd enjoyed themselves a bit too much, they could also take solace in a visit to the outhouse – a privy commode located in an outdoor shack. The problem was, the clientele were hefty drinkers and their inevitable double-vision and poor coordination frequently induced them to somehow get their lower halves stuck in the pooing hole carved into the bench. After what we can assume was one too many exasperating rescue missions, Michie decided to install a DIY option – an emergency rope dangling down so the inebriated punters could drag themselves out of their embarrassing predicament.

Louis XIV may not have liked the idea, but by the eighteenth century the notion of a separate toilet room was increasingly common, and – as well as plonking one in the backyard, as Michie had done – it was possible to have a toilet annex built into your house which dropped its contents directly into a cesspit below. In eighteenth-century London, these acquired a fine assortment of names, including the necessary house, the house of office, and the bog house, and they typically projected out from buildings, or were built into the cellar. Such privies were obviously useful, but they had various design flaws. On the simplest level, the trick was to make the buttock-hole big enough for adults to sit over, but not so big that kids tumbled arse-first into the cesspit. This, however, was not the end of the problems. If the cesspool was brick-lined, it would need regular emptying, which was both expensive and produced a foul stink that would humble even the most pungent of skunks. But such a scenario was vastly preferential to merely digging an unlined hole in the ground to store all the poop, as the raw sewage would instead seep into the water supply, or even back-up into the kitchen, which meant food and drink was essentially being prepared in sewer water.

In the 1850s, the English sanitation campaigner Henry Mayhew watched a cesspit being emptied by nightsoil men in London and said the stench was 'literally sickening', but at least it had been properly constructed to safely trap its contents. It does seem shocking that only 150 years ago, in the city where I work, such a privy outhouse might have been shared by 15 families – that's maybe 100 people.

So, how did the transition to private family bathrooms happen?

THE ENGLISH PLACE

Sir John Harington had pioneered his famous water closet in the 1590s, but had only constructed a few working models, which somewhat hampered the global spread of his fine innovation. Despite imploring his aristocratic peers to adopt his invention, Harington's smutty puns and political point-scoring annoyed his regal godmother, and his influence at court was soon tarnished. So, it was left to the French to reinvent Harington's flushing bog in the late seventeenth century.

Even as early as 1691, the architect Augustin-Charles d'Aviler was laying out floor plans for luxurious mansions with en suite plumbing. King Louis XIV might have persisted with his scarlet-quilted shitbox, but the younger courtiers were thrilled by the arrival of these dignified privies and, in 1728, the French architect Charles-Etienne Briseux declared the close stool 'a thing of the past', insisting modern people use the plumbed-in 'easy-seats' instead. A decade later, the valve-flush toilet was improved by another French architect, Jacques-François Blondel, and was soon installed with regularity in elegant homes for elegant people. Contrary to popular stereotypes, therefore, it was the French aristocracy who leapt to the front of the European hygiene league tables in the eighteenth century. And yet such toilets inexplicably picked up the euphemistic nickname of the *lieu à l'anglaise* (the English place).

Despite the French aristocracy championing the plumbed-in privy, it appears that no one told the ordinary French people how to use it. When the Scottish writer Tobias Smollett visited the French town of Nîmes in 1763, he encountered a maidservant whose life was made all the more disgusting and difficult by her mistress's installation of a flushing water closet. Apparently this hygienic device was there for the benefit of British travellers, but the French guests who stayed at the house unanimously preferred to walk into the privy, drop their breeches and crap on the floor instead. The mind boggles at how they came to this decision; were they simply baffled by the porcelain bowl? Or was Smollett just slandering the old French enemy to score some jingo points?

Apart from wrinkling our noses in disgust, what this story tells us is that the British educated classes were familiar with flushing water closets by the mid-1700s, and Lord Chesterfield – a famous wit who enjoyed writing letters of worldly advice to his son – mentioned an acquaintance who was so good at multi-tasking that he took Latin poetry with him to the toilet. The esteemed gentleman would rip out a couple of pages of Horace's odes, enjoy them while he did his business, and then wipe his bum with the pages before chucking them down the pan 'as a sacrifice to Cloacina', the ancient goddess of sewers. Presumably Sir John Harington would have been delighted to have seen his idea for toilet reading taking off, but not if his *Metamorphosis of Ajax* had been ripped off its chain, smeared with excrement and flushed away.

FLUSHED WITH PRIDE

Despite French advances, the origins of the flushing toilet that we currently sit upon are actually British. The first great innovation came in 1775 with Alexander Cumming's mechanical 'slider'. This was a lever-operated valve at the bottom of the toilet bowl that, when yanked, slid across to allow the faeces to drop away and be flushed down by a generous blast of water. But Cumming's cleverest leap forward was in his redesigning of the pipes so that they bent in an S-shape, thereby creating a stink trap – a water-filled kink which sealed the system against the rise of putrid-smelling gases. It's thanks to Cumming that you can evacuate your lunch through one end of your body without feeling so nauseous from the smell that it comes spewing out of the other.

In truth, Cumming's slider tended to get mucky as by the time the water poured in, it was already withdrawn out of the way, so it never got a good spritzing. To fix this, in 1778 another chap, Joseph Bramah, nicked someone else's idea, patented it and replaced the slider with a spring-loaded valve which was washed by the water during every flush. No longer did the homeowner have to confront their daily deposits in pans and buckets, or worry about spilling turds over the floor like the Pepys family, as these new water closets were quiet, clean and increasingly fragrant. In fact, it wasn't long before they became rather gentrified with beautiful illustrations on the inside of the porcelain bowl, in what must be the only example I've ever come across where it was expected that you would urinate on the artwork.

It's of no small significance that the arrival of plumbing coincided with the tightening of Victorian morality – the bawdy raucousness of the eighteenth century, where even kings and queens had publicly shat in buckets, gave way to an uptight world of austere privacy where one daren't even mention one's daily necessities. When it came to human excrement the water closet perfectly encapsulated the phrase 'out of sight, out of mind'. But the toilet revolution wasn't done yet. The rich may have been able to install them in their homes, but what about the masses?

THE PEOPLE'S LOO

In 1851, London played host to the Great Exhibition – technically it was an international showcase of inventions and engineering marvels from all over the world, but pretty much everyone tacitly accepted it was actually a vast advertising campaign for British imperial awesomeness. Housed in the newly built Crystal Palace, erected inside Hyde Park, the exhibition was visited by around 50,000 people per day, reaching a grand total of 6 million paying punters. With so many people milling around, consuming food and drinks, the problem of bladders and bowels requiring emptying was not lost on the organisers.

The plumber Josiah George Jennings came to the rescue, winning a contract to install toilets at the venue. These were the first public lavatories since the medieval era and came in an array of options. For ordinary men, he installed innovative urinals organised in a circular arrangement around a central column, and these were free of charge, but the real showpieces were his flushing water closets, used by 827,000 people, which were a penny per visit and inspired the toilet euphemism 'to spend a penny'. This being Victorian Britain, a place obsessed with social rank, Jennings provided two forms of water closet, depending on how many pennies you were willing to cough up.

First-class customers got to enjoy the now-traditional spring-loaded valve toilets, but in the second-class stalls Jennings had installed simplified bogs of his own design – wash-out closets which relied solely on the S-shaped stink trap to stop smells, and did away with the closing valves at the bottom of the bowl. His simplified innovation was a super-hit and these cheaper, more ergonomic devices swiftly conquered the domestic marketplace by the 1870s. But the next change to toilet design wouldn't be born of cost, it would come from scientific progress.

For two millennia the medical philosophies of the ancient Greek physicians Hippocrates and Galen held that bad smells caused disease. Then, in the mid-1850s, the triumphal cavalry of Germ Theory galloped into the fray, championed by the empirical A-Team of Ignatz Semmelweiss, John Snow, Joseph Lister, Louis Pasteur and Robert Koch. They realised that bacteria, not sinister miasmas, were causing all that frightful cholera, and, thanks to the wide dissemination of their ideas, porcelain toilets quickly became free-standing, cleanable and no longer encased in dirty wooden boxes in which germs could lurk.

The great leap forward came in 1884 when Jennings' company launched the pedestal vase toilet, which was not only freestanding but also included both an S-trap built into the porcelain itself and an overhead cistern plumbed directly into the wall. Best of all, and no doubt to the excitement of male readers, these models also introduced the hinged toilet seat so that men could use them as standing urinals. And – yes, before you ask – it's both reassuring and revolting to discover that, even in the genteel nineteenth century, women complained about their fellas splashing piss all over the bathroom floor. It doesn't matter where you are in history, the human penis just seems to have the wayward aim of Robin Hood suffering from severe conjunctivitis.

While Jennings had undoubtedly been the star in the 1850s, by the 1880s it was Thomas Crapper who had wangled a royal commission as official bog-installer to the British monarchy. There's an American urban myth that he invented the flush toilet, or that his surname was the origin of the scatological synonym 'crap' – both are false – but there is, however, some plausibility to the American phrase 'going to the Crapper' deriving from the fact that his name was stamped on British toilets when US troops were stationed here during the World Wars. The fact that Americans don't say 'I'm just heading to the Shanks' only proves that Crapper is a name that just sounds celestially destined for toilets. The poor chap seems to have been a victim of nominative determinism, though let's not feel too sorry for him as he made a bucketload of cash from it.

Crapper's biggest technological contribution was the syphon valve, which improved upon the stink trap by preventing methane gas from oozing back up the bog pan. This wasn't just to keep bad smells away; methane is also highly combustible and an errant spark from a tobacco pipe while sat on the loo could literally produce explosive diarrhoea. But toilets weren't just functional anymore. By the time Crapper reached his porcelain-wrangling peak, some had become surprisingly elegant, turning the bulky earthenware lumps into gorgeous, sinewy sea-monsters, dolphins or conch shells. Long before Marcel Duchamp tried to convince the art world that a urinal could be art, the Victorians had got there first.

But not everyone was so enamoured of plumbing's popularity. In fact, for decades this race towards mass hygiene, inspired by the Germ Theory revolution, had ironically endangered thousands...

THE ANTI-FLUSH BACKLASH

In 1858, London was struck down by a throat-rasping stench emanating from a solar-heated River Thames. The Houses of Parliament were so afflicted that the curtains inside the building had to be smeared in chloride of lime, just to stop the politicians from gagging. The entire city smelled like a sewage works, but that was only a superficial disaster. The true menace was the spike in lethal cases of cholera and typhoid. Just four years previously, the physician Dr John Snow had gathered statistical evidence to show that a cholera outbreak in Soho had being spread by a pump from which people were drawing their drinking water, but the authorities had dismissed his concerns. Now they regretted their inaction.

What had happened to turn summery London into a sweltering cesspool and harbourer of lethal bacteria? The answer, counter-intuitively, was an increase in personal hygiene; there were now too many middle-class homes with flushing toilets, and all that stinking effluent was being channelled into the city's water supply. Dr Snow had warned of this but the government had stuck its fingers in its ears, stating that a vast overhaul of the sanitation system would be prohibitively costly. But when this so-called Great Stink struck, and politicians suddenly found themselves gasping through handkerchiefs, a whole heap of cash miraculously materialised out of nowhere. Funny that, eh? This budget was hurriedly flung in the direction of the eminent engineer Joseph Bazalgette, who soon began work on his famous intersecting sewer system which to this day forms the crux of London's subterranean sanitation infrastructure.

But reasons of health were not the only concerns raised by opponents of flushing loos. For some, human waste was also an important source of fertiliser, and to wash it away was to squander a useful resource. One of the chief advocates of this early form of eco-friendly recycling was the Reverend Henry Moule, a Dorset-based vicar, whose response to the Great Stink of 1858 was to adapt the old close-stool of medieval kings and turn it into the earth closet. His discovery was that soil, when spread on a bucket of manure, had a neutralising effect on the smell, and his simple invention was widely adopted across Britain, and particularly in its overseas colonies.

These eco-toilets came in two forms. The ash closet adapted the old privy system of dropping the manure into an underground cesspit and then covering it in ashes, but this required emptying four times per year. Alternatively, the pail closet was a smaller version, essentially a bucket under a wooden seat with a sifting filter installed on the side of the device, so that soot or ashes could be poured in over the manure after each toilet trip. Rather than letting the waste sit there for months, this bucket was regularly picked up by the nightsoil men who wandered the cities equipped with specially adapted dustcarts that could carry several of these sealed tubs at once. Just like a milkman, who hands you your milk and takes away the empty bottles, a full tub of crap was handed over by the homeowner and in return a disinfected tub was thrust into their hands.

It was a nice idea, but was much smellier than the flushing water closet and only the most committed of eco-warriors, or those who couldn't afford the plumbing modifications, persisted with them into the twentieth century. Even the innovative chemical toilet of the 1920s, the Elsan closet, emitted a nose-wrinkling odour of formaldehyde and excrement. So, despite various efforts, the flushing lavatory was on an unstoppable path to victory and, though small modifications would improve the water efficiency and bowl-cleansing hygiene, it was Josiah George Jennings' simple, valveless concept which would come to dominate the West in the twentieth century.

ROLL WITH IT

Sitting on our loo, we're soon to wipe our behinds on perforated toilet paper, bought from the shops as hollowed rolls. But where did these come from, other than Tesco? While we know the Chinese were using loo paper in the ninth century, and Lord Chesterfield's friend was using Latin poems in the 1730s, it wasn't until 1857 that New Yorker Joseph Gayetty mass-produced modern loo roll, impregnated with aloe plant extract for hygienic lubrication. The beloved pre-cut perforations followed in the 1870s, and the double-ply strengthening arrived in the 1940s, although the softness of the paper may not have been terribly luxurious, as an advert from the 1930s by the Northern Tissue Company proudly claimed its product was 'splinter free', which, as promises go, strikes me as the bare minimum for a product designed for a bare behind.

But the future doesn't look so bright for loo paper. After millennia of wiping their behinds with *chugi* sticks and squatting over river houses and long drops, in the 1980s the Japanese were introduced to the Washlet, an electronic smart loo which shoots out jets of water to cleanse the arsehole and then directs a gust of warm air to dry off the moisture. This high-tech gadget, a veritable RoboPlop, literally took bottom-wiping out of the user's hands and made loo roll redundant. Given the enormous expanse of forests felled to produce our bum fodder, an environmentally friendly future will likely see the rest of the world following where Japan has led.

But that's enough toilet chat. It's time we moved on with our day so, having wiped our backside, flushed the pan and washed our hands, it's time we did something about those hunger pangs. It's time for breakfast...

A SPOT OF BREAKFAST

We plod clumsily into the kitchen, our tired limbs heavy and stiff, and ponder how best to quell our gurgling belly. The problem is that we're hosting a dinner party tonight, so don't want to ruin our appetite. Perhaps if we just nibble some cereal, then grab a sandwich at 2 o'clock, that might suffice? But, then again, those are some meagre rations and this is meant to be an enjoyable day off. So, new plan! Let's enjoy a hearty breakfast, load up on calories, and then skip lunch instead. After all, the custom of eating thee meals per day only became common in Britain by the late eighteenth century, when artificial lighting began to shove bedtime further around the clock-face.

The Romans, for example, mostly enjoyed just one formal meal per day (*cena*), and merely nibbled on snacks (*prandium*) when they got peckish. Even in the Middle Ages, most English people ate only twice, with breakfast (a fifteenth-century word meaning 'the end of the fast') following morning prayer, and dinner being served around noon. Of course, we might now use 'dinner' to mean the evening meal, and 'lunch' to mean the midday option, but 'lunch' is a very modern concept adopted in the early 1800s, and its linguistic origins are so fiercely debated that if I even try to discuss them, I'll likely get a punch in the face from a disgruntled etymologist.

So, let's swing open the fridge door and see what feast might be possible.

WHAT'S IN THE CUPBOARD?

The earliest refrigerators were invented in the 1870s, and larger houses might have owned one by the turn of the twentieth century, even though they occasionally leaked lethal gases. But many families relied on simple ice boxes until the widespread arrival of the modern electrified kitchen in the 1950s. Now, of course, it's an indispensable technology that most of us just can't live without, but for about 99 per cent of human history people somehow managed to do exactly that. They ate their food fresh, or found ingenious ways to preserve it in salt, vinegars and butter; or they stashed it away in dark larders, buried it underground or crammed it into ice-stuffed sheds to slow the spoiling process.

But, despite all these options, long-term preservation was a perennial problem. A poor harvest, crappy weather or perhaps a beetle infestation was all it took for our ancestors to be cast into the hellish jaws of famine. People in the Middle Ages were cruelly taunted by the so-called 'hungry gap' – a period in which the winter granaries were empty but the new crop was not yet ready. People could die of malnutrition, on a beautiful spring day, within spitting distance of plentiful fields brimming with tantalisingly half-grown food that, in just a few weeks, would have been their salvation.

It's no wonder medieval sources speak of desperate farmers selling their kids in return for food, throwing themselves at the mercy of their feudal masters, surrendering themselves into slavery or just foraging like pigs in the forests. One horrible story recounted by the Anglo-Saxon monk known as the Venerable Bede described how a famine in Sussex led to a desperate scene: 'forty or fifty men, wasted with hunger, would go together to some precipice or to the seashore where in their misery they would join hands and leap into the sea, perishing wretchedly either by the fall or drowning.'

Until very recently, then, the prospect of going hungry when a staple crop failed was a spectre that haunted most of our ancestors. When the fields of maize refused to materialise, the sixteenth-century occupants of Mexico were seen chewing spiders, ant eggs, deer manure and soil, while the blight that caused the Irish Potato Famine of 1844–49 claimed a million lives, and forced another million to emigrate on filthy 'coffin ships' to the USA, giving rise to the infamous Celtic diaspora that – at least in terms of self-identification on official forms – means there are seven times as many Irish-Americans in the USA as there are Irish-Irish in Ireland.

In medieval China there were at least 400 so-called 'famine foods', including tree bark and grassy herbs, but in the 1950s the country was struck by probably the worst famine in human history, as a result of Chairman Mao's cataclysmic Great Leap Forward – a collectivised agricultural policy based on extreme communist ideology that stripped food away from the farmers and handed it to the cities, causing an estimated 35 million people to perish. Tragically, the era of the famine is far from over. Parts of Africa still struggle with drought, and the North Korean crazy-train, driven by the woefully uncharismatic Kim Jong-un, is slowly trundling up the hill towards China's massive death toll, tooting its stupid isolationist horn all the way.

So we should be grateful that this morning there is food to be found inside our fridge and, as we peek inside, we notice a full carton of semi-skimmed milk begging to be opened up and guz-zled. Suddenly, inspiration dawns upon our sleep-addled mind, and a cunning plan begins to ferment... What if, while we're deciding what to have for breakfast, we enjoy a cheeky bowl of cereal, purely as an emergency interim measure to silence our rumbling tummy? As ideas go, it might be the best one we have all day, though I'm willing to concede that it's this kind of logic that's making the world obese.

A NICE BOWL OF CEREAL

The eating of breakfast cereal and the practice of masturbation might usually be assumed to be mutually exclusive activities, unless you've developed some weird Coco Pops fetish, but strangely their history is intimately intertwined. Dr John Harvey Kellogg was a physician from Michigan – a lovely rhyming epithet worthy of a Dr Seuss character – but he spent no time wearing a massive cartoon hat, because he was a serious man with a curative zeal driven not just by concerns for his patients' welfare, but also by a moralistic worldview coloured by the concept of sin. And one sin in particular really pissed him off.

To Kellogg, masturbation wasn't just a single-finger salute to the Almighty; when a person took their own genitals in their hands, they were also taking their life in their hands because, in his mind, self-abuse was the likely cause of 39 medical conditions, including cancer. So, seeing as he was the chief physician at the Battle Creek Sanitarium, Kellogg felt responsible for the wellbeing of its inmates, and, being a vegetarian, believed that a carefully regulated diet could help reduce the animalistic passions that led to all that hazardous self-abuse. He recommended bland meals devoid of taste or spiciness, lots of cereal and half-a-pint of yoghurt squirted up the bum, to keep mind and body worthy of God's good intentions.

Meanwhile, Kellogg's younger brother, Will Keith Kellogg,

had also taken a job at the sanitarium as the bookkeeper, but soon took a side-line interest in John's dietary theories and began helping out in the kitchens. One day in 1894, Will was boiling wheat, intended as an easily digestible bread substitute, when he became distracted. Upon returning to his pans, he found disaster had struck: the wheat had softened into an inedible gloop. Ever the bean-counter, Will figured he'd try to salvage the wasted food, and save a few dollars in the process, by squishing it through large rollers to squeeze out the oozing liquid. It was a bit of a long shot, but surprisingly it produced edible wheat flakes. Hoping they'd got away with it, the brothers decided to serve this odd novelty to their patients, and got an enthusiastic reply. Motivated to improve the recipe, Will began tinkering with other cereals to see if he could build upon this fortuitous accident, and, after much experimentation, he discovered that cornflakes were the superior choice.

Soon, they were manufacturing their flakes not just for the in-patients, but for those middle-class health nuts who'd checked out, gone home to their families and still hankered for it. This, to John, was sufficient, but Will foresaw huge profits in this product. Indeed, the brothers were not the only health-food pioneers and money was already being made elsewhere; Dr James Caleb Jackson had already brought granula breakfast cereal to market, and forced the Kelloggs, via legal threats, to rebrand theirs as granola instead. But this didn't impede the siblings for long, least of all Will.

In 1906, he founded the Battle Creek Toasted Corn Flake Company, and three years later he made a crucial decision to add sugar to the recipe, so as to lure in more punters. This was a betrayal of John's high-minded moral crusade against masturbation, as he believed sugar induced sexy thoughts; indeed, it proved to be a disagreement that shattered their sibling relationship. To John, they may as well have been branded pornflakes. But, sad as the familial rift was, Will was suitably compensated by the Kellogg's cereal empire swiftly growing to dominate the American market, before soon colonising the breakfast tables of Europe as well.

MILKING IT

We open up the cereal box, cram our arm into the packaging, and hunt for the free plastic toy, like a chimp fishing for termites. Triumphant, we place our gift on the table and sprinkle nutritious flakes from the carton into our bowl, then reach for the milk, break the seal and splash the cold, creamy liquid over the top. Yum! Except, it's not remotely yum if you're lactose intolerant, which is a genetic condition shared by a large proportion of the world's population.

I grew up believing that drinking cow's milk was normal, and that those who can't – because it gives them painful flatulence – are the odd ones. But, it turns out that milk-slurpers are the new kids on the block. Our prehistoric ancestors were hunting animals millions of years ago, but it wasn't until the Neolithic era that humans actually consumed their milk. Is it simply that it hadn't occurred to us before? Were we too busy hiding from cave lions? Well, maybe. But in reality it's biology that determined the success of the switchover, not lack of effort. Until about 7,500 years ago, our adult ancestors simply couldn't process the sugary lactose in milk, just as 70 per cent of the world's people can't today. It was only random mutations in the MCM6 gene that produced an enzyme called lactase that stops the uncomfortable build-up of stomach gas.

This handy genetic upgrade meant that, at some point, a European farmer washed down a jug of warm fresh milk, sauntered away and wasn't immediately converted into a methane factory. Delighted at the taste and invigorated by protein, fats and calcium, this person raised their children on animal milk too, and gradually the mutated genes were passed down through the generations and became normalised in European, Indian and African populations – where cow, goat, sheep and horse milk became a regular part of the diet. If we'd coloured in a map of the world to represent dairy consumption in the pre-Columbus era, North and South America would have been totally unshaded until the mass immigration from Europe, and the introduction of African slaves, radically shifted America's genetic makeup.

Famously, Illinois, Minnesota and Wisconsin established themselves as producers of butter and cheese, both of which could be transported safely around the country. But milk was a bigger problem. New York's enormous expansion in the mid-1800s saw demand for milk skyrocket, but it couldn't come from as far away as Minnesota, as it had morphed into rank yoghurt by the time it arrived, so specialist dairy farms were set up on the Eastern Seaboard to ship milk into the metropolis by train. But, even then, all sorts of unappealing techniques were used to preserve it for the journey and improve its appearance, including the addition of water, almonds, animal brains and even formaldehyde – an obnoxious disinfectant more commonly found in funeral parlours. What's more, hygiene standards on these farms were appalling, and until the official sanitation reforms of the early 1900s, bacteria-infested milk was one of the leading causes of urban disease. The catchphrase on the advertising billboards might as well have been lactose-lipped celebs coughing their guts out and muttering 'Got Milk? Then You've Probably Got TB!'

FROM FORAGERS TO FARMERS

So, emergency cereal ration aside, what are we going to cook for our primary morning meal? Many modern societies have their own traditional breakfasts – the Aussies smear vegemite on toast, the French munch croissants, the Israelis delight in olives and cheeses, the Alaskans plump for reindeer and pancakes – but, to me, there's only one defining breakfast of champions, and that's the heart-busting Full English, guaranteed by doctors to shorten your lifespan by a decade. Delicious!

Filled with culinary excitement, we reach into our fridge and pull out some rashers of bacon and a string of herby sausages which will shortly fill our kitchen with the salty aroma of sizzling pig, and by doing this we're continuing a tradition stretching way back into the Stone Age. Humans have eaten meat for millions of years, and at some point between 400,000 and 1.9 million years ago (the debate hasn't quite settled on when, exactly) our ancestors worked out how to control fire and thereby cook their dinners, which in turn better released calorific energy in their food and prompted the development of bigger human brains.

And if it was brains you wanted to grow, then it was brains you needed to eat. Well, sort of... Cavemen feasted on every part of the animal with the undiscerning enthusiasm of feral zombies – offal, meat, squishy grey matter and even the stomach contents were all cooked up and gobbled down – but to do this they had to catch the beasts in the first place, which required a nomadic lifestyle of constant pursuit to track the movement of wandering herds. About 11,000 years ago, however, this million-year tradition began to be gradually phased out in favour of the show-stopping razzmatazz of the Neolithic revolution in agriculture. Though the classic theory is that this sprang up solely in the Fertile Crescent of the Middle East, new archaeological research reveals farming was independently discovered in 11 different regions, including Mexico, North and South America, Africa, East India, East Asia and New Guinea.

We often hear anxious sceptics attacking genetically modified crops because 'it's not a natural way to farm', as if these newer varieties are the product of some Gothic scientist in a windswept castle. Yet 'natural farming' is an oxymoron; farming is a human-made invention and even the crops we think of as organic are themselves the product of our tinkering. Each time you nibble corn on the cob, you're enjoying the selective horticultural meddling of an ancient Mexican farmer who died 3,500 years ago. Nor was it just crops that defined this new age of food production.

The so-called Neolithic Revolution also delivered the first domestication of livestock, meaning that our ancestors no longer had to chase their dinner across the wilderness, but instead could saunter out the front door and pick from the penned-in beasts snuffling around the edges of the village. Pigs were first domesticated in the Middle East around 9,000 years ago. They were particularly easy to rear because they'll eat basically anything, don't require verdant pastures, produce big litters, and gain an extraordinary 2lb in weight every day until they reach adulthood. Other animals required greater effort, but also produced milk and fur/wool in recompense.

Counterintuitively, however, scientific analysis has shown that the increased proximity to all those animals introduced us to a bevy of new diseases, such as measles, mumps, influenza, smallpox, malaria and, worst of all, the blasted common cold – nature's most annoying illness that renders us just fit enough for work, but miserably so. So, if farming made us less robust and increased our risk of catching diseases, why did our ancestors stick with it? After all, the nomadic bushmen of the Kalahari only spend 19 hours per week hunting and gathering, and the rest they dedicate to leisure. If we told them to start growing crops, they'd stare at us in puzzlement and ask 'why bother?'

What, then, maintained the desire for problematic agriculture? The only answer that makes sense to me is the issue of food security – a life spent chasing prey over many miles, and foraging for nuts and berries, must surely have been filled with terrifying dry spells when nothing could be found, and stomachs began to shrivel. Or maybe people just really liked being able to have bacon whenever they wanted? That's certainly what would have earned my vote if I'd been there at that meeting. That, and limitless ice cream. Or even limitless bacon-flavoured ice cream! Actually, maybe not...

HAM AND HARAM

We appear to have veered off on a weird bacon tangent, but let's stick with it because pork is one of those meats with a distinctive cultural heritage. The Egyptians were occasional pig-munchers and, despite the sultry climate, found that curing the ham meant it could be preserved for year-round consumption. This is probably no surprise, after all they were well drilled in preservation techniques, having spent centuries perfecting mummification. In fact, they used the same word for both curing a pig carcass and preparing a corpse for the afterlife, which one hopes never led to any accidental cannibalism when someone mixed up the paperwork.

Similarly, as we roll a couple of sausages into our frying pan, it's worth noting that Romans also enjoyed bacon (they called it *petaso*) served with figs, wine and pepper, and gorged themselves on hot Lucanian pork sausages from southern Italy, seasoned with herbs and cured in the sharp, tangy smoke of the fire. The quality of these could be very good, or they could be little more than organic condoms crammed with guts and eyeballs. This might partially explain why, later on in the fourth century, sausages were thought to be a barbarian food unbefitting a Christian, and so were out-lawed in Roman cities. Another problem with sausage meat is that you never know what animal, or organ, you're chewing on; long before the American hotdog conquered the bleachers of baseball stadia, the great Athenian philosopher Socrates was already deeply suspicious of whether sausages were more pooch than pig.

Pork remained the defining staple meat for many medieval Europeans, including even the rural poor, thanks to the ease with which half-wild tusked pigs could be reared in woodlands. But the availability of this widespread meat didn't stop religious morality from prohibiting its consumption. In medieval Christianity, meat was banned on holy days, during Lent and on Fridays – leaving about half the year during which fish and veggies had to be sub-stituted in (though some cunning monks managed to argue that beaver was a fish because it was vaguely aquatic!). Consequently, on the eve of the 40 days of Lent, English medieval Christians enjoyed a slap-up feast of *collops*, made by frying up any bacon and eggs for a last-ditch cholesterol high before they switched to their restricted diets. This, it seems, is the origins of the English love of bacon and eggs which we are soon to enjoy ourselves.

But, of course, once Lent was done they could get back to nibbling on swine. For Jews and Muslims, however, this was never going to be okay. In Islam, ham is *haram* (a forbidden sin) mirroring the earlier tradition set forth in the Jewish faith that declares pigs to be unclean to eat. Various theories have been advanced as to why this became the case, with the most common being that pork was believed to cause certain diseases, but that seems unlikely given that the Jewish *Kashrut* laws also ban other animals from the dinner table, and the rationale for such prohibition is hard to square with what we know about veterinary epidemiology. For example, a key criteria for Jews is that an animal mustn't be eaten if it has cloven hooves, or chews its grassy cud, unless – curiously enough – it does both of these things, in which case it's perfectly delicious. This was bad news for Israeli cows.

The laws seem far more cultural than medical, and they also ban shellfish, lizards, camels, hares and most insects from the menu, all of which were readily munched by other peoples in the same part of the world, seemingly without much in the way of dangerous repercussions. The only convincing aspect of the health argument is that nothing can be eaten by Jews which has died of natural causes, an entirely sensible precaution that sidesteps the risk of consuming diseased flesh. I'm also told by a friend that road-kill is prohibited, though that's a more modern interpretation rather than a direct scriptural quote – at no point in the Torah or Talmud does it say 'you can't eat a badger squished by a truck.'

YES WE CAN!

As the bacon and sausages sizzle, we reach into our cupboard and pluck out a tin of baked beans, the very definition of comfort food for many an impoverished British student. The can is an airtight tube, sealed at both ends, and though we'll soon chuck the empty container in the recycling bin with barely a flicker of appreciation, this simple technology was once a marvellous revolution in culinary history, and the result of a strange co-operation between enemies.

For millennia, an army had 'marched on its stomach', to quote celebrity Corsican Napoleon Bonaparte, and the logistical puzzle of feeding soldiers and sailors was a head-scratcher to flummox even a chess grand master. How did one supply tens of thousands of men, miles from friendly shores or towns, with sufficient rations to fuel their gruelling demands, when the food itself spoils so quickly that it needs to be replaced every few days? If an army couldn't rely on stripping the nearby countryside of its resources, then what was the solution? In search of an answer, in 1795 the French government embraced crowd-sourcing, and offered a prize to any boffin able to solve the quandary. In 1810, after the prize money had gone uncollected for some 15 years, a cook named Nicholas Appert claimed his 12,000 francs.

The son of an hotelier, Appert had initially trained as a chef but switched to become a confectioner, a trade in which he explored the preservation of fruit in sugary jellies. For a decade he experimented with sealing food in glass jars and then boiling them for different lengths of time, and in 1804 he impressed the French Navy, and then the army, with his invention. By 1809, an official committee was called to sample his preserved foods and found them to be deliciously maggot-free. Appert clearly deserved his prize, which was handed to him on the condition that he published his theory and didn't patent it.

And so, in 1810, *The Art of Preserving All Kinds of Animal and Vegetable Substances for Several Years* appeared in print and Appert became a media darling, flogging his luxurious preserved wares from an elegant Parisian showroom. Tellingly, despite his success, he had no scientific understanding of why his techniques worked. Germ Theory, and the discovery of bacteria, was still 50 years away, and Louis Pasteur – one of the pioneering scientists to discover it – hadn't even been born yet. Appert, the new hero of food storage, had blundered his way to victory. What's more, though hailed as the 'Father of Canning', he hadn't actually invented the can. Indeed, his glass jars sometimes exploded due to the high internal pressure, were prone to fracturing if dropped, and were a bloody nightmare to open, making them less than ideal for warzones.

Instead, it was another Frenchman, Phillipe de Girard, who devised the now familiar tin can. Yet, instead of touting his invention around France, Girard pursued the healthier British market instead, though this wasn't without complications. The two nations were in the midst of the Napoleonic Wars and Britain wasn't exactly rolling out the red carpet to people with thick Gallic accents, so Girard hired an English merchant called Peter Durand to take out the patent on his behalf. But, clearly his invention was of sufficient interest to suppress any xenophobic Frog-bashing from the scientific community, as records show Girard somehow snuck out of France to make regular visits to the Royal Society in London.

Intriguingly, de Girard's involvement ended soon after as his patent was snapped up and put into production by Bryan Donkin, an English engineer, who wowed the Duke of Wellington and the British Admiralty with his long-life canned meats, preserved within the tin jacket. By 1814, these novel tin cans were sailing the high seas and trundling across the battlefields of Europe, to the delight of sailors and soldiers who wrote back to London exclaiming joyfully that their dinners were no longer accessorised with weird-smelling mould. Just five years after Appert had picked up his prize cheque from the French government, Napoleon Bonaparte faced off against the British at the infamous Battle of Waterloo in 1815, where he may have been royally peeved to discover that not only were his adversaries carrying tinned food in their wagon trains, but that a Frenchman had been the one to put them there. So much for patriotism.

Thankfully, our own can of baked beans has one of those new-fangled rings pulls on the top, and doesn't require the dreaded can-opener to be clumsily clamped over the metal lip. Still, at least the thing exists – in a weird quirk of history, the can-opener wasn't invented until 1870, a lengthy 48 years after the can itself. It seems people spent the best part of half a century frustratingly smashing the tins open with hammers and chisels as if they were the furious bone-thumping apes in Kubrick's *2001: A Space Odyssey*.

BEAN ANYWHERE NICE RECENTLY?

In 1477, a recently rediscovered ancient text by the Greek geographer Ptolemy was at last printed in Europe, some 1,300 years after it had been written. This edition came complete with a rather snazzy map of the world, allegedly drawn by a mysterious ancient cartographer named Agathodaimon. This book was one of several ancient works to have re-entered public consciousness via the libraries of the Islamic world, and they lit a fire beneath a lot of European navigators, who were eager to explore the fringes of what was surely a larger world beyond the known horizon. One of these impassioned hopefuls was the self-made, self-interested Genoan named Cristoforo Colombo, who we prefer to name Columbus, if only to avoid confusing him with the raincoat-clad crime-solving genius of Saturday afternoon telly.

Since before even Roman times, Mediterranean merchant captains had been sailing from the port of Alexandria, in northern Egypt, on a south-easterly course to the exotic lands of India, where the locals traded in luxurious spices such as pepper, cinnamon, ginger, cloves, nutmeg, saffron, turmeric and many others. In fact, recent scientific analysis of pot sherds from the Harappan ruins of the Indus Valley has shown that Indians have been enjoying their celebrated rice curries for well over 4,000 years. But, it was the Romans who prized these spices so highly, sending something like 120 ships per year to import this famous 'black gold', though not everyone was a fan. The natural philosopher Pliny the Elder lamented the vast cost of this dangerous import exercise, and angrily muttered: 'pepper has nothing in it that can plead as a recommendation to either fruit or berry, its only desirable quality being a certain pungency; and yet it is for this that we import it all the way from India!'

While it's fun to see an old man whinging about pop culture, even 2,000 years ago, Pliny was in the great minority, and remained so long after his unfortunate volcano-related death, because spices weren't just about the flavours, they were also believed to possess medicinal powers and were a splendid way of showing off. To the very wealthiest, a garnish of spices was like a gold-plated helicopter: an unnecessary extravagance for an already pricey privilege. There's a modern myth that spices were popular in later medieval cookery to cover the taste of rotting meat, but that's like saying Russian caviar might mask the acrid flavours of cheap pot noodles. No one rich enough to ship in spices from halfway around the globe would then skimp on fresh meat and veg.

So, given the demand for India's celebrated export, it's hardly surprising that the publication of Ptolemy's *Geographia* soon had navigators theorising about whether there was a quicker route to the mysterious Indies, and by the late 1480s, Genoa's own Columbus – a resident of a city built on the cash from the Spice Trade – had hatched a plan. Having studied the works of Marco Polo, Ptolemy, Strabo, Marinus of Tyre, al-Farghani, and the recent theories of the Italian astronomer Paolo Toscanelli, he was certain that all he had to do was sail west and he would bump straight into the Indies. After all, the Roman writer Seneca had cheerfully written that it was possible to make such a voyage in just a few days.

Columbus, however, wasn't entirely happy with the measurements passed on from ancient geographers, and so cobbled together his own calculations. This wasn't his best idea and he got almost everything wrong: the size of Eurasia, the circumference of the globe, the fact he later thought he was sailing uphill, and a belief that the world was therefore pear-shaped. When he finally did blunder into Hispaniola and Cuba, his knowledge of Marco Polo's travels convinced him that he was just off the coast of China – a perfectly forgivable mistake – but, unfortunately,

Columbus was also a bit of a self-aggrandising prat, and that's less easy to let slide.

He unfairly claimed the reward for first spotting land (taking credit from a sailor named Rodrigo de Triana), and when he got back to Spain, he grossly exaggerated what he had found, boasting of endless spices and eye-popping riches despite the fact that his glorious bounty, when unloaded from the ships, was actually a ramshackle assemblage of stuff, including tobacco, pineapples, some gold, a few native captives, a turkey and, least impressively of all, a hammock. The gold went down well, but I can't imagine the King and Queen of Spain were particularly enthralled by the suspended seat. Imagine if we sent a team to Mars and they came back with little more than a hovering sofa-bed?

It was all very interesting, but Columbus had set out for spices, and the ones he'd brought back didn't smell like, or look like, any spices from the Indies. In fact, one of the plants he thought was pepper turned out to be the chilli plant – the reason we call it a chilli pepper is due to his error. Not everyone back in Spain was convinced of his grand claims, but the pig-headed Columbus managed to wangle funding for another three voyages, and in the process begat the golden era of Spanish exploration that eventually bankrupted the Spanish economy and inadvertently introduced lethal smallpox to tens of millions of indigenous South Americans.

As a man, Columbus himself is certainly not deserving of heroic status in the USA. He never set foot in North America and pretty much laid the groundwork for the incalculable horrors of the transatlantic slave trade, which just makes the existence of Columbus Day seem like a bad-taste joke. But, if we separate the man from the mission, his accidental discovery of a New World really was the Renaissance equivalent of landing on Mars, and it undoubtedly changed the course of global history, including the story of food.

A Spot of Breakfast

And as we slice open our tin can, inside we find white haricot beans, drizzled in a tomato sauce, seasoned with black pepper and sweetened with sugar – all ingredients with a heritage dating back to the Spanish conquest of the Americas and the subsequent race for New World empires fought between the Dutch, French, British and Portuguese. Fascinatingly, the subsequent spread of South American plants and foods resulted in a global fusion of ingredients so emphatic that we now associate tomatoes with Italian food, rather than that of the Aztecs, and chilli peppers with Indian curry, despite them only being introduced to south Asia in the 1500s.

YOU SAY POTATO . . .

The guards stood defiantly around the edge of the fields, weapons in hand, as the local peasants peered past them, hunting for clues as to what precious luxury might be sprouting from the soil. Their curiosity inflamed, the locals patiently waited for dusk to settle and watched with eager delight as the soldiers abandoned their posts and traipsed to their barracks for the night. With no sentries on duty, these scruffy peasants scurried out into the fields, dug up the crops by moonlight, and ferried them quietly back to their own strips of land for replanting. Whatever aristocratic nosh this was, they were going to sample it first. When news of the dramatic theft reached the owner of the fields, he was delighted. His cunning plan had worked brilliantly.

As we chuck some shredded-potato hash browns into the frying pan, it may not occur to us that the story of the potato is a controversial one, and that the humble spud was once greeted with a mixture of haughty disdain and desperate panic. As with tomatoes, potatoes had been a South American food and the Incas had grown them at altitude, making use of the night frost to freeze-dry the tubers into dehydrated starch, almost like our frozen French fries, and this had allowed potatoes to be a long-life food source to fill the gap when other crops failed. Yet, upon arrival in Europe in the 1570s, the launch of such a nutritious and practical foodstuff was nothing but a spectacular PR disaster.

In 1596, the Swiss botanist Caspar Bauhin named the potato *Solanum tuberosum esculentum*, but provided a scarily dramatic drawing of the plant in his book and accompanied it with scurrilous gossip, suggesting that it caused flatulence, lust and leprosy – a holy trio of embarrassment, guaranteed to ruin any romantic encounter. We're not sure why he decided this, but perhaps he came to this conclusion due to the somewhat lumpen, gnarly shape of his sample potato, which maybe resembled the ravaged limbs of lepers. This awful write-up gave the humble spud the kind of dreaded reputation more recently witnessed with Mad Cow Disease, and despite being widely eaten in Spain and Switzerland, many Europeans soon refused to eat potatoes, even in desperate times of famine.

The owner of those aforementioned ransacked fields was Antoine-Augustin Parmentier, a French food scientist who'd formerly been a prisoner of war and who had been fed by his Prussian captors with a lowly diet of horse food – i.e. potatoes – yet had emerged after three years of captivity in robust health. Clearly, potatoes weren't some ungodly source of horror after all. Determined to prove his theory right, Parmentier began a long campaign to convince scientists, farmers, the French government and the superstitious population that potatoes were a useful alternative to bread, and not some fart-inducing aphrodisiac that made your legs fall off. In 1771, he managed to convince the scientists but still faced stiff opposition, so began plotting his clever series of promotional stunts, including serving potato dishes to celebrities, such as Benjamin Franklin; convincing Marie Antoinette to wear potato flowers in her posies; and fooling the peasants of Neuilly, west of Paris, that his heavily guarded potato crop – grown on 50 acres of sandy wasteland – was a new luxury food not intended for their low-born tummies. The reverse psychology, as we already know, was a triumph.

Parmentier is now celebrated with potato recipes named in his honour, and thanks to his efforts the starchy spud gradually shimmied its way up the nutritional ladder, from horse fodder, to emergency rations in a famine, to staple food source. Yet, tragically, in Ireland this former back-up option, there to plug the gap in times of crop-failure, ended up as the primary foodstuff and such over-reliance proved to be disastrous when the disease-prone tubers suffered a catastrophic blight.

EGGED ON

Breakfast is slowly taking shape and we're just missing a couple of ingredients, so again we pop open the fridge door and this time pluck out a fresh egg. Here in the palm of our hand we have an entirely natural food source, one pre-empting the invention of farming by millions of years, but though our Stone Age ancestors were probably stealing them out of nests, it wasn't until Neolithic farmers domesticated jungle fowl (or chickens, to you and me), in places such as Thailand, China and India, that laying hens could be kept for our purposes. In fact, the earliest definitive proof of egg-farming doesn't really appear until about 1400 BCE in Egypt. But, once we got into the habit, we never looked back.

The Romans were particularly fond of peafowl eggs, the Chinese preferred those of pigeons (choosing to preserve them in ashes and salt), the Greeks liked dainty quail eggs, and the Phoenicians went to town with massive ostrich eggs (which they also decorated as tomb goodies), but basically any sort – from any animal, including alligators and turtles – has been fair game over the centuries. If it was vaguely ovoid, and contained a potential life, our ancestors happily wolfed it down, but they didn't just stuff them into their gobs uncooked. In fact, the way in which eggs were prepared has varied immensely across time and culture.

The Egyptians enjoyed them hard-boiled, soft-boiled, fried, poached, turned into custards or soufflés, and added to breads. There was very little they couldn't do with yolk and albumen, including even using them in pharmacology. Egyptian medicine was highly sophisticated, but occasionally it lapsed into dubious superstition and it was thought that, because ostrich eggs resembled a human skull, they should be prescribed to anyone with a head fracture. By the same logic, we might treat testicular cancer with warm chestnuts, or a broken leg with a baguette.

The Roman food writer Apicius is our source on all things culinary in ancient Italy, and he wrote about a range of egg-based dinners, with this recipe sounding rather familiar to us:

Four eggs in half a pint of milk and an ounce of oil well beaten, to make a fluffy mixture; in a pan put a little oil, and carefully add the egg preparation, without letting it boil. [Place it in the oven to let it rise] and when one side is done flip it onto a platter, [fold it], and pour over honey, sprinkle with pepper and serve.

Something close to this dish remained fashionable in medieval Europe, with shredded herbs providing the flavour instead of honey, and in England this was known as *herbolace* until the French renamed it the *omelette* in the sixteenth century, added ginger to tickle the tastebuds, and bunged in loads of cheese and butter to clog the arteries with heavenly tasting fats.

That said, in medieval England the most common way to enjoy eggs was to roast them in hot ashes, poach them in boiling water or fry them on a skillet with bacon, as we are doing in our kitchen right now. But by the 1600s the famous soft-boiled egg – now so synonymous with a British brekkie – had also started to become a regular fixture on the dining room table, and in 1815 it even made a cameo appearance in Jane Austen's celebrated novel *Emma*, playing the role of the aged hypochondriac Mr Henry Woodhouse. Sorry, that's not right, is it? No, it played the role of soft-boiled egg. My mistake.

OUR DAILY BREAD

With all our varying ingredients on the go, there's just time to bang two slices of bread into the toaster, with which to later mop up the lovely bean juice from our plate.

Bread is one of the most significant inventions in human history, at least in Europe and the Middle East. It was the basic sustenance of the masses, the thing without which society crumbled like an under-baked flapjack. Just to keep the wolf from the door, around 200,000 Roman citizens received a monthly stipend of grain from the state, but this enormous food hand-out – an estimated 8 million kilograms per month – simply couldn't be sourced from the surrounding fields of Italy, and so Rome was always on the lookout for fertile fields to conquer.

Despite what Hollywood would have us believe, it wasn't just Queen Cleo's plunging neckline that lured Julius Caesar and Marc Antony across the Mediterranean. Egypt and North Africa were home to fields of enormous scale, and Rome's expanding population needed feeding. But it wasn't just left up to the state to provide the baking flour to the masses. Whoever controlled grain supply had influence over the people, and the satirist Juvenal was scathing when he claimed the Roman mob demanded only 'bread and circuses', in return for which they would support even the sleaziest of politicians.

Later centuries would see bread even further politicised. In eighteenth-century France, bread production was effectively a public service, and bakers were regulated by the state. Tellingly, in 1787 an average labourer spent half of his daily wage on bread, but two back-to-back years of failed harvest saw prices shoot up 88 per cent by 1789, helping to provoke the eruption of violent revolution. Bread riots also struck America in 1710, 1713, 1837 and 1863, while Vladimir Lenin's call to revolution in Tsarist Russia, the April Theses of 1917, came with the catchy slogan: 'peace, bread, land!'

But from where had this reliance on mass bread production stemmed? Well, as ever, it began with the earliest cities. In the Bronze Age, the invention of more intensive farming techniques, and larger irrigated field systems, meant fewer people were needed to make more food, more quickly. This, in turn, meant other careers could be invented. Where once Neolithic communities had possibly been egalitarian, and everyone had got their hands dirty, the first bread-fuelled cities, such as Uruk, witnessed the separation of the classes and the division of labour into distinct areas of expertise. Because there was enough bread to feed them, many could abandon farming and instead become priests, scholars, cart-builders, brick-makers, potters, doctors, dentists and the rest.

So pivotal was it to life, that bread became a fundamental metaphor for happiness. *The Epic* of Gilgamesh, arguably the oldest recorded story in history, quotes that the God Ea/Enki 'will bring to you a harvest of wealth, in the morning he will let loaves of bread shower down, and in the evening a rain of wheat!' In the real world, this would be an extreme weather event, with TV journalists sheltering under camera trucks as wholemeal rolls slammed into the ground around them, but as a metaphor it's a jubilant celebration of plenty. To have bread falling from the sky was the best thing imaginable.

But, if it wasn't tumbling from the heavenly ovens of nurturing deities, then who was making all this bread? The answer is that Mesopotamians had large civic bakeries churning out the huge quantities needed for soldiers, public servants and other professional types, but we shouldn't get sucked into imagining that bread's invention was purely the product of the Bronze Age; it's not as if the clock struck midnight on the end of the Neolithic era and everyone suddenly blurted out '*I've just had an idea, and it's the best thing since sliced ... er ...*' It might have stimulated the growth of the earliest cities, but it's likely that people had been baking flour in the scorching ashes of the communal hearth for many millennia beforehand.

Despite the faddish claims of the modern Paleo diet, our ancestors were eating grains and cereal crops at least 30,000 years ago, though these were from naturally occurring plants rather than carefully cultivated crops. But during the Neolithic era the most primitive form of baking required the milling of wheat and barley into flour, and this was done with a saddle quern – a tough basalt stone rolled back and forth over the grain, a sort of rolling pin hewn from the side of a volcano. Once the flour had been milled, bread could be made in three ways: it could be flat and raised just by the expansion of internal steam; it could be an organic sourdough, left to grow on its own; or it could be raised by gas-producing yeast borrowed from the beer brewery, which produced the soft, fluffy holes in the crumb.

Generally speaking, the latter of these was for the wealthier customer – flatbreads tended to be the nourishment of the poor – and, in a reversal of modern middle-class tastes, it was white bread which was the luxury food, while the hoi polloi were stuck chewing on brown loaves. The reason for this was simply that to produce white bread half of the brown-coloured bran and meal had to be chucked away, and even then it still came out fairly creamy, so it was a woefully inefficient method of using grain resources. Of course, there's nothing royalty likes more than arrogant wastefulness, which explains why King Henry VIII chowed down on white manchet bread, or what the Romans called *panis siligineus,* while most other diners at his Hampton Court Palace were served tougher, darker cheat rolls.

White bread in the royal courts of France was called *le pain à la mode* (fashionable bread), and contained butter and, sometimes, sugar to give it more of a brioche texture and taste. This inevitably became fashionable in Britain too, where the middle classes – who spent almost all their time and effort attempting to mirror those above them – began yearning for the tempting allure of white bread, even if they couldn't afford the good stuff. This resulted in a dodgy black market of artificially whitened loaves, bleached to the correct shade with the addition of chalk, plaster of Paris, alum or even arsenic. Sadly, this polluted route to paler bread inevitably gave the eater a pallid complexion too, sometimes terminally so, as alum could cause fatal diarrhoea in children. But, we shouldn't think that it was always a case of white bread = posh; brown or flat bread = poor.

Though seventeeth-century European painters used the colour of bread as a visual shorthand to suggest a person's financial status, in the 1700s rye bread was actually thought to be better for the digestion, and so trendy health-enthusiasts muddied the waters by feasting on this lower status loaf; they hoped it would keep them trim and their bowels reliably loose, though not as loose as the unfortunate purchasers of alum-laced bleached loaves. To add yet more confusion, the poor people's lowly flatbreads, including crepes and the Russian blini, were adopted as fun aristocratic delicacies in the early 1800s, and these days we're much more likely to have blini served with expensive smoked salmon and Prosecco than with a thin gruel of mashed turnips.

But our bread this morning is a simple slice of wholemeal, clamped in the electric toaster for a couple of minutes. We're all aware of the phrase 'the best thing since sliced bread' but it's a fairly recent catchphrase, and a probable example of American marketing at its best. After all, the bakery slicer was the brainchild of an Iowan jeweller called Otto Frederick Rohwedder, who began tinkering with the idea in 1912. After pouring his life-savings into the research, and suffering various setbacks, he eventually sold his working prototype to bakeries in 1928. Within just five years, it's thought that 80 per cent of American bakeries were pre-slicing their bread, probably because toasters were increasingly popular. Funnily enough, the greatest thing until sliced bread was apparently pre-wrapped bread, but we only know this because the launch motto for Rohwedder's novelty was: 'the greatest step forward in the baking industry since bread was wrapped'. Don't ask me what the greatest thing was before that ... I have no idea.

Anyway, as our toast pops triumphantly out of the toaster like a stripper bursting from a giant birthday cake, we snatch it up, lay it onto our plate, and begin ladling the other ingredients over the top – first the sausages, then the bacon, then the egg, a dollop of baked beans and then the hash browns. We settle down at the table, switch on the TV for some mindless background entertainment, and tuck into our delicious feast. Admittedly, some of the baked bean juice finds its way onto our chin, and our hair now smells faintly of burned pig, but that's why we invented showers ...

JUMPING IN THE SHOWER

Having gobbled down an early breakfast, it's time we return to the bathroom for a quick wash. Admittedly it's only been 24 hours since last we belted out that Whitney Houston ballad in the shower, but we humans are natural filth sprinklers, unrelentingly pumping out waste like an amoral energy corporation in a dystopian sci-fi novel. We are constantly in need of a good cleansing. Despite our society's current state of über-sanitation, the story of human hygiene is not one of linear progress. This chapter will not read like one of those *Ascent of Man* drawings with a shit-caked bloke on the far left, various increasingly cleansed chaps in the middle, and then us standing in glorious posture at the far right, soap suds on our limbs and a flimsy plastic shower cap perched on our bonce. No, definitions of hygiene varied immensely through the ages.

The reason for this historical see-sawing is that hygiene is, at its most basic core, a war with dirt, and when we think of dirt we imagine children rummaging gleefully in mud and emerging triumphant with blackened fingernails. But, to anthropologists, dirt is merely 'matter out of place'. Ancient Greek philosophers used the term *katharsis* to describe the idea of purging the soul and body of bad stuff, but defining exactly what constitutes the good and the bad has frequently been a question of ever-changing cultural tastes, and there will be definitions of 'clean' in this chapter which will literally make you want to throw down this book and disinfect your whole body with bleach.

So, where should we begin? How about with something unequivocally bad...

LOUSY BEGINNINGS

While it's fun to ponder what life would be like as Tarzan or Mowgli, leaping about in trees, we're just not cut out for jungle loneliness. Much like our distant chimp cousins, who wash in water and smother their bodies in sweet-smelling forest fruits, we are social animals who keep clean for the benefit of others, knowing that they'll expel us from the group if we start to reek of raw sewage. After all, it only takes one filth-monger to spread disease among a whole community. Famously, apes also groom each other's fur, diligently plucking out the unwanted lice and parasites – it's part of an intense socialisation process that may even have spawned the development of human speech, and we still perpetuate such social grooming today. Is it any coincidence that a trip to the hair salon is often sound-tracked by a ceaseless outpouring of gossip about our romantic heartbreaks, holiday plans and the shocking exploits of that bloke off the telly who bonked some pop star in the back of a taxi? There's just something about a fellow human's touch which unleashes our inner chatterbox.

Of course, unless our kids have come home from school and inadvertently catapulted them in our direction we're hopefully lice-free – but our ancestors were much more susceptible. The ancient Egyptians were so bedevilled by head lice that they shaved their heads and wore wigs, but even as recently as in the First

World War soldiers cowering in filthy trenches found themselves utterly covered in hundreds, sometimes even thousands, of body lice which had to be picked off one by one and sizzled on the fire. We can assume with some confidence, then, that Stone Age people were also blighted by tiny unwanted passengers.

Human lice are similar to those that annoy chimps but are better suited to our furless bodies and come in two distinct clans: head lice and pubic lice, the latter of which we acquired from gorillas around 3.3 million years ago. Both of these have clung tenaciously to us for millions of years and pestered every incarnation of the *Homo* species, but, fascinatingly, about 170,000 years ago head lice evolved into a third species specially adapted to a new terrain – fabric. These body lice are thereby useful archaeological timestamps that date the invention of clothing; that's great for archaeologists, but they also carry dangerous diseases, which is less good for humanity at large.

It's likely, then, that our Stone Age predecessors not only groomed themselves, like the soldiers in the First World War, but also bathed regularly. After all, many of the famous Spanish and French caves that boast beautiful prehistoric art are also within walking distance of natural hot springs. We popularly think of cave dwellers as dour types who sat huddled in the dark, glumly chewing lumps of auroch flesh, but it's equally likely they spent their weekends sploshing about in warm geothermal bubbles and giggling gleefully like toddlers in a paddling pool. After all, I would... wouldn't you?

WATER, WATER EVERYWHERE

An extraordinary quirk in humanity's story is the speed at which we transformed ourselves from small packs of nomadic hunter-gatherers into vast societies of city-dwelling sophisticates. It's as if *Homo sapiens* spent 190,000 years chugging slowly up the steep incline of a vertiginous rollercoaster, making only the subtlest of progress – a new hand axe here, a javelin there – and then, out of nowhere, the Ice Age ended and we suddenly found ourselves hurtling with cheek-flapping acceleration towards the Neolithic era, screaming in terror as we corkscrewed through the invention of houses, agriculture and urban planning, all in just 10,000 blisteringly paced years.

But, for all the Neolithic's innovations, it was in the Bronze Age that public sanitation properly began. In modern Pakistan and India, the ancient Harappans were devotees of mass hygiene. Keeping clean was their thing, just as passive aggression and fanatical queuing is Britain's thing. As we've already discovered, underpinning Harappan cities were sprawling sewer systems built of gypsum-coated bricks, comprising a combo of subterranean pipes and roadside gutters that collected the waste water pouring from run-off pipes installed in homes. Even multi-storey dwellings were catered for, as they cleverly housed interior flues running through the walls, or plug holes in the floor, so that water could exit from every level. In the plumbing hall of fame, the Harappans were definitely up there with Mario and Luigi.

Such an elaborate drainage system might lead us to believe the Indus Valley was constantly vanishing beneath torrential downpours of rain, and that these must have been flood defences, but nothing could be further from the truth. Annual rainfall was a measly 13cm, barely enough to drown a poodle. So where was all this water coming from? The answer is from underground. Among the 1000+ settlements in the Indus Valley was the city of Mohenjo-daro which boasted an estimated 700 brick-lined wells, dotted every 35 metres, that produced clean water in limitless quantities for public consumption.

Water was the life-blood of a Harappan settlement, a free-flowing resource elevated to sanctified status. Mohenjo-daro's

Great Bath – a brick-lined indoor pool of 12 x 7 metres, housed in a building of daunting proportions – stood at the peak of the city as a symbolic declaration of water's revered potency. Rather than a communal lido full of shouting kids 'bombing' into the deep end, it may have been a source of ritual purification for more important members of society. Certainly, it wasn't the only washing facility available – the rest of the population washed in rectangular brick-built dipping pools installed across the city.

In comparison to such jaw-dropping infrastructure, the ancient Egyptians in this rare instance are something of a disappointment, but the quality of their historical records makes them worthy of mention. When it came to cleanliness, their priestly caste was particularly careful to avoid the curse of lice infestation by regularly shaving every inch of skin, and washing the body in cold water up to five times per day. To men who inhabited the sacred temples of the revered gods, corporeal purity was every-thing – there was nothing more insulting to the heavenly deities than sporting hirsute limbs more befitting a Halloween werewolf costume.

Today, we wash our hands frequently, and bathe fully probably once a day, but how does that compare to the washing customs of ordinary people in ancient Egypt? It seems they too washed their hands before and after a meal, but there was no running water. Instead, it had to be fetched from the Nile by women who carried the heavy, sloshing vases upon their heads, perhaps returning several times per day to service the needs of the rich who weren't going to jeopardise their elaborate hairdos by doing it themselves. Though water wasn't available at the touch of a button, the rich could smugly show off their en suite bathrooms, featuring waterproof stone floors and shallow run-off channels, which allowed them to strip-wash quickly in the morning and bathe fully at dusk. But more meagre facilities didn't stop the poor from keeping clean either, and even lowly farm labourers had access to rudimentary soap made of animal and vegetable fats with which they could wash in buckets, or down by the Nile while keeping a watchful eye out for hungry crocodiles.

The Indus and Nile Valleys are often justifiably celebrated as cradles of glorious civilisations, but when it came to scraping away the day's grimy sweat there was another Bronze Age culture that was equally keen on a good wash...

CLEAN LIKE A CRETAN

Discovered on the northern coastline of the Mediterranean island of Crete, the huge ruins at Knossos were once a dazzling sight: a massive complex of 1,300 interconnected rooms and buildings that would have induced envy in even the blingiest of Russian oligarchs. Such impressive scale led the site's first excavator, Sir Arthur Evans, to theorise that Knossos was the ceremonial residence of the legendary King Minos, the unfortunate custodian of the man-eating Minotaur lurking at the heart of the famed labyrinth. Evans may well have overstated his case, but it does appear that the grounds were a ceremonial palace for the Minoan people (later named in honour of Minos) and what remains of the buildings tells us they were pretty nifty engineers.

As we enter our modern bathroom we are faced with a choice: have a quick blast in the shower, or run a deep bath and bask luxuriously until our skin wrinkles. You might suspect that the latter is the older technology, and you'd be right, because the ruins of Knossos – the dizzying scale of which may have inspired the labyrinth legend – played host to a beautiful 5ft-long terracotta bathtub, possibly dating to around 1500 BCE. It probably sat alongside pedestal basins in a special bathing room that drained excess water out through a hole in the floor, but that's unfortunately the extent of our knowledge. We might like to imagine an elegant queen soaking in the tub with a mug of red wine in her hand and a lit candle perched on the edge, listening to the Bronze Age equivalent of Lionel Richie's *Greatest Hits,* but there's no evidence to support such a charming fantasy.

Unlike the Egyptians, here there was no need to fetch water by hand. Instead, it was delivered down from the nearby hills by manmade aqueducts, and there's a fair possibility it came in a range of temperatures. Archaeological excavation at Akrotiri – a neighbouring Minoan island settlement, buried by a torrential downpour of volcanic pumice from an erupting Mt Santorini – revealed the locals had installed dual water pipes, suggesting one was for cold water and one for geo-thermally heated spring water. It seems then that although the volcano annihilated the town with devastating airborne savagery, at least it had made prior efforts to be sociable. Crucially, Santorini's explosion probably battered Crete with a terrifying tsunami, but the island didn't vanish beneath the waves like legendary Atlantis; a much more likely culprit for Minoan collapse in the mid-second millennium BCE was a marauding bunch of aggressive Greeks called the Mycenaeans who would soon after besiege the legendary city of Troy.

DID A GREEK REEK?

Being something of a human disaster-magnet who's managed to piss off the vengeful god of the sea, Odysseus is shipwrecked for a second time. Exhausted, naked and bruised, he falls asleep in the secluded safety of some shady trees, but is discovered the following day by a young princess and her handmaidens who've come to the beach to wash their clothes. Quizzed by this royal rescuer, the heroic Odysseus – a mighty king, down on his luck – decides to keep schtum about his identity. Despite looking like he's been in a fight with Mike Tyson, this knackered tramp is offered King Alcinous's hospitality which includes a hot bath in a copper pan heated over burning logs. Odysseus clambers into the tub, is scrubbed and oiled by the princess's maid, and emerges a shining, sexy paragon of masculinity. The princess takes one look at him and thinks 'cor!' – or ancient words to that effect – and, by the end of the dinner, no one is that surprised when Odysseus reveals his regal identity. He may have looked like a hobo on the way in, but a quick scrub in the tub has been the equivalent of Clark Kent taking off his glasses and ripping open his shirt. The transformation from schmuck to superhero is immediate and impressive.

If you don't know already, Odysseus was the legendary protagonist in Homer's epic poem *The Odyssey*, which was the sequel to his blockbusting super-smash, *The Iliad*. (I say 'his', but some scholars doubt Homer's existence. He may have been an invented figurehead, a collective noun for many poetical traditions.) After surviving the ten-year Trojan War, Odysseus is homeward bound but gets disastrously waylaid for another decade by an exhausting conveyor belt of magical islands, terrifying monsters and gratuitous romantic entanglements that make even the ludicrous plot of the TV series *Lost* seem like a haiku scribbled on the back of a napkin. Yet, thanks to Homer's poetic elaboration, we get some fascinating insights into early Greek bathing customs. Despite the obvious potential for eyebrow-raising naughtiness, there's no suggestion that Odysseus being washed by a woman leads to any sexual impropriety. Instead, the simple act of bathing is ascribed transformative power. A guy goes into the tub a dirty, tired mortal but emerges a gleaming demi-god. But there was logic to this: achieving cleanliness was a quasi-religious triumph of purity over the body's filthy nature, and I suspect the Greeks would have rather liked the phrase 'Cleanliness is next to godliness'.

Scrolling forward a few centuries, we arrive at the triumphal peak of Greek civilisation, the Classical era of the mid-fifth century BCE. With the city state of Athens at its powerful zenith, few could expect an oily rubdown from a nubile handmaiden, but it does seem that being washed by another remained customary. But how was this washing happening? Was Odysseus enjoying rare luxury in that hot tub, or could less illustrious buttocks also have been permitted into the warm water? If the ancient ruins of Olynthus – found in the far north of Greece – are anything to go by, then it's very much the latter. Here, archaeologists have discovered that a sizable proportion of homes came equipped with terracotta bathtubs which were probably heated by the kitchen fire, though they weren't designed for full immersion; people sat in them with their legs outstretched, but the water barely came up to their waist.

Those who owned a tub would also have probably possessed a wall-mounted washbasin called a *labrum*, or a tall free-standing pedestal vase called a *louter*. Like the Egyptians with their stripwashes, these were probably used early in the morning and again before dinner to wash the hands, face and necessary zones of pungency. But when it came to a thorough body wash perhaps the most common preference was to head down to the public baths (*balaneion*) made famous in the Classical *polis* of Athens. These were large, rectangular buildings, but their interiors were commonly arranged so that the shallow individual hipbaths, just like those found at Olynthus, were installed in a sociable circle so visitors could natter with their pals while a servant scrubbed them down with *rhymma,* a soap made of fuller's earth or ashes. The hipbaths were the main attraction but they were not the only facilities on offer, as visitors could also stand under a rudimentary shower nozzle with cold water dribbling onto them from a large cistern, or could sweat out their filth in a sweltering steam bath before leaping into the chilly plunge pool for a cool-down session.

In Athens, women and men were forbidden from bathing together, but the fact that all strands of society shared their water was symbolic of civic identity. The inventors of democracy may have been woefully undemocratic when anyone mentioned the rights of women, slaves and the landless poor, but they weren't morally disgusted by the idea of sitting in a bath formerly occupied by someone lowly – there was no such thing as contagious poverty.

Not everyone was so delightfully in love with the relaxed nature of Athenian hygiene. A satirical play by the comic playwright Aristophanes, *The Clouds*, laments the prissy preening of the young men attending the baths, and it's true that there was a certain degree of camp theatricality in these youths exercising nude in public and then washing and oiling their toned physiques afterwards. We might assume this was macho peacocking for passing ladies, but in gender-repressive Athens women were barely permitted to leave their homes, let alone ogle naked dudes. That said, Aristophanes' criticism was mild compared with the outrage of Athens' austere neighbours, the Spartans, whose militaristic society demanded almost impossible levels of stoic ruggedness from men, women and even kids. These warriors, who pretty much wrestled wolves for fun, stared in disgust at any man who dared fill an entire bathtub with water when a modest basin would do. Yet, somewhat hypocritically, these same Spartans were also famous for fastidiously combing their hair before battle – an oddly effete ritual for such rugged blokes.

Of course, if I asked you to tell me a famous Greek-in-the-bath story, you'd probably recount the tale of Archimedes who suddenly realised how to measure the volume of a gold crown through water displacement when he lowered his ageing body into the public baths on his native island of Sicily. His excited shriek of '*Eureka!*' ('I have found it!') has gone down in history as the ultimate declaration of discovery, but it's said that he also ran naked through the streets in delight, a proud tradition sadly ignored by modern scientists. Alas, Archimedes' passion for science was also his downfall. Having put up something of a one-man defence against an invading Roman fleet, by building various ingenious gadgets to hold them at bay, the Greek geek was unable to stop the conquest of the city and ended up being horribly stabbed by a Roman soldier sent to arrest him. I mention this because, according to the writer Plutarch, the Romans had actually planned to capture Archimedes alive and make use of his magnificent brain. They were more than happy to exploit Greek ideas for their own ends, and the *balaneion* was no exception.

A DIP IN THE ROMAN BATHS

Like those of the Greeks, Roman baths (*thermae*) also used the *hypocaust*. This was an under-floor heating system in which, between stacked pillars, super-heated steam billowed from slave-manned furnaces and wafted upwards to heat the rooms and pools above. Such elaborate plumbing meant that most baths provided a range of temperatures, but the crucial thing about the *thermae* was that absolutely everyone was welcome, though not necessarily at the same time. Traditionally, men and women bathed separately, although – unlike Athenians – they were allowed to share the same building. Ladies, slaves and servants tended to be morning visitors, while male citizens sauntered along in the afternoon for a long, leisurely dip.

There was no hard and fast rule about how the baths were to be used, but commonly the visitor would first enter the exercise courtyard (*palaestra)* where they would exert themselves in sport until sweaty and puffing for breath, which in my case would have taken about eight seconds. Then they'd have walked through to the changing room (*apodyterium)* and hired a slave to guard their toga from thieves – or else they'd shamefully walk home naked that evening – before stepping into the main atrium of the baths.

From here they might move through zones of increasing temperature, beginning with the chilly plunge pool (*frigidarium*) and followed by the gentle warmth of a room called the *tepidarium*. The next stage was to get sweaty, so some bathhouses featured a sauna (*sudatoria*), but more common was to take a dip in the *caldarium* – a room with a hot pool – in which a slave masseur might also oil them up and scrape the dirt from their body with an iron *strigil*. Cool water splashed from nearby basins closed up the bather's pores, and then they went out into a dry resting room called the *laconium* to end the process. I probably don't need to point out that our five-minute shower is a bit quicker than a full Roman dip.

These days we tend to be private in our washing habits, closing the bathroom door to shut out even our closest family members, but the Romans were a communal bunch and were happy to let it all hang out. Bathers were surrounded by hundreds of naked people and, as well as being hygienic cleaning stations, the *thermae* also functioned as a social hub where people could gossip with pals, network with business partners, or even just sulk in the corner and enjoy some quiet introspection. Going to the baths was the ancient equivalent of combining a gym session with a swim, a spa treatment and a friendly natter in a café, but with the added bonus of flopping genitals.

Given that these were communal buildings provided for the benefit of the masses, there was an obvious prestige to sponsoring such a public gift and a few bathhouses were truly astonishing in scale, to better glorify their generous patrons. The Baths of Caracalla, built in the early third century, could comfortably house 1,600 people and even the main bathhouse alone, which sat in the centre of a vast complex, was twice the length and width of a modern football pitch. They also included two lavishly decorated libraries for Greek and Latin texts, which brings a whole new meaning to reading in the bath.

Such a huge structure reveals how integral bathing was in Roman society. In many ways it defined Roman identity – everywhere the Empire went, baths followed. Though Caracalla's Baths were a grand engineering feat, elsewhere the scale didn't matter so much as the intent: hygiene was integral to the civilising process, and was the advertising campaign that lured terrifying, uncouth barbarians into dropping their axes and opting into the Roman way of life. But just because access to water was an essential right for every citizen and slave doesn't mean it was distributed equally. In the first century, water flowed into Rome via aqueducts and was divided up hierarchically – 10 per cent to the emperor, 40 per cent to those wealthy enough to pay their water taxes, and the remaining 50 per cent to communal facilities of baths, troughs and fountains. This meant that the poor did not have running water in their homes and had to traipse out into the streets to get it, though they didn't have to walk far: at its peak, Rome had around 900 bathhouses to choose from.

NEXT TO GODLINESS . . .

As a young boy, Bindeshwar Pathak's natural curiosity got the better of him. Standing close-by was an 'untouchable' – a person from the lowest rung of India's caste system, believed to be born innately dirty – and the youngster, who would one day become a leading sociologist and sanitation campaigner, couldn't help but touch this intriguing outsider. Though his flesh didn't melt like that of the Nazi villain in *Raiders of the Lost Ark*, nevertheless he was now polluted. Horrified to learn what he'd done, Pathak's grandmother forced him to take a ritual bath to cleanse his body from contamination. But the bath was not like our own. His cure was to gargle the urine and excrement from a cow . . .

In Hinduism the cow is a sacred animal so, despite scientific evidence to the contrary, its waste products are hallowed. It may seem strange that the antidote to merely touching a fellow human was seemingly much, much filthier, but that's the curious thing about cleanliness – it's a cultural construct. If we go back to the ancient Holy Land, the ancient Israelites spilled *hatat* blood from a sacrificed animal to purge a sanctuary and cleanse holy altars of impurities, yet this did not mean that *all* blood was 'clean'. A Jewish woman could not have sex until she had waited seven days after the end of her period, and had purified herself in a sacred bathtub called a *Mikveh*, which was also used as a baptismal font for new converts or to disinfect utensils or crockery purchased from non-Jews, like some sort of holy dishwasher.

The *Mikveh* is just one cultural example of how washing could have a potent cleansing effect upon not just the body but also the soul. In fact, the cleansing power of water is central to almost all the major world religions, bar one. The pagan ancient Greeks washed their hands before prayer and their bodies before marriage, Hindus bathe in the sacred Ganges to shed their impurities, Buddhism and Shintoism also declare water as integral to cleanliness, and so does Islam. But Christianity? Not so much...

Christianity began its meteoric rise from minor cult to official state religion in a period when public bathing was, as we've heard, integral to the Roman Empire, but early Christian thinkers found it decadent. Initially, their opposition to it began rather gently. Clement of Alexandria, a second-century moderate, opined that there were four reasons to attend a bath – pleasure, warmth, health and cleanliness. Of these, he declared that only the latter two were permissible for Christians. He thought it was all right to wash, provided you didn't enjoy it, and you didn't stare at all the hot nudies, but the talismanic St Jerome wasn't standing for any of that. Living mostly in the fourth century, he was alive to see the Roman Empire wobbling on the verge of collapse, and would have been delighted to imagine the famous baths falling into disrepair.

In his eyes, warm water excited lust in the loins, and encouraged virgins to shame themselves, but – even more than that – he saw no justification for any Christian to publicly bathe at all. His catchy maxim for men: 'he who has bathed in Christ needs not a second bath' was mirrored by the advice of his friend, St Paula of Bethlehem, given to female virgins: 'a clean body and a clean dress mean an unclean soul.' As odd as it seems to us, to be clean was to commit the sins of pride and vanity. St Jerome's writings, particularly his translation of the Bible into Latin, were hugely influential in early Christianity, but so was his withdrawal from public life. Ascetics tried to emulate Christ in the desert, turning existence into a spiritual battle against even the most basic of comforts. Some withdrew so completely from society that they barely saw another face.

The outright champion of such solitude was surely St Simeon Stylites the Elder who became so infuriated by newbie Christians quizzing him about their faith that he chose to live for 37 years balanced atop a tiny platform, some 15 metres off the ground, like some archaic precursor to David Blaine. But most ascetics were more likely to end up in monasteries, where codes of conduct were drawn up to regulate behaviour, including washing arrangements. St Benedict, founder of the Benedictine order, permitted occasional washing – 'Let the baths be allowed to the sick as often as necessary; but baths should only be rarely allowed to the healthy, and especially to the young'. However, most of his monks were likely to enjoy a full dip only at the holy periods of Easter, Christmas and Pentecost. For the rest of the time, a small basin of cold water sufficed.

This practice of acquiring sacred filth was known as *alousia,* but while it became the ultimate gesture of holiness for Christians, Muslims found it a disgusting habit. The Prophet Muhammad had declared cleanliness as 'one half of faith', so the rituals of washing became crucial to the daily life of all Muslims, beginning with the *wudhu* ablutions, performed prior to the five daily prayers, that cleansed the hands, mouth, nose, face, right arm, left arm, hair, ears, right foot and then left foot. This elaborate protocol was, and still is, also deployed after visits to the toilet, or any unhygienic discharge of bodily fluids, such as a bleeding cut. But Islam's greatest contribution to hygiene was to extend the Roman tradition of public bathing with their glorious *hammams*, or what are more commonly now known as Turkish steam baths.

Here the more immersive full bath – *ghusl* – could be completed, thereby restoring purity to the body after sex, menstruation or any of the other major causes of impurity. Even a thousand years ago, Baghdad was claimed by medieval chroniclers to have 60,000 baths. This was surely an enormous exaggeration, yet it shows how pivotal good hygiene was to everyday Islamic society. As with the Greeks and Romans, religious custom dictated that men and women bathed separately, and so did Jews and Muslims, but the Islamic faith also strictly prohibited public nudity, so the licentiousness, so despised by St Jerome, was not revived. That restriction aside, however, all were welcomed to bathe, and children and servants paid no entry fees, ensuring the general population was universally clean.

GETTING STEAMY

This morning we've elected to enjoy a brisk shower instead of the long bath, and as we step under the hot spray the soap foams on our limbs and the heat gradually awakens our snooze-dulled mind, readying us for the day ahead. But if we'd wanted even more oppressive heat – the kind that makes your hair stick to your face like it's been glued on by a naughty child – then we could have popped out to the gym and sat in a sauna, and in doing so we would have been following an archaic custom.

We already know *hammams* made good use of steam, and still do all over the world, but the Vikings of the chilly north were also ardent sauna lovers. We're very used to their popular depiction as filthy barbarians – intent on raping, pillaging, and setting fire to stuff for no good reason – but Vikings were actually fastidious neat freaks intent on raping, pillaging and setting fire to stuff for no good reason. Males were said to set aside each Saturday (which they named *Laudag*, or 'washing day') for a good sprucing, a custom that Saxon men found really weird and Saxon women rather liked, for more obvious reasons. The merchants and mercenaries of the Swedish *Rus* – who wandered through Russia, and reached Constantinople – were even more scrubbed, being said by the Islamic emissary Ibn Fadlan to have had their face and hair washed for them daily by servant girls.

The Vikings were the first Europeans to discover North America, five centuries before Columbus stumbled into the history books, but they spent most of their brief stay in Newfoundland fighting with the neighbours rather than documenting their lifestyles. If only they'd made friends rather than enemies, they might have seen that these indigenous peoples were also big fans of a therapeutic sweating session. Indeed, according to the seventeenth-century Dutch traveller David De Vries, the Algonquian tribes of the Atlantic coast used sweat baths (*pesa-punck)* to purify their bodies of sickness, dirt and impurity. De Vries described this sweat lodge as a small wooden oven, covered in clay and built near lakes and rivers so that the people inside could rush out of the heat and fling themselves into the cooling water, which doesn't sound so dissimilar to the Roman practice of leaping into the *frigidarium*.

In a charming, and less violent, sequel to the medieval encounter between Vikings and American Natives, two ships full of

Finnish and Swedish settlers turned up in the Delaware River valley in 1638. Although their vessels and houses were not pre-assembled in flat-pack form, they were decent enough to conform to at least one Scandinavian stereotype. Their native neighbours were greatly cheered to witness the building of a sauna, happily declaring that these newcomers were also 'sweat lodge men' like them. Meanwhile, on the other side of the world, another set of European merchants – the Dutch – were regular visitors to Japan, where the culture also prizes cleanliness, and these travellers discovered that the island's inhabitants made full use of their volcanic inheritance by frequently bathing in hot springs called *onsen,* or public baths called *sento.*

So, next time you visit a sauna, remember that you're partaking in an ancient and intercontinental tradition.

CLEANSED CRUSADERS

What do you think were the key tenets of being a medieval knight? Athleticism, courage, fine horsemanship? Yup, yup and yup. What else? Well, knights had to be deeply religious yet not remotely bothered by the prospect of stabbing a fellow human in the face, which is hard but, apparently, manageable. They also needed a willingness to fight for their king, no matter the cause, and were supposed to uphold the virtues of honesty, civility and charity towards the vulnerable, which they probably found trickier than the ultraviolence. Oh, and one last thing... they probably needed clean testicles.

After many centuries of celebrating religious filth in monasteries, and tolerating civic stench on peasants and lords alike, something rather surprising happened in the West during the twelfth century. While a controversial period in Christian history, the Crusades to reclaim the Holy Land from Islamic control had the unwitting effect of introducing thousands of unwashed soldiers to the benefits of not smelling like a dead dog rotting in a ditch. Suddenly, *hammams* seemed like quite a good idea after all, and knights in particular took note. They were bound together by the Chivalric Code, which placed a great emphasis on the romantic treatment of women, so it wasn't long before courtly literature started rejecting grim, grimy *alousia* in favour of noble cleanliness – unwashed hands, nail dirt, sweaty armpits and pungent genitals were suddenly deemed inappropriate for a first date.

Of course, it wasn't just the guys getting intimate hygiene hints. *The Trotula*, a medieval compendium of feminine medicine allegedly compiled by an Italian female physician, advised well-bred women on all manner of grooming, including how to deal with their odorous vaginas and pubic lice, recommending that their downstairs parts be washed in scented astringent and treated with a mixture of ashes and oil. Knights and ladies cleaning their naughty bits was obviously a step in the right direction, but what of the malodorous masses toiling in the fields and towns? Well, their noxious aroma was also becoming something of a hot-button issue. Thomas Aquinas, the brilliant thirteenth-century theologian, was a strong advocate of mirroring the Middle Eastern custom of using purgative incense. It was a sweet smelling metaphor for God's divine grace – a reminder of the heavenly paradise awaiting well-behaved mortals – but it also went some way to fumigating the gathered church congregation that inevitably reeked like the arse-end of a warthog.

So, what was the solution to the problem of the poo-smeared poor? Baths, of course! In a rejection of St Jerome's militant ban, medieval versions of the Islamic *hammam* soon sprung up across Christian Europe. However, these baths were not used every day and numbered far fewer than in Baghdad – there were only 26 in Paris by the 1290s – suggesting that a good number of the lower classes probably didn't see much in the way of soap for months at a time. But what baths lacked in capacity they made up for with nudity. Retaining much of the leisurely reputation of the ancient *thermae,* English bathhouses acquired the naughty nickname 'stews' which almost instantly connoted sexual impropriety. This was perhaps inevitable given that mixed bathing was permitted. In truth, it wasn't all sordid kinkiness as wealthy couples could share a romantic meal in a hot tub, while the medieval equivalent of a mariachi band serenaded them, but if that sounds rather innocent, it doesn't quite tell the whole story...

Though these married women were supposed to protect their modesty with veils, single men may well have enjoyed more than just bubbles when being scrubbed down by the unmarried bath girls, many of whom were reputedly willing to do more than wash a chap's stinky pits. The Italian humanist scholar, Gian Francesco Poggio Bracciolini, noted in his travels that the baths of Baden, in Germany, were very liberal in their morality: 'If pleasure can make a man happy, this place is certainly possessed of every requisite for the promotion of felicity.' Moralists were outraged to discover that in Germany and Switzerland full frontal nudity was the accepted norm for bathers of both genders, who were barely kept separate at all. So, while it's hard to know just what level of debauchery went on in stews, we can assume there was enough to warrant a drama series on HBO in which women wander around topless for no reason whatsoever – which is basically all HBO dramas, isn't it?

Baths had already fallen out of favour once, and then – like an ageing rock band lured out of retirement – had enjoyed a triumphant comeback. But, the revival was to be brief. When the Black Death swept mercilessly through Europe in the 1340s, annihilating something like 30 per cent of the continental population, fear of contagion led to the strict suppression of communal bathing. Not long after, even private washing would be chucked out with the bathwater, as a new trend rolled into town.

THE AGE OF LINEN

In the sixteenth century Queen Elizabeth I of England installed an opulent steam bath in her palace, and famously declared that she bathed every month, probably during menstruation, whether she 'needed it or not' – a somewhat redundant phrase by modern standards. Not to be outdone, her cousin, Mary Queen of Scots, also erected a bath house at Holyrood Palace, but her standards of hygiene were not passed onto her son, King James VI, who came to the throne as an infant when she was booted out of Scotland for having unbelievably terrible taste in men. And I mean really, really bad: her first husband died of an ear infection, her second brutally murdered her private secretary, and her third hubby likely murdered her second...

Though it would be another 20 years before Mary's head was hacked from her body on Elizabeth's orders, in her maternal absence the young James had already developed some less-than-charming habits. By the time he added King of England to his already impressive CV in 1603, he had completely abandoned washing his body in favour of gingerly rubbing his fingers in a bowl of water. This wasn't a personal quirk but was a response to novel medical advice coupled with the promotion in Europe of a certain wonder-fabric: linen. At the beginning of the seventeenth century, when James was doing his best to not be terminally exploded by the Catholic conspirator Guy Fawkes, French thinkers were claiming that baths were needless because linen was a cleaner, better alternative to washing. The practicality was simple – change your outer layer regularly and there would be no need to wash beneath it.

But the popularity of this clothing revolution was also boosted by a strange new belief that made washing sound more dangerous than roller-skating into oncoming traffic. Scientific thinkers began proclaiming that the skin's job was to protect the body by producing vital secretions to block up the pores and stop nasty stuff getting in. Clearly, stepping into a bath of water rubbed away this layer of protective sheen and could therefore cause dizziness, sickness, and muscles to loosen themselves into slack uselessness. It was even feared that pregnant women might prematurely give birth if they took a dip, as if the womb might catastrophically relax, allowing the foetus to slide out and dangle between her knees like a tiny bungee-jumper swinging from an umbilical cord.

To prevent such bizarre tragedy, an eminent English polymath developed a complex safety bath. Francis Bacon, who would later suffer one of history's strangest deaths when he caught hyper-thermia by stuffing a chicken with snow, conjured up a curious 26-hour bathing process that treated humans like a garden fence in need of creosoting. Here's a brief run through his extraordinary technique, in case you want to try it at home:

1. Rub the bather in oil.
2. Wrap them in a waxed cloth impregnated with resin, myrrh, pomander and saffron.
3. Bathe them for two hours while they wear this protective garb.
4. Empty the bathwater, but make sure they keep the cloth on for a further 24 hours.
5. Does the skin feel hard, and the pores closed? Good! Proceed to the next step.
6. Now remove the cloth and coat the skin in oil, saffron and salt.
7. Congratulations, you have waterproofed your first human!

It sounds less like preventative medicine and more like an elaborate recipe for marinating an oven-baked chicken, but hot bathing wasn't entirely banned. It could sometimes be prescribed by anxious doctors in need of a cure when other remedies had failed, but was viewed as a highly risky procedure. Before patients could do anything as dangerous as sitting in a warm tub of water, their bodies were prepared with vomitous purging and colonic enemas, and only then were they permitted to wash themselves under careful medical monitoring. Considering that they had just leaked foul fluids from both ends, a bath was surely necessary anyway.

In 1610, King Henry IV of France sent for his finance minister, the Duc de Sully, but the messenger arrived to find the minister wallowing in a bathtub. Hearing this worrying news, the king was seized with panic and ordered Sully not to leave his house under any circumstances – such was Sully's vulnerability, the King would wait. I can't imagine any modern political leaders cancelling a cabinet meeting every time a minister takes a shower, but it highlights the genuine fear in the seventeenth century of water's potential treachery. With baths off the agenda, the French in particular took the linen revolution to heart, proudly ignoring the hygienic progress of their forebears. Henry IV's son, King Louis XIII, followed in dad's bath-shunning footsteps and proclaimed triumphantly 'I take after my father, I smell of armpits'. The illustrious King Louis XIV agreed to install baths at Versailles, but was reluctant to take them himself, while his sister-in-law, the Princess Palatine, felt it significant enough to record in her diary that she'd been forced to wash her face in water after a dusty carriage journey.

But it wasn't just the French aristocracy who let themselves develop a thick crust of dirt. The English toff Lady Mary Wortley Montagu was almost heroically filthy, with hair that was visibly lank and greasy. When someone was brave enough to comment on her dirty hands she rather wonderfully retorted: 'What would you say if you saw my feet?' She was clearly a sharp conversationalist, and famously introduced an early form of smallpox inoculation to Britain, so we should rightly applaud her brassy confidence. But, saying that, you probably wouldn't have wanted to share a carriage with her on a hot summer's day.

WHEN HOT WATER WAS COOL

So, if kings and queens smelled of body odour mixed with perfume, and recoiled in horror at the prospect of washing their faces, why are we so keen to bathe our bodies and scrub our hands today? Well, the see-saw tipped back the other way in the eighteenth century when a tag-teaming duo of new ideas arrived to demystify this curious cult of dirt. Firstly, the old theory about sealing up the pores was chucked out. Medical experts began explaining that rather than being vulnerable flaws in the human system – the body's own Death Star weak spot, vulnerable to Luke Skywalker's proton torpedo – pores were actually little valves that filtered good and bad air, so it was crucial to keep them unclogged.

Allied to this scientific rethink was a new attitude towards cold water that saw philosophers like John Locke, and the physician Sir John Floyer, promoting the value of river swimming, claiming that a 'cold regimen' invigorated the body and hardened it to life's many knocks. This also chimed rather nicely with the burgeoning naturalism espoused by Jean-Jacques Rousseau and the radical English Methodists – one of whom, John Wesley, popularised the phrase 'cleanliness is next to godliness'. Water was a key part of the natural world, so how could it possibly be a bad thing?

Having been first a useful aid to washing, then a fearful threat to human health, water was now labelled as a therapeutic cure. It became popular for the wealthy to visit the seaside and splosh about in the waves, or to drink from natural springs in such places as my hometown, Royal Tunbridge Wells. Medical tourism became a boom economy, and water was a miracle product. But most importantly, it wasn't just cold water that got the green light. Napoleon Bonaparte frequently plotted the conquest of Europe while soaking languorously in his own private tub of warmed water, probably due to the influence of European colonial expansion into Africa, Asia and the Middle East, which was once again reminding people of the joys of *hammams*. Indeed, the notoriously filthy Lady Mary Wortley Montagu was fascinated by Turkish baths when she travelled abroad, while the Indian entrepreneur Sake Dean Mahomet brought traditional Indian *champu* head massages and vapour baths to Regency Britain, becoming 'shampooing surgeon' to King George IV.

So, hot water was cool again, and – after an absence of more than two millennia – the Greek and Minoan domestic bathtub could now return to the home where, soon, a specialist room would be required to house it.

THE VICTORIAN BATHROOM

In 1851, Charles Dickens, already extraordinarily famous, was forced to move house after his lease expired quicker than he'd expected. Annoyed at the inconvenience, he decided that he would move into a grand new home in London's Tavistock Square and transform it into his ideal abode. But he found the slow renovation process hugely frustrating, as revealed by the increasingly desperate letters he wrote to his brother-in-law, Henry Austin, who was overseeing the work: 'P.S. NO WORKMEN ON THE PREMISES! Ha! Ha! Ha! I am laughing maniacally.' Every room was to receive a makeover, and in one of his most fascinating letters to Austin, Dickens attached 'an elegant drawing' of his ideal shower-bath, writing: 'I don't care for the possibility of a Tepid shower. But what I want is, a Cold Shower of the best quality, always charged to an unlimited extent, so that I have but to pull the string, and take any shower of cold water I choose.'

Cleanliness was important to the neurotic writer, but he was also a firm believer in the healing powers of the cold-water regimen. Dickens, you see, had recently attended the Malvern 'clinic' of Dr James Gully whose hydrotherapy techniques involved wrapping high-profile celebrities in wet blankets and dunking them in chilly baths until their chronic health conditions improved. So, eager to stay clean, and determined to shock his body into prime condition with daily Arctic blasts, Dickens figured he'd reconstruct the clinic in his own house.

The famed novelist was wealthy, but he wasn't the only person to be investing in sanitary plumbing. In imitation of regal tub-lovers like Napoleon and Josephine, by the mid-nineteenth century the newly affluent middle classes began installing portable tin or wooden bathtubs in their tasteful homes. At first these squatted obtrusively in the corners of bedrooms, but, as Dickens discovered, it soon became possible to create bespoke new rooms given over entirely to hygiene. These 'bathrooms' were bedecked with all-in-one shower/bath units, sink basins with hot and cold taps, and toilets – all fed centrally from a water cistern. Sounding familiar yet?

In truth, not all of these glamorous mod cons were entirely practical at first. While Dickens' shower (nicknamed The Demon) was permanently plumbed in, the first modern shower had arrived in 1767, having been designed by William Feetham, and featured a pump to draw the water up to a tub, suspended over the bather's head, which could be upturned with the simple yank of a chain. Surprisingly, such early models were sometimes portable and could be wheeled about, so users had to take care in locking its position or else find themselves careening naked down the corridors on what was essentially a moistened skateboard. Other curious contraptions included personal steam baths – indoor sauna-boxes that encased the entire body apart from the head, like a sort of steampunk torso sarcophagus.

But surely the most baffling invention was the Victorian *velo-douche,* a pedal-powered shower unit attached to a bicycle that paradoxically demanded the user get sweaty in order to get clean, as the shower only gushed water when you started pedalling. But apparently this wasn't necessarily a problem for the Victorian homeowner. *The Habits of Good Society: A Handbook for Ladies and Gentlemen* recommended that the average man do ten minutes naked exercise immediately after a bath, with the explicit purpose of sweating profusely. Curious, I gave this a go myself, but my wife's reaction to my post-exercise perspiration was a wrinkled nose and an instruction that I 'go and have another shower!'

Dickens loved bracingly cold water, but the greatest innovation for middle-class bathers was the ability to heat their water automatically, without the need for servants to drag buckets from fireplace to tub, yet it didn't come without its perils. The water could be heated from below by igniting a gas stove under the tub, but if it was too small then the bath took ages to heat, and if it was too big, then there were serious dangers of over-boiling. Indeed, many cases of agonising, even fatal, scalding were attributed to people clambering into baths that were hot enough to poach an egg. If this wasn't risky enough, the gas could also prove deadly. Benjamin Waddy Maughan, a painter by trade, invented the geyser in 1868. This device passed small jets of cold water through super-heated gas, thereby producing a torrent of instantaneously hot water. It was a fine idea, but leaking gas could make the device explode.

A more common fix for sending hot water to multiple rooms was to install a large downstairs boiler heated by the kitchen fire. Again, this was hugely dangerous – something of a recurrent theme in nineteenth-century domestic appliances – as the 'tank system' positioned the water reservoir in the roof, instead of next to the boiler. This could result in high-pressure steam building up in the flow pipes, which then literally blew the boiler to smithereens, flattening the house in the process. If that happened, you didn't need a plumber, you needed a funeral director. But, the deaths were clearly too few and far between to dissuade the ever-growing tide of people choosing to wash themselves at home, and soon a new industry was born – one designed to flog us a never-ending supply of bathroom products.

THE HARD SELL OF SOFT SOAP

Having washed our hair, and bellowed the heartfelt lyrics to *I Will Survive*, we reach for the fruit-scented body wash and lather it on to our skin, sluicing away the dirt and replacing it with the extracted essence of guava. This, on the face of it, is a very modern way to wash. Since the Bronze Age, most people had scrubbed themselves with little more than water and herbs, or soap made of ashes and animal fats. Indeed, in the ancient Mediterranean, the word 'soap' referred to a type of Celtic hair dye, and the Romans and Greeks instead preferred to oil themselves, and scrape off the residue, rather than smear the skin in burned ash and tallow. The hard soap cake made from olive oil was a medieval Islamic invention, and entered Europe through Moorish Spain, which is how it became known as Castile soap.

Yet this remained a luxury item from the twelfth century until the massive industrialisation of the nineteenth century finally allowed for commercial products to be churned out cheaply. At London's Great Exhibition in 1851 soaps abounded in huge number and some were even gently perfumed, an enticing novelty at the time. Worryingly, some contained bleaching chemicals like arsenic and lead, to whiten the skin to a ghostly shade of alabaster, but the medal-winning Pears Soap was much less abrasive, being made from glycerine and natural oils, and is still to this day said to be the oldest continuously marketed brand in British history, having been founded in 1789 by a hairdresser named Andrew Pears.

The lengthy catalogue of exhibited soaps at the Great Exhibition attests to a sharp-elbowed rivalry between producers which was already simmering by 1851, but in 1898 a high-quality soap – which now floated, due to a fortuitous manufacturing accident – made from a combination of palm and olive oil, was introduced to the market and lit a fire beneath that rivalry. Its brand name was Palmolive and it immediately sold like hot cakes (or is that soap cakes?), kick-starting a ferocious soap war between corporations, as everyone realised there was a goldmine to be plundered from the Victorian obsession with cleanliness.

Looking to expand their range of products, these companies soon began targeting chronic sweaters who needed a solution to their pongy pits, with early deodorants appearing on the market in the 1880s. But these worked in a very simplistic way by trying to shut up the pores with wax, a bit like Francis Bacon's bizarre safety bath, and the real breakthrough only came in 1907 when a surgeon invented his own chemical deodorant based on aluminium chloride. Having dubbed it Odorono (as in 'odour, oh no!'), he allowed his daughter, a shrewd young woman named Edina Murphey, to market the product exclusively to ladies. It was messy to apply, often staining clothing, and sales were sluggish because it was marketed as a temporary medical cure. Determined to boost sales, Murphey hired a young copywriter called James Young to convince women they needed Odorono in their lives. In 1919, Young brilliantly exploited our dread of social embarrassment, suggesting to the advert's readers that they were probably being secretly shunned for their sweaty armpits.

It was a brutal campaign, one of the earliest deployments of paranoia pressure in marketing, and magazines that carried the ads reported female subscribers cancelling their subscriptions in disgust at the emotional blackmail. Yet, Odorono's sales soared and soon many other adverts began flogging miracle cures to anxious women, but none with catchphrases as marvellously monstrous as Odorono's 1926 slogan: 'the ugly half-moon stain under her arms means a woman just doesn't belong', and 1934's image of a woman rubbing her pits, allied with the headline 'the woman nobody wants to be!' Such advertising was as subtle as a brick smashed over the head, but it worked a treat.

As the twentieth century progressed, the 'hard sell' increased in its impact, and epic battles over customer loyalty broke out between brands. The most obvious repercussion was the naming of the televisual 'soap opera' in honour of the pervasive dominance of soap adverts broadcast during these popular shows, but a more subtle result was a dramatic shift in human behaviour towards not just cleanliness, but artificial sensory identity. Whereas once we had smelled of sweat and dirt – the insufferable stench of urban humanity, or even just of smug French kings – these days our hands give off the gentle waft of lavender and our hair smells of jojoba and coconut essences. Our bodies have become billboards for beauty products, to the point that it's easy to forget what we naturally smell like beneath the creams, scrubs, moisturisers, deodorants and shampoos.

Every time my wife emerges from the shower she smells like Willy Wonka accidentally built a chocolate factory in the middle of a tropical rainforest; it's a blend of cocoa-buttered skin and citrus-infused shampoo. It makes me slightly dizzy, and also weirdly hungry. The irony is, I suppose, that washing our bodies in water and then smearing our skin in a bodily mask of sweet-smelling fruits and plant extracts is exactly how wild chimpanzees mask their bodily odour. Millions of years may have passed, but it seems we're still just animals at heart.

Oh, and speaking of animals...

WALKING THE DOG

We're nicely scrubbed, have hurriedly flung on some clothes, and are en route to the lounge when a drooling fur-ball bounds up to us, its tail wagging and eyes glistening. We stare into the begging face and realise that, despite our dog's lack of speech, he's basically saying 'May I remind you that there are damp tennis balls to retrieve, and some idiot – I'm not naming any names – has locked the front door?' Annoyingly, he has a point. It's not just a new day for us: our pets also have their own routines.

PETS: WHY BOTHER?

To be blunt, owning a pet is a pretty illogical thing to do. They're constantly hungry, their medical care is often pricier than our own, they need plenty of supervision, they'll ruin your furniture, they're always trying to shag stuff, they're monosyllabically in-articulate and you can't even eat them – they're basically human teenagers. In fact, even the English word 'pet' referred to a spoiled child in the sixteenth century, being a probable abbreviation of the French word *petit* (little one).

There's plenty of scientific and psychological evidence to suggest our bond with animals can be a powerfully parental one. Some people really do love their pet as they would a child, and this is only further exemplified by the reports from early anthropologists who observed indigenous women from Guyana and Australia breastfeeding baby mammals, including monkeys and deer, in order to nurse them to strength when their own mothers couldn't. Similarly, St Veronica Giuliani, an eighteenth-century Catholic mystic, used to breastfeed a 'lamb of god' as a rather literal demonstration of her faith, and in Europe the reverse principle applied well into the twentieth century, with impoverished human children going full 'Romulus and Remus' by suckling from a goat or donkey in order to receive their necessary calcium and fat intake.

Humans nursing animals is a pretty extraordinary thing to witness, I imagine, but it shouldn't really be so unexpected. The Nobel-Prize-winning zoologist Konrad Lorenz argued that all baby vertebrates share uniformly 'cute' physical traits – soft bodies, big eyes, oversized heads, endearingly clumsy move-ment – and we're suckers for this Disney-esque physiology. We project our genetic drive to nurture our own young onto similarly proportioned creatures, which perhaps explains why the internet is essentially just a digital shrine for kittens.

But when did animals stop being food and starting being friends? As ever, the answer lies in the Stone Age.

IT'S BAD MANNERS TO EAT YOUR FRIENDS

It's thought that the emergence of *Homo sapiens* in the Stone Age contributed to the extinction of about 85 per cent of large land animals (*megafauna*), including giant sloths, giant wombats, giant beavers, giant kangaroos and... er, mammoth-sized mammoths.

So why, if we were busily wiping out anything with a heartbeat, did our cave-dwelling ancestors decide to spare some animals to keep as pets? The likely answer is that canines were indeed our earliest companions, probably due to their dual abilities to hunt and act as danger-spotting sentinels. A skull found in Belgium's Goyet Cave has been scientifically dated to 31,700 years ago, and DNA analysis suggests this animal was the product of a deliberate breeding program – it wasn't a wolf, so it must have been Dog v.1.0.

As we slip our feet into some trainers, fetch the leash from the rear porch and swing open the front door, our loyal hound bounds off in pursuit of passing cars. Worried he's about to get run over, we shout 'Stay!' and those powerful limbs come to an immediate halt. Our dog may be disappointed with our censorious rules, but he's still going to abide by them. This is actually pretty astonishing; somehow our ancestors invented an animal willing to obey our orders. But how? It wasn't a case of shouting 'roll over, play dead' at a fully grown wolf – that's a recipe for getting your throat savaged. A new theory suggests wolves essentially domesticated themselves, by snacking on leftover food from human camps, but the traditional theory is that our ancestors grabbed very young wolf cubs and socialised them into the human tribe before breeding them with another equally 'tamed' wolf. By constantly selecting the least aggressive breeding pairs, the genetic offspring would have been less instinctually prone to slaughtering everything in sight, and after many generations the howling wolf would have evolved into the barking dog, able and willing to communicate with humans, fetch slippers and harass postal workers.

Surprisingly, it may not have taken long to produce this transformation, as evolution can move pretty rapidly if given a firm shove. In 1959 the Russian scientist Dmitri Belyaev showed that after just ten generations of experimentation with feral foxes, his tamed breeds weren't just less aggressive, they had biologically altered in both appearance and reproductive cycle. It seems the process of selecting for personality traits accidentally selects for physical ones too.

PET CEMETERY

Sad as it is to imagine, one day our beloved pooch will pass away and we may feel compelled to bury him in our back garden. This might seem a tremendously modern custom, but nothing could be further from the truth. At Uyun al-Hammam in Jordan, in a grave dating back 16,500 years, a man's skeleton has been found deliberately buried alongside fox remains, with both his corpse and that of the fox having been posthumously relocated from another grave. Was there a special connection between person and animal? Was the fox a pet? It does seem that way, or why else would both bodies be so carefully moved? If so, clearly Belyaev wasn't the first to tame foxes.

More tellingly, dogs were also given respectful burials in the Stone Age, not only alongside their human masters, but individually too – presumably because dogs live shorter lives than their owners. This act of burial suggests a close symbiotic relationship between human and animal. If the dog had merely been functionally useful in life, but un-mourned for in death, might we not have expected it to have been eaten for dinner or chucked in a ditch for the vultures to snack upon?

MAN'S BEST FRIEND

The panicked animal strained at its chains, desperately tugging at the post to which it was tied, but there was no escape. The sky was thick with black smoke and hot pumice was raining down.

The whimpering animal's master was nowhere to be seen, a victim perhaps of the noxious gas settling from the mountainside, and so the dog barked and barked for someone else to release it from its shackles. But no one came. A thermal blast-wave of 500 degrees centigrade blew through the town, killing every living thing in its path, and within hours the corpses and buildings had vanished beneath 22 metres of volcanic ash.

Today a tragic plaster cast of this Pompeian dog, curled despairingly around the post, remains as a reminder of Mount Vesuvius's devastating eruption in 79 CE. But it's not the only canine to be found in the excavated ruins of Herculaneum and Pompeii, for there's a beautifully preserved floor mosaic depicting a large black hound, held by a leash, with its teeth bared threateningly and its legs fringed with long dark fur. For the Romans, as with many other societies, the dog was a familiar presence. We know, for example, that it played a key role on Roman farms – the agriculturally minded writer, Lucius Junius Moderatus Columella, advised that sheepdogs should be aggressive 'to pick quarrels and to fight', and preferably white, so they weren't mistaken for wolves in the dim light of the dawn and therefore killed.

We're out in the park playing fetch when some nefarious mugger leaps out from a bush to snatch a nearby lady's handbag. If we'd been throwing a Frisbee for our pet cat, then its response to the assault would likely have been to stare with bored disdain, but our dog leaps into action, charging at the ne'er-do-well with snarling teeth and a piercing bark, and, alarmed at the inbound Exocet of teeth heading his way, the criminal drops the bag and flees in terror.

Whether it's scientifically true or not, we perceive dogs to be steadfastly loyal, and protective of the vulnerable. This is nothing new. Medieval stories told of how dogs would refuse to budge from their dead master's corpse, and in rare instances their 'testimony' was even permitted in the resulting murder trials.

More recently, it's been reported that Adolf Hitler patronised an animal-training school in the Second World War, in the hope that hounds could be trained to speak, count and spy upon the enemy. This proved a slightly over-optimistic wish – the most notable achievement was one dog's ability to bark 'Herr Hitler' when asked 'Who is the Führer?' though, in all likelihood, it probably sounded more like... well, basically, a dog barking.

Not all dogs in the past were working animals required to snap at intruders' ankles, herd livestock, or spy on the enemy. Ancient Egyptian tomb illustrations from Beni Hasan depict several species of hunting canines: racy greyhounds, ferocious mastiffs, stumpy-legged quasi-dachshunds and what look like slender, bushy-tailed foxes – all of which presumably had physical characteristics ideally suited to their varying purposes. But that's not to say our ancestors didn't also own useless pooches for whom an energetic afternoon involved pootling from one cushion to another. Roman aristocratic women were particularly fond of furry little snuffle-moppets that nestled in their bosom like sleeping babes, the classical equivalent of the pampered lapdog peeping out from the Hollywood handbag.

The fact that we've bonded so closely with our dogs is perhaps because we have to spend so much time caring for them. But when we wash them, or take them to the vet, we're walking in the footsteps (and paw-prints) of many dog owners before us. European aristocrats kept their hunting hounds in top condition, as depicted in a French medieval illumination in *The Book of the Hunt*, where we are shown men cleaning dogs' paws, grooming them with a brush, laying out their straw bed and checking their teeth – these were certainly not low-maintenance mongrels fed on scraps and banished to windy sheds. Still, it's not as if the aristocrats were the ones getting their hands dirty, and you wouldn't have seen a mud-covered Earl struggling to keep an excitable puppy in the bathtub.

The variety of roles given to medieval English dogs is attested by John Caius in his 1570 tract, *De Canibus Britannicus*. As well as the ferocious *mastive*, one might also encounter the door-guarding *dogge keeper*, the dog *messenger*, the lunar-barking *mooner*, the water drawer who turned well-wheels, the *tynckers curre* which carried a bucket on its back; the barking *warner* that yapped at anyone approaching, the *turnspete* walking on a tread-wheel to turn the kitchen spits and, most enjoyably of all, the *daunser* which performed to music. Such an array of hounds required an array of names, and in the early 1400s Edward, Duke of York suggested 1,100 possibilities in his book, *The Master of Game*. There are too many to mention here, but I rather like Nosewise, Swepestake and Smylefeste, though I pity the poor pooch that ended up being called Nameless. Charmingly, a century later, Anne Boleyn – Henry VIII's ill-fated second Queen – had a favourite canine companion called Purkoy, apparently because it had a ceaselessly quizzical expression, and 'why?' translated to *purkoy* in medieval French.

One notable dog-lover, who tellingly had no kids, was George Washington. The names he gave his numerous hounds were equally varied, including Sweet Lips, Truelove, Tipsy and Drunkard, which sound more like profile names on a dating website for slightly desperate singles. Washington was the typical eighteenth-century gentleman, obsessed with hunting and fascinated with animal husbandry. He had many breeds scurrying about his Mount Vernon estate, including spaniels, sheepdogs, terriers, Newfoundlands and Dalmations – one of which was called Madame Moose, for reasons I wish I understood. He also created his own American foxhound breed by partnering up his English foxhounds with some French foxhounds sent to him by the Marquis de Lafayette to produce 'a superior dog, one that had speed, sense and brains'. I too am the product of an Anglo-French breeding programme, and was a fast runner in my youth, but I don't think I'd qualify for the 'sense' bit, seeing as I once drove a ride-on lawnmower into a pond. True story.

FELINE FRIENDS

If dogs are a man's best friend, then cats are his adolescent child that lazes about the house, wanders off on a whim and only shows interest when it wants something. There's some debate as to whether we even domesticated cats, or whether they domesticated themselves. The earliest evidence for their being welcomed into our lives is at Shillourokambos in Cyprus, a Neolithic site dating to about 9,500 years ago. Here a cat was found buried only a few inches from a human male, which, as with the aforementioned canine burials, suggests the body was treated with certain care. Though it was young, possibly only eight months old, the cat's bones were much longer than those of a modern moggy, meaning its ancestry was probably wild, because domesticated animals tend to be dinkier.

Presumably this cat, or its recent ancestors, had sauntered into the camp one day, slaughtered a few mice, received an affectionate stroke from the grateful farmers, and realised it was onto a good thing. By lurking around human settlements, and munching on the rodents lured in by the grain silos, cats accidentally became pets. Though there are five species of wildcat in the world, all domestic moggies are descended from African Wildcats (*Felis silvestris lybica*) – the type discovered at Shillourokambos – so the housecat is directly related to that cunning kitty from 9,500 years ago, which explains why they wander next door for a second dinner when we're not looking.

Though the internet has made us unhealthily obsessed with kittens, it was the Egyptians who truly worshipped cats, burying their mummified moggies in the sacred city of Bubastis, and mourning each loss by shaving their eyebrows. Because cats were symbolic of the goddess Bastet, killing one warranted a death sentence: the Greek writer Diodorus Siculus described how a Roman soldier accidentally ran one over with his chariot and was fatally lynched by an angry mob. Such was the Egyptian cat reverence that the Persian ruler Cambyses II allegedly instructed his soldiers to carry cats into the Battle of Pelusium, knowing that the enemy Egyptians would be morally prevented from shooting their arrows into the midst of all the innocently mewing kitties.

In Hinduism and Islam, cats were vastly preferred to dogs due to their fussy cleanliness, and they were occasionally tolerated in medieval Christendom because they were expert mousers. In Geoffrey Chaucer's *The Miller's Tale*, a character drops to his knees to peek through a door: 'an hole he foond, full owe upon a bord, Ther as the cat was wont in for to crepe'. This is one of our earliest references to a cat-flap, and there's a slightly later real example to be enjoyed at Chetham Library, built in Manchester, England in 1421. The seventeenth-century cat-flap in the door to the belltower in England's Exeter Cathedral was used by the cat that was introduced there to hunt the blasted rodents nibbling on the bell-ropes and is thought to have inspired the nursery rhyme that begins 'Hickory, dickory, dock, the mouse ran up the clock'.

But many medieval people disliked cats intensely. The German abbess Hildegard of Bingen thought they were furry mercenaries (fur-cenaries?) loyal only to those who fed them, while other writers commonly associated them with feminine sexuality and prostitution. Cats were also scapegoats whenever plague broke out, or a witch-hunting craze erupted, as they were associated with demonology and heresy. The Cathars – a persecuted medieval cult from southern Europe that espoused the duality of twin gods (one good, one evil) – were accused of kissing a feline's puckered arsehole as part of their religious rituals. This was an extension of the Kiss of Shame *(osculum infame)*, where witches were alleged to greet the Devil by snogging his exposed arse, and Satan was thought to often take the form of a black cat.

Though feral dogs were commonly whipped or drowned on St Luke's Day, cats were treated far worse. On any day of the year an unfortunate moggy might be roasted on a spit (as happened in Ely Cathedral in 1643), hung from a pole, skinned, tortured or drowned. On one gruesome occasion in 1677, English Protestants stuffed live cats into the belly of a burning effigy of the Pope, so as to give the impression that the Pontiff – who they clearly didn't like very much – was screaming in agony as he burned to death.

In a superstitious era when science and reason went hand in hand with biblical rhetoric, cats were also witches' familiars – demonic animals not to be trusted – and earned this reputation because they enjoyed toying with their prey, as did Satan himself. Perhaps it was for this reason that the people of France took an almost sadistic delight in capturing cats in nets and lobbing them onto mass bonfires held on the Midsummer solstice. King Louis XIV even had the honour of igniting the Parisian pyre in 1648, before spending the evening dancing and feasting as the living creatures were scorched to a horrific death for the delight of the crowd.

But despite being routinely purged in the Middle Ages, cats clung on and became increasingly popular house pets. Isaac Newton was said to have been fond of his feline companions, and – though they were often described as womanly pets in America – the celebrated writer Mark Twain was a definite ailurophile whose moggies were cheerfully named with such lovable monikers as Sour Mash, Apollonaris, Lazy, Abner, Famine, Fraulein, Buffalo Bill and Cleveland. He and George Washington had a lot in common, it seems.

DO ALL DOGS GO TO HEAVEN?

Why were animals treated with such thoughtless cruelty? Though people have always loved their own pets, Christian theology dictated that animals were not sentient creatures with souls. Aristotle's Great Chain of Being had plonked gods and then men atop the natural hierarchy, and placed animals (and women – Aristotle was something of a biological misogynist) purely in the service of man. St Augustine of Hippo had agreed with this, saying 'thou shalt not kill' didn't apply to 'irrational living things', seeing as 'it is by a very just ordinance by the Creator that their life and death is subordinated to our use'.

Jumping on the bandwagon, Bartholomeus Anglicus wrote in his *De Proprietibus Rerum* that all animals had a purpose: deer and cattle were for eating; horses, donkeys, oxen and camels for helping; peacocks, monkeys and songbirds for amusement; bears, lions and snakes to remind us of the power of God; and lice and fleas were to remind humanity of its fragile mortality. So, if animals were useful but unthinking creatures, did they have souls? It was a problematic question.

Certainly, many medieval saints, including St Francis of Assisi, were famed for protecting animals, seeing them as part of God's creation. But the thirteenth-century theologian Thomas Aquinas was happy to follow Aristotle's lead in declaring that animals had vegetative and sensitive souls, which gave them the powers of biological growth, memory, emotion and sensation, but that they did not have mankind's rational soul. Yet, despite these intellectual heavyweights admitting that animals were more than just inert lumps of flesh, the concept of their existence being for our benefit went unchallenged until the French writer and philosopher Michel de Montaigne arrived on the scene in the 1570s.

Montaigne was an intriguing chap, a supremely well educated

125

courtier to the king, and a key bureaucrat in regional government, who decided, aged 37, to jack it all in and spend a decade living in a tower, surrounded by books, like some scholarly wizard from a fairy tale. Here he scribbled his famous *Essays*, brilliantly readable ponderings on grand themes, filtered through anecdotal experiences, and when it came to discussing animals, Montaigne relied on his own beloved pets for insight. Famously he wondered if when he was playing with his cat, his cat was actually playing with him – a genuinely revolutionary thought that pre-supposed a cat's agile intellect – and he also pondered whether his pets could dream, or communicate between themselves. Montaigne didn't know it, but he was setting forth the philosophical underpinnings of Disney's *The Aristocats,* though it's unlikely he foresaw the possibility of a trumpet-tooting, scat-singing, feline jazz band.

Montaigne's musings are much closer to our modern views of assigning personalities to our pets, but they wouldn't hold sway for long. Unlike Aquinas, who took the Aristotelian view of the soul and body being inseparably intermingled, the seventeenth-century philosopher René Descartes – the bloke who wrote 'I think, therefore I am' – was a dualist who stated that the mind and body were separate, and therefore animals didn't even possess consciousness, because they don't even compensate for their lack of speech, like deaf humans do, with sign language. For him, dogs might howl if you kicked them, but they were just fleshy automata programmed to do so by a pragmatic god.

PAMPERED PETS

It was the hottest ticket in all of India, the celebrity wedding that would be more spectacular than Lady Gaga wrestling a unicorn in the Grand Canyon. The groom arrived by train, decked out in a glorious cummerbund and gold necklace, to be greeted by a guard of honour, a full military band, and 250 guests sporting golden brocade. There was even an elephant parading up and down. As the lucky groom entered the marriage hall to wait for his bride he was greeted by some of the most important politicians and royals in all of India. Then the Maharaja of Junagadh, Nawab Sir Mahabet Khan Rasul Khan, arrived with the bride by his side, her jewels gleaming as she walked up the aisle to tie the knot. This magnificent 1922 wedding had a budget of £22,000, which in modern money is about £1,000,000. Was it worth it? Well, it depends on how you feel about dogs...

Yes, the Maharaja was something of an animal lover, who owned 800 dogs – each with its own room, servant and private telephone – and, for fun, he frequently dressed them in doggy-sized evening jackets and had them driven around the city in rickshaws. But even by his standards, marrying off his dog Rashanara to a golden retriever called Bobby, in front of India's premium celebs, and a huge entourage of his other pets, was quite a bold move. These days we commonly spoil our pets with all manner of silly accoutrements, and as we re-enter the house, kick off our shoes and pack away the Frisbee, our slobbering hound – fresh from his outdoor escapades – settles down in his basket to chew on one of his vibrantly coloured toys, a Christmas gift from us. But if you think this is a modern trend, inspired by bored Hollywood celebs with nothing better to do, you'd be wrong. It wasn't just the Maharaja who went slightly overboard with his pooch pampering.

Privileged pets at the Chinese imperial court had a heritage extending back to 1000 BCE, when special dog-feeders called *chancien* were tasked with caring for the royal dogs. It wasn't an entirely unbroken line of canine aristocracy, though, as dogs were evicted from the palace in favour of cats during the Ming Dynasty (1368–1644), but, when the Manchus returned, Pekingese dogs were once again elevated to the status of princes, with some puppies even being breastfed by human wet nurses. Such imperial pooches were also bathed and perfumed, and even their turds were the subject of a ritual ceremony which, to modern eyes, would be more befitting of the birth of a royal baby.

Pet pampering was common among the wealthy in Europe as well. Mary Queen of Scots dressed her dogs in blue velvet suits, while the eccentric English politician John Mytton (who rode his pet bear around his living room) furnished his cats with cute little uniforms. Isabeau of Bavaria – the wife of Charles VI of France – was often seen with her pet squirrel which sported a custom-made collar sewn with pearls and gold filigree, and she also kept exotic birds in silver cages, draped with green velvet cloth, and used the same fabric to line the comfy-cushioned bed for her cats.

It's understandable why so much attention was lavished on posh pets, as the pressure of being a royal could be a painfully lonely experience. From a very young age, the political importance of continuing the lineage sometimes meant heirs and heiresses were packed off to distant houses to be raised by distant relatives, or virtually quarantined against the outside world for fear of contracting some awful disease. Sometimes the simplest way to soften the cold luxury of such a childhood was to trust in the loyal companionship of pets. A young prince could even learn to ride at only three years old by being mounted on the back of a hunting dog and having it scamper about the courtyard with him clinging on. Even better, as a boy, the future Louis XIII of France harnessed two of his pet dogs to a miniature carriage and had them pull him around the palace in what sounds like a thrilling cross between a husky sled and go-kart.

In the hurly-burly of realpolitik, queens could be equally as neglected as their children, particularly if an arranged marriage had forcibly united two individuals in a passionless union. Elizabeth of Bohemia, the daughter of King James I of England (and

VI of Scotland), surrounded herself with an entourage of 16 or 17 dogs and monkeys, and was said to vastly prefer their company to that of her own kids or hubby. Of course, some royals just loved animals. Charles II of England and Scotland was a spaniel-obsessive who even had a breed named in his honour, though his courtiers weren't always as keen on the tiny yapping fur-balls, and one exclaimed 'God save your majesty, but God damn your dogs'. On at least one occasion, the King found himself grumpily posting a notice in a newspaper demanding the return of one of his pet pooches which had been villainously dognapped! One wonders if that same grumpy courtier might have been on the suspects list.

Queen Victoria was equally devoted to dogs and was particularly keen on her Dachshund called Dachel – a gift from German relations in Coburg – which was an exceptional rat-destroyer, despite its big brown eyes and floppy-eared cuteness. Other than chewing on rodents and waddling around the palace looking adorable, such diminutive lapdogs might appear to have been almost entirely useless, but they could have their special talents. The medieval Dukes of Burgundy pioneered the food-tasting, poison-detecting *chiens-goûteurs*, a line of work with some delicious perks for a loyal puppy, provided the king wasn't unpopular. The fearful King Henry III of France carried three fluffy Bichon Frises around with him, suspended in a basket hung around his neck, and they were trained to bark at anyone they didn't trust. Sadly, he was still murdered – fooled by the assassin's monkish disguise.

During the English Civil Wars, Prince Rupert of the Rhine also had a much beloved dog with an unusual talent, though it would be hard to classify it as a lifesaving skill. Apparently, his pet poodle, Boye, was trained to cock his leg and urinate on cue whenever the name of the enemy commander, Pym, was spoken. Boye was also popularly rumoured to possess sinister magical powers but, for me, an evil dog needs to be some sort of slobbering Rottweiler, or a ghostly Hound of the Baskervilles, not a pissing poodle – honestly, it's like they weren't even trying! Still, if you were looking to impress your friends and enemies, an allegedly demonic poodle wasn't much cop compared with having panthers, cheetahs and lions sauntering about your palace looking murderous. The twentieth-century Abyssinian Emperor Haile Selassie was brave enough to enjoy exactly this, undoubtedly leaving visitors to mutter desperate prayers that the prowling predators had been well fed that morning.

But, that's enough pet chat. Our trusty dog has already nabbed too much of our morning, and it's time we checked our emails. Who knows, perhaps there's a Nigerian prince offering us millions of pounds if we would only be so kind as to send him our bank details? Let's hope so!

KEEPING IN TOUCH

With the morning's necessities completed, it's time we engage in a bit of Saturday leisure. After all, it's been a long week at work and we could do with a few hours of cheerful idling to recharge the proverbial batteries. With nothing scheduled until our friends join us for dinner and drinks, let's kick back and engage with the wider world. And so we fire up our gadgets – we switch on the telly, unlock our smart phone, log in to our laptops and open up our digital tablets – and welcome in a tsunami of information.

HANGING ON THE TELEPHONE

While happily scrolling through photos of other people's lunches, we're suddenly startled by a ringtone piercing the silence. Glancing at the name on the screen, we smile in recognition and lift the phone up to our face. A familiar voice chirps into our ear, swiftly pursued by its own tinny echo – a latent ping from a satellite 22,236 miles above the Equator – but neither of us stops to consider the practicalities of Space Age techno-wizardry; not when we'd much rather gossip about our mutual friend who changes girlfriends more than we change our pants.

Ours is the age of the mobile phone, with more SIM cards in existence than humans on the planet, and we've adapted so swiftly to its essential, portable genius that modern children are utterly bemused by my teenage tales of phoning up my mates on their parents' landlines and agreeing in advance to meet at a certain time and place – apparently, this sounds like some archaic fable from the murky Middle Ages, rather than 1999. And while a phone attached to a plastic cord appears rather quaint to youngsters, for the rest of us it's been an ever-present technology in our homes and offices. But there was once a time, back in the late nineteenth century, when the telephone was just an idea percolating in the brains of two brilliant rivals.

Alexander Graham Bell was a Scottish-born inventor whose lifelong obsession with communication technology stemmed from his mother's deafness, and his desire to help those like her. Yet, after having moved to Boston and aiding deaf people with their inter-social skills, Bell found himself tinkering with a totally new contraption – the electrical speech machine. Having joined forces with a talented electrical engineer, Thomas Watson, their device for sending sound frequencies through an electrical wire was re-volutionary, but it wasn't unique; in 1876, Bell unknowingly found himself in a desperately tight race, complete with photo finish, when he submitted his patent application just two hours before his rival.

Elisha Gray had not enjoyed the easiest start in life. Raised on an Ohio farm, his father's untimely death had forced him out of school early, and he'd stumbled into an unfulfilling career as a carpenter, boat-builder and blacksmith. Basically, he was good with his hands. But, aged 22, Gray instead decided to tax his brain by enrolling at Oberlin College to study physical sciences, specialising in electricity. Though undoubtedly handy with a hammer, it was soon evident that electrical engineering was his true métier and he swiftly conjured up prototypes for various gadgets. Crucially, on Valentine's Day 1876, he submitted a caveat – a confidential placeholder for a yet-to-be perfected design – detailing his plans for a telephone. Had he filed it the day before, he'd now be world famous, but his submission was added to the clerk's in-tray on the same day as Bell's, who has since been accused of benefiting from a dash of legal chicanery to ensure his patent was seen first. In the race between these two jostling geniuses, the umpire – or rather the law courts required to arbitrate between them – called the photo finish for the Scotsman, even though recent experiments have proved Gray's was the superior design. The conspiracy theory appears to have merit.

As the official victor, Bell had little time to break out the bubbly and party. Instead, he was soon swatting away a swarm of copyright-infringers, all of whom were intent on nicking his idea, and the biggest of his 600-odd legal cases came early. Soon after his breakthrough, and struggling for cash, legend tells that he'd wafted his patent under the noses of the Western Union Telegraph Company, America's largest corporation, but they'd refused to meet his $100,000 price tag. This large sum is quoted in many history books but is possibly apocryphal. It seems that a deal was indeed offered, and Bell very nearly ended up selling out to the corporate giant, but negotiations failed because Western Union's president, William Orton, bore a grudge against Bell's chief backer (and father-in-law) Gardiner Greene Hubbard. Ultimately, Orton was a proud, brilliant tycoon and Bell was small-time. Western Union knew that if they needed telephone technology, they could hitch their wagon to Elisha Gray instead. Like the high-school quarterback able to snare any pretty cheerleader he wants, there was no need to chase the kooky girl in the glasses. But, over the next couple of years, the bookish Bell took off his glasses, let down his hair and revealed himself to be quite the business hottie – in short, his telephone proved to be a hit.

Cursing their bad decision, Western Union hired the superstar inventor Thomas Edison, and Bell's affronted nemesis Elisha Gray, to try to circumvent the copyright law by tinkering with Bell's design just enough to not have to pay the Scotsman a penny. Bell and his associates challenged the legal infringement, but probably assumed that they were about to get royally shafted, seeing as Western Union was so rich it could have hired every lawyer in America and then got those lawyers to dance a conga around Washington DC while burning dollar bills. And yet, if you'll pardon the continued high school analogy, the US Supreme Court's famous ruling of 1879 revealed it too was sporting a Team Bell t-shirt.

Such an upset might be dubbed a David and Goliath scenario, except what happened next was tantamount to Goliath repeatedly smashing himself in the face with his own weapon, rather than being felled by David's dinky pebble. Frustrated by the ruling, and desperate to protect their telegraphy monopoly, Western Union decided to make a deal with the upstart. This policy adjustment stemmed from the death of William Orton, the company president, of a huge stroke in April 1878. Without his leadership, and his animosity towards Bell's father-in-law, the corporation made a huge blunder. It handed over 84 separate patents and ownership of 56,000 telephones that they'd installed in 55 American cities, and also agreed to exit the phone business until 1896. This gave Bell 17 years of free rein, or – rather – free reign, as it essentially allowed him to dominate the telephone market like some lustrously bearded imperial prince. In focusing solely on their sacred cash cow – the telegram – Western Union's executives had inadvertently unbolted the cage door and released its natural predator. It was the historical equivalent of a multi-billion-pound company saying 'you can have all these new-fangled mobile phones, so long as we get to keep making pagers'.

It wasn't just Alexander Graham Bell's genius, or Western

Union's reflexive crotch-punch, that changed the world. The celebrated Edison, for example – himself, almost entirely deaf – made at least two crucial contributions to the telephone's swift ascent to popularity. In 1878 he had invented a super-sensitive microphone from granular carbon which would allow the phone user to abandon red-faced bellowing and instead speak at normal volume, even when making long-distance calls. If only someone would tell that to the obnoxiously loud businessman on your commuter train. But Edison's other suggestion had nothing to do with scientific jiggery-pokery. It was simply a word.

YOU HAD ME AT HELLO!

Apparently, when Edison first witnessed a demonstration of Bell's contraption, America's leading inventor exclaimed 'hullo!' in total amazement that it actually worked. 'Hullo' was the nineteenth-century version of 'fancy seeing you here!' – the kind of disbelieving greeting we'd blurt out if we met our dentist at the top of some remote volcano – but, with our sceptic's hat on, this story sounds a little too charming to be true. However, it was definitely Edison who pushed a slightly amended version, 'hello,' into the public consciousness as the official telephone greeting.

He thought that 'hello' had strong, clear syllables, and this was important because he envisaged telephones would primarily be used between businesses, and that the lines would remain permanently open rather than there being a ringing sound for each call. In short, 'hello' was chosen specifically because it wasn't a familiar word used in ordinary office chat, so hearing it would immediately notify someone that there was a call for them. While Edison's greeting is now one of the most recognisable words on the planet, I must admit I'm slightly disappointed that Bell's alternative suggestion, borrowed from nautical terminology, wasn't picked up instead: just imagine the musical majesty of Lionel Richie singing: 'Ahoy, is it me you're looking for?'

Yet, 'hello' wasn't immediately welcomed into the English lexicon. Initially, only the well-to-do could install phones, and Edison's novel ice-breaker was considered uncouth, so a respectable caller would open a conversation with the bluntly functional 'are you there?' or the fantastically passive–aggressive 'well . . . ?' It wasn't just the novelty of 'hello' that made people uncomfortable. Protecting one's privacy was an immediate concern, and many an upstanding gent dreaded the prospect of poor people phoning them, or having to field unwanted calls from businesses touting for new clients. Another fear was the potential for social embarrassment caused by not knowing who was on the other end of the line, and then there were the wrong numbers, the children using the receiver as an amusing toy, and the technical glitches when crossed lines or signal failure caused people to confess their secrets to strangers, or blather cheerfully into an empty void.

Affordability and practicality rendered some solutions a less-than-ideal compromise. In rural areas, particularly, it was common even up until the 1970s to share a single party line with one's neighbours, which easily allowed for eavesdropping and soon gave rise to reports of phone-hogging housewives 'visiting' each other over the phone, rather than in person, and blocking the communal line for way beyond the customary two minutes. Even those wealthier women who had their own lines were firmly requested by telephone companies to restrict their chatting to the evening, when special cheap rates were offered as an incentive, due to the need for businesses to take priority during the day.

Etiquette had dictated for centuries how one was to behave in person, or when writing a letter, but the puzzling newness of the telephone revolution saw people inundate newspapers and magazines with what we might perceive as the strangest of questions: 'Should a man only make a call while standing upright, as a mark of respect? Was it deeply immoral for men and women to converse on the phone if either wasn't fully dressed? Could diseases be caught down the wire?' In France there were scandalous murmurings that women were using phones to conduct illicit affairs – phone sex clearly isn't all that modern – and men soon feared that aural intercourse in the front room might well lead to oral intercourse in the bedroom ...

But it wasn't just the way we communicated that changed. For this new-fangled telephony to work, there needed to be central exchanges that would put a caller through to the right number. But who would take such a job – one in which the operator would be required to occasionally listen in on the conversation? Adolescent boys proved too untrustworthy, and so the role was offered to young unmarried females (instigating a watershed in the history of women's employment) and such exchange workers were dubbed the 'Hello girls', confirming that Edison's new greeting, so reviled by snobs, had wormed its way into popular culture. 'Hello' was here to stay, and so was the telephone.

We've been chatting away to our friend for ages, and have undoubtedly used up our free call minutes, so – to avoid a hefty phone bill – we hang up the phone and switch to texting instead. By doing this, we're transliterating our previously spoken words into written symbols, a rather brilliant party trick well beyond the capabilities of our Stone Age heroes, Ug and Nug. Or, at least that's how we used to see it. Now, we're not quite so certain ...

IN THE BEGINNING WAS THE WORD

There aren't many students whose research gets reported in international science journals, mostly because they're busy putting traffic cones on statues and stumbling around with dangerous levels of vodka in their bloodstream, but Canada's Genevieve von

Petzinger was something of an outlier. In 2009, she submitted her MA thesis in anthropology, and immediately made headlines.

Her focus was on some of the lesser-known art of the Stone Age – geometric symbols scribbled on the walls of French caves – and though archaeologists had known about them for 150 years, these curious squiggles had often been ignored in favour of the more bewitching cave paintings of bison, lions and bears. Von Petzinger, however, noticed that no one had compiled a complete catalogue of all the symbols, so she and her supervisor, Dr April Nowell, built a database of the 146 French cave sites in which the art had been found, and then analysed the results. They soon discovered that these weren't just random doodles, but a roster of 26 recurrent symbols: a crosshatch, hands, lines, dots, spiral whirls, serpentine waves and many other shapes. The evidence virtually leapt out of the computer screen: thousands of years ago, long before the Bronze Age invention of writing, there may have been a very primitive form of symbolic proto-alphabet in use across western Europe.

Pictographic symbolism is everywhere in the modern world. If we peered into our kitchen cupboards we'd find packets plastered with little drawings telling us whether the cardboard is recyclable, or warnings to say that dunking our face in boiling water is inadvisable. And, as we put down our phone, and go to check today's emails, the button we push to load the relevant software is probably a little digital envelope, a pictogram alluding to the former glory days of written communication. In the West, particularly with the menu screens on electronic gadgets, pictograms – i.e. artistic representations of a thing – have returned to their former prominence, but in east Asia they never went away; the Chinese alphabet is almost completely based on pictograms and ideograms (depictions of an abstract idea). It makes one wonder: if pictograms were good enough for both the Stone Age and modern Asia, how come the West ended up with alphabetic letters? Well, strap yourself in! This section is not for the faint-hearted...

There's a cartoon I recall seeing on a birthday card that made me chuckle and then immediately tut like a tedious pedant. It depicts an archaeologist in an Indiana Jones hat joyously clutching what seems like a priceless Egyptian vase decorated with hieroglyphs, but at the bottom of the card we get to enjoy the humorously banal translation, 'dishwasher safe'. It's a lovely gag, but one that's symptomatic of a widely held misunderstanding. Yes, it's true that hieroglyphs, along with Sumerian cuneiform, were probably the earliest fully developed writing system, having originated about 5,200 years ago. However, the word hieroglyph is a later Greek one meaning 'sacred engraving', and that's because they were only ever used in religious contexts – there were no 'please queue here' signposts decorated in these holiest of symbols. Instead, everyday writing was in a cursive script called hieratic (later replaced by demotic), and hieroglyphs were as unintelligible to most Egyptians as a restaurant menu written in binary code would be to us.

Speaking of binary code . . . As we type out our email, it's obvious to us that the lucky recipient of our witty bons mots won't receive a physical message, but a digital facsimile comprising electronic 1s and 0s, catapulted through cyberspace. Yet, when it comes to jotting down our thoughts, some of us still prefer to use a physical medium, if only because paper allows us the cathartic pleasure of scrunching up unwanted junk mail and joyfully hurling it at the bin. Confusingly, paper gets its name from ancient Egyptian scrolls made from interlaced strips of papyrus reed, a technology dating back about 4,500 years.

But paper itself was a much later Chinese invention – it's perhaps only 2,000 years old – and requires the pulping of cellulose fibres, rather than the latticing of plant strips. Paper and papyrus are therefore quite separate, but the blurring of etymologies is understandable. After all, we modern writers have much in common with ancient Egyptians and, though they wrote from right to left in a choice of either black or red ink made from crushed minerals, their quill – made from a reed brush which had been sliced diagonally at the nib – wasn't so different from our fountain pen.

By contrast, in Bronze Age Mesopotamia, the Sumerian language was written using a system called cuneiform, etched into soft clay tablets which were then baked for permanence. Cuneiform seems to have evolved out of an inventory system dating back to the Neolithic era, in which little clay tokens of varying geometric shapes probably represented numerical values of traded goods. As the budding Sumerian empire stretched out its vast tendrils, the complexity of its trade arrangements quickly required a more comprehensive method of recording who owed what to whom. Instead of hoarding mountains of tokens, by 3200 BCE the information was being recorded with cuneiform writing. Depressingly, this means the romantic medium that preserved the genius of Shakespeare, Molière, Sun Tzu and Aristotle was invented by tax accountants – that's a bit like discovering Margaret Thatcher invented rock 'n' roll...

But not all great empires embraced writing. Until the arrival of the Spanish conquerors in the sixteenth century, the South American Incas used a fascinating system of coloured string knots called *khipus*, woven from cotton or llama hair, to convey information via knot placement. Just like a written letter, a *khipu* could be brief and contain just ten bits of string or it could be a set of complex instructions with 2,000 strands that resembled a Hawaiian grass skirt. Puzzlingly, it probably wasn't based on their Quechua language, either, and was more likely encoded numerically with a Base 10 system, meaning Incan string theory is proving to be a knotty problem for researchers (a double-pun for all you physics fans, there...).

But let's get back to cuneiform. Initially, Sumerian scribes used a very sharp reed to carve the strokes, but this dragged up the wet clay so instead a pen with a triangular tip was adopted, creating a linguistic system based on wedge shapes squished into the tablet, perhaps as a pictographic representation of the abandoned tax token. But unlike the 26 Stone Age pictograms found on those cave walls, these soon grew in number as each subtle change of shape came to represent one of thousands of words, names, places or actions. So, if a person bought three cows, the scribe didn't just draw three cow symbols in a row any more. Instead, there was a symbol for cow and a separate symbol for the number three, and to avoid confusion a system called determinatives gave clues to the context of the word. For example, imagine if floating above the English word 'witch' there was a tiny doodle of a green-skinned lady on a broomstick to prevent confusion with its homophonic counterpart, 'which'. Put simply, cuneiform meant each distinct idea could be represented in writing.

AS EASY AS 'A, B, C'

Okay, so that's the tricky origins of writing out of the way, but we still haven't addressed the birth of the Western alphabet. Anglophones can thank the vital contribution of the Phoenicians for that, as they were a maritime people from what is now Lebanon, and, when not bobbing around the Mediterranean, established trade colonies on the coastal edges of North Africa, southern Spain, Sicily, Sardinia, the Greek islands, Cyprus and the length of eastern Mediterranean. Yes – much like The Beach Boys – they got around, and wherever they went they carried with them their improved version of cuneiform which was a new alphabet of 22 consonantal letters.

Once introduced to the Levant, this morphed into the Aramaic alphabet, which itself then split into Hebrew and, later, Arabic writing. Meanwhile, the Greeks acquired the Phoenician system and then added the novelty of vowels, presumably to better mirror their own spoken language, and this iteration seemingly reached Italy, where it was picked up by the Etruscans, who were then obliterated by the all-conquering Romans who ended up with the Latin alphabet of 23 characters, including vowels and consonants, but no letters J, U or W. The Romans then dedicated themselves to annihilating their Libyan rivals, the Carthaginians, who just happened to be settled Phoenicians – well, that's gratitude for you!

Stick with me, I promise we're nearly done... When the Roman Empire swelled to an unwieldy size, it found itself being forced to recruit Germanic mercenaries to patrol its expansive lands. These tribes then took the Latin alphabet back to the windswept north with them, where it possibly inspired the emergence of the Norse and Saxon runic alphabet, which was believed to be vaguely magical if scratched into swords and other stuff. As if all that wasn't enough, in around the year 900 the Greek alphabet was updated for Slavic speakers by the Bulgarian disciples of St Cyril and St Methodius (two missionary brothers who brought eastern Orthodox Christianity to the region). This new alphabet, which has since lost a quarter of its initial 43 letters, is therefore named Cyrillic. It is the basis of writing in Russia, Ukraine, Serbia and, of course, Bulgaria, where my inability to decipher it on a business trip to Sofia once caused me to mix up toothpaste and foot cream, with dire results.

All the while, as the Catholic Church foisted Latin upon the unruly Germanic tribes, the Roman alphabet grew to suit the needs of nascent European languages that were slowly deviating from standard Latin to become modern French, Spanish, Italian, etc. This, of course, finally led to the English alphabet of 26 letters, which I am currently using to bore you to tears. Sorry about that. Anyway, to make it really simple, without the Phoenicians there would be no 'Alphabet Song' on *Sesame Street,* and I think we can all agree that would've been a tragedy.

It's time we finish that email and do something useful around the house – maybe some DIY? After all, that unhinged cupboard door isn't going to magically improve on its own. But as we stand up to fetch our hammer, we spot the paperboy dragging his over-stuffed satchel up our driveway. Ah, yes – the weekend paper, how could we forget? Suddenly, the cupboard door doesn't look *that* broken after all – certainly not now there's the prospect of lounging on the sofa with a warm mug of coffee, and catching up with global events. Ooooh, and there's the crossword, too! Right, decision made. We pop the kettle on, claim our newspaper from the welcome mat, and start glancing through the headlines.

A NEW PAGE IN HISTORY

Print journalism is just about clinging to life, but digital media is hovering impatiently at the foot of the hospital bed, waiting to switch off the life-support machine and inherit the family business. Newspapers have had a good run and, before we get sentimental, let's remember that all things are eventually superseded. After all, when was the last time you read a scroll?

Two thousand years ago, the book (or, codex to be technical) was a huge leap forward in writing culture. It was a lot more portable and, unlike unravelling a massive scroll, allowed the reader to easily flip to a specific section – wonderfully handy when trying to preach pertinent lessons from the Bible to a crowd of shrugging pagans. Indeed, it's no coincidence that the spread of Christianity, a religion based upon a holy text, mirrored the rise of the book. Back in the first century, when Christianity was just another weird Eastern cult, the apostle St Paul was a strange hipster, carrying a kind of folded notebook in an era when none of the texts recovered from Pompeii or Herculaneum were codices. Instead, Romans wrote on papyrus, wax, broken bits of pottery or – as was the case at Vindolanda, a fort on Hadrian's Wall near the border with Scotland – on thin wooden tablets. Yet, by the fourth century, when the Empire had officially embraced Jesus, the codex was as popular as the scroll, and, within 200 years, it had roundhouse kicked its rival off the roof of the moving train into the ravine of historical obsolescence.

Despite the codex being the shiny new technology, texts still had to be laboriously written line by line. The book was special because it required enormous effort to produce a single copy, and proof of this can be seen in the charming margin doodles scribbled by medieval scribes – my favourites are the hopeful: 'Thank God, it will soon be dark!'; the weary: 'Writing is excessive drudgery. It crooks your back, it dims your sight, it twists your stomach and your sides' and the hilariously unpoetic: 'Ow! My hand!' But, rarity aside, the value of these texts could also be aesthetic. Administrative documents, such as William the Conqueror's Domesday Book census of 1086, might be jotted down with minimal flair, but sacred gospels – often etched onto animal-skin parchment – could transcend mere utility to become gorgeous illustrated artworks whose oversized opening letters demanded hours of careful design, during which time they were imperilled by even the slightest of sneezes.

For obvious reasons, restrictions on book production meant that literacy rates were extremely low in western Christendom. Whereas you and I get our news from all manner of external sources – radio, telly, email, blogs, newspapers, etc. – in medieval Europe ordinary people mainly received their information via the pulpit of the local church, or from gossip brought through the town gates on market day. There were few paths to self-education, or political radicalisation, without expensive tuition in the mysterious art of reading. The Church and the Crown controlled society by possessing the only powerful modes of communication, and that power would have to be prised from their cold, dead hands. But, fittingly, there was a man in possession of exactly the right kind of crowbar...

You've possibly never heard of Johannes Gänsefleisch, which is understandable, because who's going to celebrate a man called John Goosebumps? He sounds like a mediocre children's entertainer. Clearly, Johannes thought the same thing, and adopted a family surname more befitting his lofty ambitions, to become Johannes Gutenberg: once a German goldsmith from Mainz, but now a titan of global history. If the 2005 press release for Apple's iPod Nano – a tinier version of a quite good gadget – can use the word 'revolutionary', then Gutenberg's printing press was nothing short of an über-mega-super-revolution... to the max.

Gutenberg's innovation is worthy of enormous admiration. It's true that he didn't invent printing as a concept, as the Chinese had been carving wooden block templates to produce facsimile copies since the eighth century, but Gutenberg's fifteenth-century spark of genius was to create tiny metal letters which could be limitlessly rearranged to spell anything at all, and endlessly reused for new works. Basically, he invented the precursor to those alphabetic fridge magnets that can be cheekily scrambled to spell rude words. Previously, books – the product of monks toiling in snug scriptoria, or professional scribes beavering away in universities – had been tediously scrawled at a leisurely pace of five pages per day, per scribe. But, thanks to the mechanical press, probably adapted from a winemaker's screw-press, 3,500 pages could be churned out in a single session.

What this did, of course, was to flood the market with hitherto unattainable knowledge. In 1517, 50 years after the inventor's death, the German monk Martin Luther published his *95 Theses* – a list of complaints against what he perceived as the institutional corruption of the Catholic Church. Where once such rants might have gone unnoticed, or bubbled locally for a brief spell, the book-loving people of the numerous German states had become increasingly literate, and Luther's ideas spread like a virulent contagion, disseminated by Gutenberg's press. The age of unimpeded control by Church and State was gone. Finally, the people had a voice, and – like a straight-laced colleague who suddenly lets it all go at the office karaoke party – they were determined to prove just how loud it could be.

I READ THE NEWS TODAY, OH BOY

We slump on the sofa, waiting for our coffee to cool, and begin to methodically plough through the weekend newspaper, digesting the carefully crafted opinion pieces and sifting through the sections with ruthless efficiency: 'Fashion supplement? Who has £380 for a velvet hat?' But, if a major story were to break in the next half hour, we'd hurl the paper to one side and switch back to our digital screens, where the eternally updating BBC website would flesh out the drama, line by line, as it breaks. We devour such rapid journalism with ravenous appetite, yet we shouldn't assume that our ancestors weren't equally hungry for news. They were just as curious, but lacked the infrastructure for regular newsgathering.

Two thousand years ago, even in the glorious zenith of the Roman Empire, the best they could muster was a sort of daily gazette called the *Acta Diurna* that provided a brief round-up of headlines – political acts, scandals, battles, legal cases … that sort of thing – but though there was tremendous interest in acquiring this new information, no official thought to distribute multiple copies. It was, quite literally, a single engraved tablet pinned up in the Forum, like a drab notice in a school canteen, and if someone wanted to know what was happening in the Empire, they had to send their slave to jot down the good bits, and report back.

The genesis of proper news, then, wasn't until the sixteenth century when the alliance between Gutenberg and Luther fuelled the birth of the pamphlet, which was effectively a single-story blog post that was printed up cheaply and sold to eager readers. Initially pamphlets covered the religious furore stoked by Luther's anti-Catholicism, but when the fuss died down publishers switched to current affairs, though journalistic integrity wasn't yet sufficiently developed to risk pissing off the authorities. It wasn't North Korean standards of propaganda – no one claimed the Pope frequently sunk 18 consecutive holes-in-one at golf – but the sins of omission meant pamphlets were more 'all news is good news' than 'no news is good news'.

So, what was the first actual newspaper? Fittingly, perhaps thanks to Luther's influence, it was written in the German language, in the town of Strasburg, and was printed by a local senator called Johann Carolus in 1605. His idea was to collate handwritten reports from across the Holy Roman Empire and then print them once a week for the benefit of his 150–200 readers. Some of these people were undoubtedly rich types in castles, but a sizeable proportion were probably merchants seeking vital intel on the health of foreign markets. At the end of the year, Carolus collected the 52 sheets into a book – the catchily monikered *Relation aller Fürnemmen und gedenckwürdigen Historien* – as a historical account of the year's events, much like the end-of-year retrospectives we see from modern magazines in December. Given this early success, other European newspapers soon followed, often communicating updates from the brutal Thirty Years War that was tearing Germany asunder.

In Britain, foreign news was being reported in eight-page corantos by the 1620s, but unfavourable winds in the English Channel could delay the arrival of news packets for weeks, so the 'new' news might be old news by the time it turned up – even in the rosy aftermath of the printing revolution, logistics remained a serious problem. Another headache was that readers were baffled by newspapers keeping the same name on the masthead every week, because pamphlets changed their title to suit each new idea. The editors of the *Weekly Newes from Italy, Germanie, Hungaria* patiently had to explain to their readership that the latest edition was different to the one before, even if the name was the same. In any case, though the newspaper was up and running, these early broadsheets didn't much resemble the one we're reading on our comfy sofa – there were no emboldened headlines, celebrity gossip or adverts, and illustrations were less frequent. What's more, the news was delivered in dispassionate, decontextualised accounts that relied on the reader making their own judgements. There were no editorials assigning blame.

The key watershed for the British newspaper industry was the violent eruption in the 1640s of the Civil Wars between Crown and Parliament. As the war became increasingly frenzied, journalism started looking inwardly at British politics, and both sides published their own partisan titles to rubbish the other, with the success of the Cromwellian *Kingdome's Weekly Intelligencer* inspiring a royalist rebuttal – the *Mercurius Aulicus*. Into this maelstrom leapt the debonair publisher Marchmont Nedham, who was just 23 when he cranked out his scathingly anti-royal *Mercurius Britannicus* in 1643. This enraged King Charles I, and Nedham swiftly found himself grovellingly promising to issue his pro-royal *Mercurius Pragamaticus* instead. Of course, King Charles then lost the war, and – more permanently – his head, leaving the victorious Parliamentarians to chuck Nedham into prison for sedition. But, ever the pragmatist, the journo-jailbird then flip-flopped his way out of the gaol by printing *Mercurius Publicus,* the official mouthpiece of Oliver Cromwell's authoritarian regime.

In barely a decade, the once-innocuous broadsheets crammed with Hungarian weather trivia had turned into scurrilous polemics bestrewn with adverts and illustrations to catch the eye. A good 350 years before the left-wing/right-wing polarity of our modern tabloids, news titles were already taking ideological stances and hectoring their political enemies. To us, this is a sign of a healthy democracy, but in the tumultuous aftermath of a savage Civil War this was seen as destabilising. When the monarchy was restored in 1660, the new king – whose dad had publicly endured that nasty head-lopping – did not welcome all these muck-rakers stoking up rebellion. Charles II may have gone down in history as the hedonistic populist blessed with the common touch, but he came down on press freedom with the crushing force of an elephant dropped from a helicopter. Still, he shagged a lot of women, so the English are strangely fond of him.

Though censorship blunted journalism's rapier, the burning desire for news remained, and soon special venues popped up to cater to this need. In the 1650s, London's newly erected coffee houses became the fountains in which people quenched their intellectual thirst. For the admission price of a penny, men (women weren't all that welcome) could hang out, read the newspapers and indulge in an exotic hot beverage, newly imported from Turkey. This seventeenth-century coffee wasn't comparable to the aromatic bean we're currently slurping from our favourite mug, rather it was a disgusting sludge – a sort of burned, nutty coal-tar gloop – but, in an era when most people were perennially tipsy, the intense caffeine shot jolted woozy brains out of dull hangovers and into excitable overdrive.

Not content with just reading the newspapers, those gathered inside coffee houses hunted for novel information from every source. It was customary to greet anyone entering through the front door with the refrain 'what news have you?' in the expectation that they knew something you didn't. Nor were these places only crammed with bored slackers, or pals just shooting the breeze – the bewigged equivalent of Ross, Rachel, Phoebe, Monica, Joey and Chandler – instead, they were the meeting places for London's most eminent poets, philosophers, writers, capitalists and scientists. Regulars at the Grecian Coffee House might have witnessed Isaac Newton and Edmund Halley dissecting a dead dolphin, which really isn't something you'll see in a local Starbucks, and Jonathan's Coffee House became so stuffed with rude, bellowing merchants, tracking the price of commodities, that it gradually evolved into the London Stock Exchange.

As all these clever radicals bonded over a hot mug of joe, King Charles II became increasingly anxious that coffee houses were turning into hotbeds of dissent. In 1675, he tried to close them – just as he'd crushed the press – but it's never wise to deprive a caffeine addict of their daily buzz, and the chastened King was swiftly forced to execute a foppish U-turn. But, while he admitted defeat here, he didn't let up on the newspapers. It required the death of Charles and the deposal of his brother, James II, for the English press to be unshackled of royal censorship by the expiration in 1695 of the restrictive Licensing Act, and this sparked a huge outpouring of popular journalism.

In 1702, England's first daily paper, *The Daily Courant,* was launched, and the idea soon spread to the colonies. Here, a young Benjamin Franklin spent his teens working as an apprentice in his brother's New England print shop, and – as we know – exploited this connection to prank the *New-England Courant* into thinking he was a crotchety old woman named Silence Dogood. His fortnightly letters, which were humorous satirical rants on popular culture, became a hit with gullible readers and his whingeing widow received several marriage proposals from those captivated by her relentless capacity for disappointment.

By 1800, when Franklin had helped lead America to independence, there were a healthy 200 newspapers on sale nationwide. Not bad. Yet, by 1880 – when the Tenth Census of the United States compiled a massive study on the newspaper industry – that figure had leapt to over 11,000 periodicals, with an estimated 32 million copies being shifted anually to readers eager to make sense of their life and times. Just as the first newspaper revolution had required printing technology, now this huge expansion was carried on the back of the game-changing electric telegraph machine. Its spider's web of cabling joined up local, regional, national and international journalism into one big syndicated news-stream shared across the vast sprawl of the American continent. We'll get to that shortly, but first let's explore where so-called telegraphy (which literally means 'faraway-writing' in Greek) had first originated. As ever, it's further back than you might expect.

SENDING OUT THE SIGNAL

The ruler of the mighty city has succumbed to madness. As vast enemy forces encroach, he refuses to beg help from his allies and instead sends his son on a suicidal mission to recapture a fallen outpost. But a wise councillor, seeing the stricken leader's irrational despair, tasks a young hero to sneak past the guards and defiantly light the beacon, for there is still hope. The beacon erupts into glorious flame and, moments later, a mountain promontory on the far horizon also bursts into orange light. Along the snow-capped mountains, a chain of fires spark into brilliant life, one by one, until, hundreds of miles away, in the city of the allies, a watchful figure spots their golden glow and, elated, bursts into the king's chambers shouting 'the beacons are lit! Gondor calls for aid!' Not missing a beat, the King responds with the immortal lines: '. . . and the Rohan will answer!' At this point pretty much everyone in the cinema punches the air with relieved joy, showering ourselves in popcorn and Diet Coke. Hooray for Gandalf the Wizard!

Okay, so the *Lord of The Rings* movie trilogy isn't exactly history, but it perfectly illustrates an ancient form of telegraphy dating back to the Bronze Age. A network of flaming beacons was much quicker than sending a guy on horseback – it was their version of instant messaging. That said, beacons only delivered a pre-agreed message. We, for example, might smash the glass in a fire alarm if we saw smoke billowing out of the kitchen; but we wouldn't do it if we'd only run out of milk and fancied a cuppa; to us, the fire alarm only means one thing. Similarly, beacons weren't much use for long-distance day-to-day chats, and instead functioned as an urgent klaxon. In ancient Assyrian cities, one beacon meant 'this is worrying' and two beacons was basically '*holy shit, send help!*' But, not all signals were desperate pleas for aid. In the ancient play *Agamemnon*, by the Greek tragedian Aeschylus, a watchman waits for the beacon to confirm the fall of Troy, while in 1588 beacons were lit along the English coast as an alarm system triggered by the invading Spanish Armada looming into sight.

Beacons, in theory, were a simple system but they weren't glitch-proof. The Sumerian city of Mari, in modern Syria, was wiped off the map by the all-conquering Babylonian King Hammurabi in 1759 BCE, but when it was rediscovered in the 1930s, among its ruins were something like 25,000 cuneiform documents, including reports of torch signals from neighbouring cities. One in particular revealed that there'd been a bit of a hiccup: 'My lord wrote to say that two torch signals were raised; but we never saw two torch signals... my lord should look into the matter...'. This was the Mesopotamian equivalent of 'hey, I sent you a text. Did you not get it? Weird!'

Long before the naval flag semaphore of the nineteenth century, there was a clever suggestion by the ancient Greek historian Polybius which allowed beacons to facilitate more flexible messaging across great distances. For him, a letter's position in a 5 x 5 grid system could be communicated with flaming torches. So, if 'A' was found 1 along and 1 down on the grid, then the letter 'P' was 4 along, 2 down. Therefore, to spell the letter 'P', four torches were lit to the left of a marker, and two to the right. It was an excellent concept, but was probably too unwieldy to use in practice, as each torch would have needed to have been some considerable distance from the next, so as to be inter-distinguishable to the human eye from miles away. Ironically, therefore, the guys doing the messaging would have needed their own messaging system to make sure they were all working in harmony, and the fact that the Romans didn't bother to adopt such a clever system, despite their huge empire, suggests implementing it was like founding a synchronised gymnastics team made up of kittens – a lovely notion, but a nightmare to actually organise.

Understandably, beacons weren't the answer and practical telegraphy only emerged in the late eighteenth century thanks to the network of towers built by the Frenchman Claude Chappe and his brothers. Established in the wake of the French Revolution, these telegraph towers had a tall mast poking out the top, upon which balanced a horizontal beam called the regulator. This could be moved like a see-saw into one of four positions, and on both ends of the beam were indicator flaps that could each be set in seven positions, allowing for 196 (7x7x4) possible configurations which were then allied up with three code books. Cleverly, instead of spelling words letter by letter, as Polybius had suggested, the operators worked from dictionaries and, by sending just three signals, could convey a specific word, from a specific page in one of the three specific code books – so, a semaphore message of '2, 22, 67' meant 'the 67th word on page 22 of book 2'.

By 1846 it became possible to send a theoretical list of 45,050 words – a vocabulary beyond even the memory of Stephen Fry – to the 534 relay stations dotted around France. This was obviously tremendously useful for military communication, and Napoleon Bonaparte was understandably a fan, but for ordinary citizens it provided nothing more than a regular dose of crushing disappointment because all it did for them was speedily deliver the national lottery results, and nothing is more depressing than continually not winning a truck-load of cash. The British, on the other hand, invested in similar technology – first with Lord George Murray's shutter semaphore which, like Polybius's system, communicated letters not words – and then opting for something closer to the French telegraph. In 1827, merchant shipping companies were permitted to send telegraphs via Liverpool, initiating the dawn of high-tech commercial communications technology. However, bad weather and nightly darkness rendered these line-of-sight signallers totally useless which, when you consider the dreary climate in Britain, meant they were probably little more than massive eyesores for large portions of the year.

If only there were a system that worked 24/7, come rain or shine, that was available to all...

WIRED UP

It was the manhunt that stole the headlines and captured the imagination of the British nation. On New Year's Day 1845, Mrs Ashley of Salt Hill, near Slough, heard a series of spine-chilling groans through her wall. Fearing something was very wrong, and noticing a man hurriedly exiting from next door, she went to investigate and found her neighbour, Sarah Hart, frothing at the mouth from a fatal dose of poison. Panicked, she raised the alarm and, among the first to react was a vicar, the Rev. E.T. Champnes, who took down Mrs Ashley's description of the suspect and immediately pursued him to the nearest train station. Frustratingly, our daredevil in a dog-collar arrived just in time to see the culprit climb into a first-class carriage and pull away from the station. So close, yet so far... or was it? Luckily, Champnes was up on his cutting-edge tech – he was obviously a zeitgeist-surfing vicar vigilante – and had the stationmaster send a telegram through to Paddington Station, alerting the police to the suspect's whereabouts.

As the train puffed into London, a Sergeant Williams was waiting, not to arrest the man, but to follow him home. The next day, having reported back to the Metropolitan Police, Williams was involved in arresting John Tawell – a respectable Quaker – for the murder of Sarah Hart, who turned out to be his ex-mistress. The trial was a sensation and the verdict, inevitably, produced a death sentence. In response, *The Times* was certain that: 'had it not been for the efficient aid of the electric telegraph, both at Slough and Paddington, the greatest difficulty, as well as delay, would have occurred in the apprehension [of Tawell].' Unfamiliar with the speed of electrical telegraphy, the Victorian public was utterly enraptured by this quasi-magical gadget whose cables were christened with their own superhero soubriquet: 'the cords that hanged John Tawell.' But from where had this crime-fighting gadget originated?

In Britain, the electric telegraph was only eight years old by this point, being the shared brainchild of William Fothergill Cooke and Charles Wheatstone. They had engineered a way of harnessing the push/pull nature of electro-magnets to point in different directions, and therefore to be used as directable indicators on a rhomboid-shaped board on which letters were written. By linking up such boards with cables, it was possible to send written messages at 186,000mps, day or night and in all weather conditions, making wired telegraphy far superior to its line-of-sight predecessor. Just like the Kellogg brothers, the two men immediately fell out over whether to commercialise their invention, but Cooke bought out his high-minded partner's share and launched the device to instant success.

But it wasn't just a fun gimmick, thrillingly handy in criminal pursuits. The electric telegraph transformed global communications. In 1856, the journalist W.H. Russell, who had gone out to the Crimea to cover the Anglo-French war with Russia for *The Times*, was able to have his battle reports published in London the next day. By contrast, in India – where no cables had been laid – news of 1857's infamous mutiny didn't reach Britain for 40 days. Such greater connectivity would have a huge impact on ordinary lives, but it would also increase the pace of journalism. The Reuters News Agency, established in 1851 by the German-born Paul Julius Reuter, was the first major news-gathering organisation to acquire scoops and sell them to other newspapers, relying on carrier pigeons and the electric telegraph to deliver the reports speedily. In the nineteenth century, when people were acclimatised to waiting days or weeks for coverage of an event, to have updates within 24 hours of their occurrence was truly marvellous.

In America, the telegraphic boom exploded almost overnight thanks to government support. In 1846, there were merely 40 miles of experimental lines between Washington and Baltimore. By 1853, that had increased 600-fold to 23,000 miles – an unprecedented rate of expansion. Yet this huge expanse of cabling wasn't designed for the Cooke and Wheatstone device, but for a similar gadget invented by the portrait painter, and part-time inventor, Samuel Morse. His machine relied on a tapping code of dots and dashes which operators could 'sound read', allowing them to decipher ten words per minute.

As we browse our Saturday newspaper, we spot an article on violent computer games and the moral decay of the selfie-generation. Our modern phalanx of opinionistas is often determined to tell us that the internet is fracturing healthy society, and we're all going to end up fat and miserable. This anxious hand-wringing, however, is nothing new. When the passenger steam train was invented, some doctors feared the outrageous speeds of 20mph would cause brain damage; and when the bicycle became popular with women in the late 1800s, medical men claimed ladies' expressions would permanently contort into so-called 'bicycle face' due to the exertion. And, as the telegraph began to dominate in rapidly industrialising America, the neurologist Dr George Miller Beard popped up with his book, *American Nervousness,* to argue that each human was born with a finite supply of nervous energy, and the relentless buzz of modernity was whittling it away far too quickly, resulting in a delirious, headache-inducing fatigue called neurasthenia that struck even the best-educated minds in the country.

For Dr Beard, pretty much everything was an exhaustive drain on the feeble brain, but:

> **The telegraph is a cause of nervousness, the potency of which is little understood. Before the days of Morse and his rivals, merchants were far less worried than now... now, prices at each port are known at once all over the globe. This continual fluctuation of values, and the constant knowledge of those fluctuations in every part of the world, are the scourges of business men, the tyrants of trade - every cut in prices... becomes known in less than an hour all over the Union; thus competition is both diffused and intensified.**

Neurasthenia became more popular when it was snappily redubbed by the eminent psychologist William James (brother of the novelist Henry James) as 'Americanitis'. Yet such panic wasn't confined to just the USA. In 1901, an editorial in the *London Star* newspaper read: 'we have minimised and condensed our emotions... we have destroyed the memory of yesterday with the worries of tomorrow'. Technology was rocketing our ancestors forward at unprecedented speeds, but it seems quite a few wanted to stop the ride and get off as it was making them queasy.

And yet, sitting here in a room filled with numerous electronic gadgets, we've done the exact opposite, and have clung on for dear life as the ride gets faster and faster. Gutenberg liberated people by giving them a voice, and now the digital revolution is doing the same again. But with governments able to scoop up endless tranches of data on every tiny aspect of our lives, it won't be long before conspiracy theorists start hankering for the good old days when messages often had to be delivered by hand. But, a word of warning to them: it had its own downsides...

LONG-RUNNING NEWS

A top-100 list of history's most dramatic deaths would likely feature Pheidippides. In 490 BCE, intent on glorious conquest, a vast Persian army stomped into Greece brandishing a pincushion of bristling spears. Understandably alarmed, the people of Athens craved help from their Spartan neighbours but, sadly, there was no red telephone hardwired to the office of Sparta's two co-ruling kings, nor a bat signal projected into the night sky. Instead, a runner – Pheidippides – was dispatched to carry the plea in person. Two days later, having dragged his weary body 150 miles, the lone saviour of Athenian independence delivered the city's desperate cry for aid. But the Spartans were in the midst of a sacred festival and, despite the seriousness of the threat, offered only the polite brush-off – essentially a dressed-up version of 'Oh, we'd love to come, really we would, only it's a religious festival, yeah? How about next week? Are you free then?'

A despondent Pheidippides ran home to find his city's troops about to engage in an epic battle at Marathon. Having failed to motivate the Spartans, he expected to be a glum-faced witness to the inevitable slaughter of his people and the ensuing destruction of his city. And yet, somehow, the Athenians emerged from the carnage as the unexpected victors. Despite presumably suffering the world's worst ever case of jogger's nipple, poor Pheidippides was once again packed off to Athens to share the glorious news. Moments after entering the city to proclaim the heroic triumph, however, the knackered runner did what most of us would have done about a hundred miles further back along the road – he dropped dead.

Until the glamorous arrival of the electric telegraph in the mid-1800s, sending a message a long way often required a human or animal to physically deliver it and, for a lone messenger, the expansive scale of an empire could render that task more arduous than pushing a piano up the internal stairs of a skyscraper. Pheidippides' existence is debated, so don't take that story at face value, but he's a useful stand-in for a very real profession – the *hemerodrome*. These runners were expected to cover something like 80 miles in a day, over mountains and hills, to deliver top secret missives, and though the messages didn't self-destruct after five seconds, as in *Mission Impossible*, the cautionary tale of Pheidippides suggests the same may not have been true of the runners.

THE SOCIAL NETWORK

Every day, we send phone texts, emails, tweets, instant messages, etc. when we want to communicate quickly. In Rome, the equivalent was a human courier dubbed a *tabellarius,* who'd be seen scampering back and forth between parts of the same city, delivering brief messages between friends and co-workers on hastily etched wax tablets that could be wiped clean and overwritten. Yet, sending messages between cities was much harder. For example, the Persian Empire had boasted a postal network so impressive that Herodotus wrote: 'neither snow nor rain nor heat nor darkness prevents the swift completion of their appointed rounds' – which is quite the company motto – but Republican Rome lacked such a centralised system.

Soon, Caesar Augustus – the first and greatest in the bulging catalogue of Roman tyrants – realised that running an empire in which legal decrees, news of important deaths and rumours of usurpation plots could all go unheeded for weeks was putting his rule at risk. By the time reports of an invasion reached the capital, the enemy army would already be camped outside the palace sharpening its swords. So, Augustus nicked the Persian idea and established a massive courier network, the *Cursus Publicus*, linking an array of relay stations. Now, messages could be sent throughout the Empire at speed, carried over Rome's sprawling road network by animal-drawn carts and chariots, and – as the name suggests – the *Cursus Publicus* was open to the public too.

One particularly celebrated user was the notebook-loving apostle St Paul of Tarsus, who was a shoo-in for Best Supporting Actor in the New Testament, and a guy who wasn't remotely embarrassed to address his open letters to the Christian congregations of entire cities, in what must be history's earliest known mass mailshot. St Paul expected that his epistles (the books of the New Testament are predominantly collections of letters) would be read, copied out and passed on to other congregations; he was trusting in an effective system of duplication and transmission to save him from having to traipse across the Empire, performing the same thing in every city, like a jaded pop star on an exhausting global tour.

Other evidence for the system comes from the Vindolanda tablets, discovered by archaeologists in the ruins of the Roman fort on Hadrian's Wall. These documents are a fascinating insight into the daily lives of soldiers dispatched to the windy fringes of the Empire, but they also reveal how frequent and banal messages could be. Tablet 291 is a charming invitation to a birthday party, sent by the garrison commander's wife; Tablet 310 is from a soldier writing to his comrade Veldeius – who appears to have been temporarily deployed to London – asking if his buddy can arrange for those shears he'd already paid for to be sent up north. Tablet 311 is from another soldier, this one somewhat peeved that his pal won't write back to him: 'I am in very good health, as I hope you are in turn, you neglectful man, who have sent me not even one letter.'

In truth, the lazy recipient may not have been so lazy. Though official communication travelled via the *Cursus Publicus* in Britain, meaning a letter could get from Vindolanda to London in just a week, it seems lowly soldiers had to entrust their letters to travellers going in the right direction, and that was less reliable. For instance, in Tablet 343, an anxious Octavius writes to Candidus:

> **I have several times written to you that I have bought about five thousand modii of ears of grain, on account of which I need cash. Unless you send me some cash ... I shall lose what I have laid out as a deposit, about three hundred denarii, and I shall be embarrassed ...**

While it's possible Candidus was a dodgy shyster, it's possible those previous letters had not reached him.

It wasn't just Eurasian empires that had to communicate across epic geography. At its peak in the early 1500s, Incan lands sprawled over 750,000 square miles, stretching 2,500 miles along the Andean range from Colombia to Chile. That's quite a postal area. Communication between cities was obviously a logistical nightmare, but the Inca had an excellent solution – a huge chain of messengers stationed in little huts. So, rather than the Greek model of one bloke covering 150 miles, and arriving on the verge of a heart attack, the Incan *chasquis* sprinted as quickly as they could over much shorter distances and then, when they saw the stopping post ahead, blew their conch shell horn to alert the next messenger to their imminent arrival. He would then carry the message to the next waypoint. Oh, what fun it would be to have similar trumpeting in the 4 x 100 metres relay at the next Olympics!

Of course, some animals are quicker than humans and so it made sense to co-opt them into the messaging industry. Horses are the natural world's swiftest courier, mostly because no one's been stupid enough to try to saddle a cheetah, and, in April 1860, America's Pony Express was launched as an equine version of the Incan *chasqui* relay. In just ten days, anyone could send a letter from newly settled California over 1,900 miles to Missouri by a courier who swapped between a series of 400 galloping horses, picked up every ten miles. The Pony Express was revolutionary, it was thrilling, it was era-defining... and it was short lived. Just 18 months after its launch, the electric telegraph swaggered through the saloon doors of history and instantly rendered the brave riders of the American West superfluous. As careers go, theirs was almost as brief as that of a runner up on a TV talent show. Or, come to think of it, also the winner.

But horses, camels and humans are only blessed with legs – in the past, if you wanted really quick service, you needed to get yourself a homing pigeon. Scientists still don't really understand the biological mechanism that allows pigeons to find their way back, but, whatever natural wizardry it might be, it is dramatically impressive. We know, for example, that during the Crusades, besieged and blockaded Muslim soldiers used pigeons to carry messages over the frustrated heads of their Christian enemies, who were powerless to intercept them. Even further back, over 2,000 years ago, the results of the ancient Greek Olympic Games were delivered to the cities of the Aegean by cooing winged mercuries, with messages attached to their feet so they could flap homewards at 50mph, covering a range of some 1,100 miles.

Pigeon couriers also played a vital role in the First World War, with 100,000 sent by the British to the frontlines to compensate for the chaotic failures of the radio network. There, remarkably, pigeons had a 95 per cent mission success rate, even when their mobile lofts were moved after they'd taken off. A few even became proper medal-winning heroes, surviving bullet wounds and savage attacks by squadrons of German hawks trained to intercept them, to deliver their blood-stained, feather-strewn pleas for back-up from desperate soldiers pinned down in deadly trenches. More recently, criminals have been caught using pigeons as literal jailbirds to deliver contraband goods, with wardens in South America having caught knackered birds waddling around yards with mobile phones strapped to their backs. I look forward to the heart-warming animated film about the plucky pigeon who, despite the odds, manages to deliver his consignment of heroin to the drug-lord with the face tattoo.

Messenger pigeons haven't always taken off under their own power, though. In September 1870, Paris was surrounded by a vast Prussian army of 200,000 men, and its telegraph cables were severed. To break the blockade, and send word to the rest of France, Gaston Tissandier – a scientist trained in aeronautical meteorology – volunteered to float out of the city in an old battered and bandaged hot air balloon, carrying 30,000 letters that had been lovingly scribbled by anxious Parisians who didn't know if they would live or die. Also on board was a crate of carrier pigeons – if his mission succeeded, they would deliver the news to the capital. At 9:50 a.m., Tissandier's balloon floated high above the formations of Prussian Lilliputians, whose attempts to shoot him down were met only with Tissandier's cheeky sprinkling of German-language pamphlets designed to demotivate France's enemy.

After drifting for more than two hours, the balloon crashed dramatically next to the village of Dreux. Amid the jubilant locals, the heroic Tissandier dragged his sacks into a nearby carriage, enjoyed a lunch provided in his honour – there are always perks to a job, no matter how dangerous – and set off for the local post office, carrying the hopes of a city by his side. Amazingly, those 30,000 letters would reach their destinations. And, thanks to the returning pigeons, Paris would know it.

PEN FRIENDS

Looking up from our newspaper, suddenly we hear a noise at the front door as letters, brochures and magazines are stuffed through the letterbox and plummet gently onto our welcome mat. The postman turns away and vanishes up the street, not having disturbed us. But imagine if he'd stood in our doorway and demanded a fee for his morning's work. Now imagine that he returned another 11 times today, each time with the expectation of payment. As strange as it sounds, that's exactly how the British postal system used to function – regular door-to-door pickup and delivery meant homeowners had to find enough small talk to get through up to 12 visits per day. No wonder the rich had servants to answer the door for them; there's only so much weather chat one person can muster...

So, how had this curious system come into being? As we know, Rome had got the postal ball rolling 2,000 years ago, and though its Western Empire collapsed like a house made of soggy waffles, in Constantinople it doggedly continued as the glorious Byzantine Empire. At the same time, the Arab Caliphate to the south could also boast 930 postal stations, overseen by an ever-loyal postmaster. So, in the East, the *Cursus Publicus* was in safe hands. Sadly, Western hands were considerably clumsier, and the only communication network in medieval Christendom was an intranet between the monks, bishops, clergy and cardinals of the Catholic Church, meaning people like us didn't get a look in. In fact, in the Middle Ages – as with the Romans legionaries at Vindolanda – sending a letter often meant entrusting it to some anonymous bloke you'd met in a tavern. It's an extraordinary thought that intimate secrets, urgent requests or important business news would be left at the mercy of rogue travellers and the myriad perils that they could face. Would you feel comfortable filing your tax return via a stranger you met in a petrol station queue? No, me neither.

Even the respectable Paston family, Norfolk gentry in the 1400s, were not immune to the problem. Though a great deal of their letters survive – testament to many having been hand-delivered by a trusty servant named Juddy – communication lapses did still occur, and could be cause for alarm in the midst of the brutal Wars of the Roses. Who could blame Margaret Paston when she anxiously wrote to her husband:

> I sent you a letter by Bernie's man of Witchingham which was written on St Thomas' Day in Christmas; and I had no tidings or letter of you sin the week before Christmas, wherof I marvel sore . . . I pray you heartly that ye will vouchsafe to send me word how ye do as hastely as ye may, for my heart shall never be in ease till I have tidings from you.

With such unreliability in the makeshift postal system, we can appreciate why letters were deeply cherished. They might be bound together for safe-keeping, or even transcribed and printed, and these collections often remained in the family long after the deaths of the correspondents.

One of the most extraordinary eighteenth-century examples was the friendship maintained over 46 years between Horace Mann, a British diplomat in Florence, and the illustrious writer Horace Walpole – son of the Prime Minister, Robert – who was based in England. They had met in Italy as young, glamorous men and stayed pen friends for the next five decades, racking up 1,800 letters that are now preserved for posterity. The odd few undoubtedly got lost over the years, but the much more common obstacle was the sheer mileage between the men – the equivalent of three weeks journey per letter. In 1745 Mann enquired about the health of Walpole's father, not knowing that Sir Robert was already decomposing in his grave. An emotional Horace Walpole wrote back: 'I wish I had received your letters on his death, for it is most shocking to have all the thoughts opened again upon such a subject. It is the great disadvantage of a distant correspondence.' As bad as that was, spare a thought for those nineteenth-century pen-pals with contacts in Australia: there was no point asking 'how's your headache?' when a reply from the other side of the world wouldn't arrive for eight months – four months there, and four months back.

PENNY FOR YOUR THOUGHTS

Long before Walpole and Mann were getting inky fingers, Britain's medieval postal service had been a government prerogative – what Henry VIII had dubbed his Royal Mail – but this centralisation had also served a darker purpose: both domestic and foreign letters arriving into the Tudor court were secretly opened, read, resealed and sent on by shady spies hunting for nefarious plots. Henry's daughter Queen Elizabeth I was particularly prone to such grand snooping, and her rabidly patriotic spymaster – Sir Francis Walsingham – was a sinister genius more than happy to call upon his clandestine network of spooks and torturers. Mary Queen of Scots famously lost her head due to his cunning trap, but there were undoubtedly many more victims.

Yet the postal service couldn't simply remain a tool of national security, not if Britain wanted to become a prosperous commercial nation. In Europe, speedier communication between cities had sired the rise of the newspaper, and invidious British merchants could only watch from afar, with their faces squished up against the glass, excitedly pointing at all the continental progress and shouting 'why can't we have that, Dad?'. And so, after much lobbying, the Royal Mail opened its doors to the public in the mid-1600s. Nevertheless, government mail interception and censorship continued unabated in Britain until 1844. Now it's our emails that get read instead – *plus ça change!*

Inevitably, the government's monopoly was soon challenged by the sharp-minded merchants Robert Murray and William Dock-wra who established a London penny post in 1680. This allowed customers to drop off their package at one of six dispatch offices, and have it delivered that same day for a flat fee of a mere penny. This was a brilliant idea, which meant it was doomed to fail. The grumpy Duke of York, brother to King Charles II, had wangled a cushy arrangement in which he skimmed the profits from the Royal Mail and was rather affronted by Dockwra and Murray daring to piss in his revenue stream. Not one to share nicely, he had them shut down and fined, and then promptly launched his own London version of their idea. The Royal Mail, therefore, bumbled on unhampered by the nuisance of fair competition, and immune to progressive reform.

Now, if you happen to dwell in a vast country with more than one time zone, you'd be well within your rights to mock the paltry expanses of British soil. However, getting mail up to Scotland or north Wales from London wasn't merely a case of a quick jog up the road; it could take a fortnight – that's literally enough time for a modern astronaut to fly to the Moon, have a week-long holiday playing lunar golf, and fly home again. Something had to be done, but what? In 1782, a theatre impresario from Bath named John Palmer sold his business and began badgering the government about postal reform. He had previously instigated a high-speed carriage system to ferry his actors and props around the country, and was convinced that mail coaches could go quicker. In 1784, he was permitted to run an experiment; his pimped-out mail coach left Bristol at 4 p.m. and arrived 16 hours later in London. By our standards, this was as speedy as an arthritic tortoise, but the previous record had been 38 hours, so it was declared a resounding triumph!

Soon the red-liveried mail coaches of the Royal Mail were bouncing along the cobbles in all corners of the nation, but no one had learned from Dockwra and Murray. Costs still varied wildly depending on where you lived, how far a letter was travelling, and how verbose you were. Charges were levied per sheet, causing poorer people, and skinflint Scrooges, to scribble their letters with lines running both horizontally and vertically across the paper, in a space-saving tactic called 'cross-writing' that resembled a completed crossword puzzle. On the other hand, wealthy show-offs left massive margins on the paper, in a smug expression of deliberate wastefulness. But, most significantly of all, while newspapers and parliamentary correspondence between high-ranking bigwigs travelled for free, everything else was paid for upon delivery by the recipient, not by the sender.

With no money-grabbing Duke of York to hamstring reform this time, the mood had changed in favour of designing a better system. Stepping out from the shadows to push through the crucial changes was the progressive educationalist Rowland Hill, who published a pamphlet in 1837 advocating the standardised payment of the penny post, no matter the distance it travelled and paid for up front by the sender. Despite two years of political opposition from harrumphing conservatives, Hill was appointed to run this bold scheme, which also required the invention of the adhesive pre-paid stamp. This innovation, what Hill called: 'A bit of paper just large enough to bear the stamp, and covered at the back with a glutinous wash' required the bearer to lick the back of Queen Victoria's head, the novelty of which must have felt vaguely treasonous to some.

The Penny Black stamp, launched in 1840, is now hunted by keen-eyed philatelists and changes hands for crazy amounts of money, but back then they were somewhat less rare; 68 million went on sale in the first year alone. After a few months, it was found that the red ink used to cancel the validity of a used stamp was rubbing off too easily, and people were cheekily recycling stamps, and so in 1841 the Penny Black was replaced by the Penny Red. Imagine the excitement for all those budding philatelists – there were now two entirely different stamps to collect!

The next step in the system overhaul was to ensure the sender's privacy by introducing the envelope, and by 1853 people no longer had to contend with those red-coated 'bellmen' flitting relentlessly back and forth between front doors like hyperactive humming birds. Instead, now they could simply pop a letter into the newly installed letterboxes in the streets, an idea borrowed from the French by the well-travelled novelist Anthony Trollope, who just happened to have a job with the Post Office. One person to fully embrace the postbox was Oscar Wilde who, much like the medieval optimists entrusting secrets to strangers, would allegedly fling a pre-addressed letter out of his window into the street, confident that someone would pick it up, assume it had been dropped, and post it for him. I still can't decide if that's utter genius or sheer stupidity.

Rowland Hill's reforms were a triumph and the British became obsessive letter writers. In 1839, 75 million items were posted, which sounds like a lot, but by 1850 that had already more than quadrupled to 350 million. With the British Empire spanning the globe, and generations of colonial emigrants living abroad, never had it been so hard to keep in touch with loved ones back home. Yet, conversely, the establishment of national postal systems in other countries, and the subsequent co-operation between them, meant that, despite the ever-growing distances between people, communication was actually getting easier.

Still, it wasn't all uplifting loveliness. We may think ourselves terribly modern in our struggle with dodgy spammers ungrammatically asking for our bank details, but criminals, trolls and pranksters have been around for longer than we may think, and they took full advantage of the nineteenth-century postal revolution. Fraudulent begging for cash by men imitating destitute ladies was one such popular scam, while others discovered a sinister joy in anonymously sending abusive postcards to strangers; but perhaps the highest profile fraud was *The British–American Claim Agency*, set up by two unscrupulous Brits living in New York. In 1887 they wrote to innocent citizens teasing them with the possibility that unclaimed inheritances could await them, if they would only pay the modest search fees. Of course, there was no fortune to be had, and the 'fees' went straight into their pockets. By the time the police caught up with them, they were raking in $500 per day, the modern equivalent of having a brand new Mercedes delivered to their driveway every 24 hours.

Throughout history, wherever new technology has gone, exploitative criminals have soon followed, swooping on the naïve like rapacious vultures. But, being social creatures that have lived in complex societies for thousands of years, there was never any chance of people giving up on communicating with their fellow humans; sharing our lives is just too important to us. And, on that note, it's probably time we get dressed for tonight's big social gathering. The hours have flown by, and we're suddenly in danger of not being ready in time!

6 p.m.

PICKING AN OUTFIT

Tonight we're hosting a few friends for dinner, so it's probably incumbent upon us to abandon the comfy jogging trousers and T-shirt in favour of our sexiest party apparel. Or, at the very least, clothes unsullied by baked-bean juice. Entering the bedroom, we swing open our wardrobe's doors and gaze at the static array of fabric – some neatly folded, some dangling from hangers, but most bundled up and hurled in with careless disregard. The range of colours and styles is a reminder that clothes serve more than just a practical purpose; in fact, they transmit our social status, perceived gender, our wealth or lack thereof, and even our social and tribal allegiances. What we wear is a message to the world, though it may not be one we realise we're broadcasting.

But, in the very beginning, clothes probably began as little more than sensible outerwear to stop our nipples freezing off.

SHE'D RATHER WEAR FUR THAN GO NAKED . . .

When we talk about Big History, the obvious revolutions get a lot of airtime: the wheel, fire, metalworking, agriculture, mass communication. These are the heavy hitters of textbooks, but to that list we should add one more: the String Revolution. Unlike our ape cousins, most humans aren't quilted in heat-insulating fur. While that gives us the useful advantage of being able to sweat, and therefore run great distances without overheating, it does leave us in a bit of a pickle come winter time. And so, our ancestors began wearing clothes.

The oldest discovered sewing needles (thus far) date back 60,000 years and are slender bone tools, poked through with tiny eyelets, that allowed animal furs – previously worn as little more than a shoulder blanket – to be fastened together with sinew thread into tight-fitting clothing that snugly insulated torso and limb. It might not sound as thrilling as punch-ups with sabre-tooth tigers, but needlework prevented humans from freezing to death in the last Ice Age. So, when movie producers showed us Raquel Welsh sporting a fur-lined bikini in *One Million Years BC*, they weren't entirely wrong (well, apart from the presence of marauding dinosaurs).

With the gorgeously buxom actress parading around in furry knickers, the movie undoubtedly gave rise to many a schoolboy's masturbation fantasies, but what it sorely lacked was mastication, because Welch should have spent parts of the movie sat on her shapely bum, gnawing on her clothes like a puppy chewing a slipper. Why? Well, because one of the oldest known techniques for softening up leather is to break it down using the teeth and saliva. This is a low-tech solution to the inevitable hardening of the animal hide as it dries out, and it's a technique still practised by Inuit traditionalists whose caribou-skin parkas keep frostbite at bay.

But a better Stone Age process was to tan the skin into leather by soaking it in animal brains, thereby sluicing it with lubricating oil, or to bathe it in a mushy paste of water and acidic tree bark. This kept the skins soft and flexible, meaning clothes could be worn for more than just a few days before they dried up. And, extraordinarily, some of these prehistoric clothes are now preserved in museums.

PREHISTORIC FASHION (VICTIM)

About 5,250 years ago, in the Ötztal Alps that now separate Austria and Italy, a man lay dying, but this was no unfortunate skiing accident. A flint-tipped arrow had lodged violently in his torso and now he lay prone in the snow, drifting into fatal unconsciousness as the warm blood seeped from his wound. Our murder victim's name is forever lost, but he's globally famous thanks to his accidental discovery by two hikers in 1991 who spotted the upper parts of his mummified body appearing to try to haul itself out of thawed ice. To the archaeologists who've studied him, Ötzi the Iceman is the human equivalent of Pompeii – a time capsule literally frozen in time – and his clothes froze with him.

So, was Ötzi proudly showing off his bikini body? Sadly, the opposite – and who could blame him, frankly, seeing as he was stuck halfway up a snow-capped mountain? Instead, his loincloth and jerkin were of goatskin, with the latter made of cross-stitched panels of scraped fur, and, seeing as he'd already killed the goat anyway, he quilted his legs in goatskin too, fashioning a furry set of partial leggings of which even Mr Tumnus would have been jealous. To keep his head toasty, Ötzi wore a bearskin cap, and around his waist he sported a fetching belt of calf leather, while his shoes were fastened to his leggings with laces of deer hide. Clearly, for Ötzi to survive the winter, several animals had to do the opposite. But that's not to say all Stone Age clothing necessitated the spilling of blood.

There's strong evidence dating back perhaps 40,000 years for our Stone Age ancestors weaving plant fibres, having twisted them on their fingers to create yarn; but organic evidence of cords, string or fabric are rare, and no one's yet found a pristine Palaeolithic cardigan, so instead archaeologists have turned to artistic clues to corroborate their hunch. Across Europe and Eurasia, many ceramic and stone figurines depicting curvaceous women have turned up at Stone Age sites. These beautiful objects are among the earliest examples of human art, and their consistent form, no matter where they are found, suggests some cultural continuity across great expanses of territory.

But what catches the eye of fashion historians is that these so-called Venus figurines appear to be wearing woven fabrics. The Venus of Lespugue, from France, is perhaps showing off a string skirt with low-slung hip belt, while the Venus of Willendorf appears to be rocking a knitted cap on her head, the kind of headgear Bob Marley might have donned had his recording studio been located in an Austrian cave. So, it seems that even tens of thousands of years ago, humans weren't just draped in animal carcasses, they were also wrapped up in knitwear.

WE ARE LIVING IN A MATERIAL WORLD

In 1881, a man named Mohammed al-Rassul betrayed his two brothers. For the previous decade, the trio had been illegally flogging ancient Egyptian antiquities from a secret tomb which they'd stumbled upon when chasing down an errant goat (as you do...). But after suspicions were raised by officials, and an investigation led to the brothers, al-Rassul decided to shop in his two siblings and claim the reward for himself. Such betrayal suggests he had a crappy personality, but the world was undoubtedly grateful to him when he led archaeologists to the site of more than 50 ancient mummies, including that of the greatest of all the Pharaohs – King Ramesses II.

But, how's this relevant to clothing? Well, Ramesses was wrapped in perfectly preserved linen, a fabric woven from the flax plant – one possibly worn as far back as 30,000 years ago – and it was the Egyptians who really took to linen because it's a cool, lightweight fabric which can be easily bleached back to its pleasing creamy tone. More importantly, it was hygienic in a culture that prized cleanliness. Ramesses may have been a semi-divine king, but he wasn't shrouded in gorgeous silks, velvets and furs; no, his funerary garb was the same as that of any plough-wielding peasant smeared in ox shit. Linen was for everyone.

And, as we now know, linen shirts and slips were also the most common type of underwear in seventeenth-century Europe, where the fact they could be regularly rotated, and laundered clean, was much preferred over applying soap and water to the body itself. Crucially, though, when washing made its big comeback, linen didn't go quietly into the night, and many a Victorian housemaid found herself engaged in a never-ending battle to keep clothes and bedding looking white. These days, we tend to wear less of it, and prefer to stretch it over tables and mattresses rather than our shoulder blades, but it still goes everywhere with us, lurking in our wallets, because linen – along with cotton – is a constituent part in some modern banknotes. That doesn't mean you can put them through the washing machine, though . . . 'Money laundering' isn't a literal thing.

Cotton, of course, is also an ancient fabric. When Herodotus wrote 'And further [In India], there are trees which grow . . . a wool exceeding in beauty and goodness that of sheep. The natives make their clothes of this tree-wool', he was describing a custom already two millennia older than him, and that's really saying something because he was an ancient Greek who died 2,400 years ago. So, who were these Bronze Age cotton farmers? No prizes for guessing that it was those trendsetting Harappans who began cotton's journey to becoming the most influential fabric in world history. But cotton wasn't just confined to Asia, as it was also the primary fabric of the advanced South and Central American cultures, such as the Incas and Aztecs, the latter of whom – not possessing steel – made their battle armour (*Ichcahuipilli*) from nothing more than a dense padding of quilted cotton soaked in saltwater. Surprisingly, it was highly effective against sharp weapons, but I don't recommend you make your own armour and embark on late night vigilante sprees against knife-wielding muggers. You're not Batman, and I don't want your death on my conscience.

Cotton is the Meryl Streep of fabrics: it is endlessly versatile. Posh hotels crow about the 400-thread bed-sheets in their rooms, but that's a feeble level of softness compared with the 'white gold' of Royal Muslin, a hand-spun variety which achieved almost legendary status in ancient India, with its shimmering fineness topping the charts at a whopping 1,800 threads per square inch. As the medieval poet Amir Khusrow wrote: 'it is so transparent and light that it looks as if one is in no dress at all, but has only smeared the body with pure water.' It's tempting to wonder whether such sheerness had any influence on the moral tale of the Emperor's New Clothes, or whether it might be a useful excuse for nudists arrested for public indecency, 'No, I am wearing clothes, officer, they're just hand-woven by Indian spinsters . . . honest!'

Imported from India in the seventeenth century, cotton had a huge impact on European fashion. Chintz – a rough calico printed with busy floral patterns – became highly prized by the lower middle classes and, among other things, provoked the rise of Britain's own cotton industry that transformed the city of Manchester into nineteenth-century 'Cottonopolis'. By importing American-grown cotton and spinning it in huge power-looms chuntering away in noisy Lancashire factories, Britain outcompeted the Indian market and made this cheap fabric the clothing of the masses. It also fuelled Britain's ascent as an economic powerhouse that straddled the globe.

Previously, however, Britain – or rather England – had been a nation obsessed with wool. Sheep ambled across much of the rural landscape, and their fleeces were exported at lucrative prices to Italy and Flanders. It's a point emphasised by the seventeenth-century bishop and satirist (a weird combination, I'll grant you) Joseph Hall, who wrote: 'There were wont to be reckoned three wonders of England, *ecclesia*, *foemina*, *lana* – churches, women and wool.' Obviously English men were somehow deficient in Hall's eyes. Indeed, so pivotal was wool to medieval England that King Edward III demanded that his Lord Chancellor be perched upon a wool-stuffed red cushion (the Woolsack) whenever addressing the king's council. This was meant to remind everyone of where the nation's cash came from, and the Woolsack still remains in the British House of Lords, though – rather brilliantly – it was discovered in 1938 to have actually been crammed with horsehair. Dishonesty in politics! Who would have thought it?

Much like cotton, wool could be a coarse cloth suitable for a peasant's breeches or a sumptuous, scarlet robe fit for a princess – it's a warm, hard-wearing fibre but can vary wildly in quality, and so its use was widespread throughout ancient and medieval Europe, though in Asia it's likely that the coats of other animals, such as yaks and goats, might have been woven as well. But one material that we can confidently ascribe to Chinese origins is silk, a fabric produced not by wandering, bleating ruminants, but from the larval stage of a rather ugly moth.

The legend goes that about 5,000 years ago, the wife of China's Yellow Emperor, the Empress Léi Zǔ, was having a nice cuppa in her garden when a weird blob tumbled from an overhanging mulberry tree and splashed into her tea like an incompetent Olympic diver belly-flopping from the high board. Reaching to pluck out the interloper, the Empress found it was unspooling in her hands because a silkworm, when boiled alive, loosens its thread. Delighted at her discovery, she asked her hubby for a mulberry tree of her own and began experimenting with spinning and weaving silk, single-handedly kick-starting a major Chinese industry. It's a nice story, but it's probably rubbish. In fact, archaeological evidence for Chinese sericulture – the technical term for the silk industry – extends far beyond her lifetime to an estimated 7,000 years ago.

Though silk was strictly prohibited for ordinary folk, the Chinese didn't hoard their secret. Instead, its lucrative value in the West meant finished silks were transported 4,000 miles by caravan along the difficult Silk Road between eastern China and Damascus, from where they were shipped onwards to the eager Romans, Persians, Byzantines and Arabs, who regarded silk to be more valuable even than gold. Though eager to monetise their export, the Chinese were also careful not to let the secret of sericulture slip from their grasp, and made its smuggling a capital offence. But, by the fourth century CE, Korea, India, Japan and Persia all seem to have developed their own industries, and, a century later on, two monks working for the Byzantine Emperor Justinian pulled off an ingenious heist by smuggling silkworms out of China inside bamboo canes. The Byzantines also then sat on their newly acquired secret, flogging their wares for exorbitant prices, until eventually the methodology of silk production drifted westwards into Europe, and then was brought to Britain in the 1600s by the French Protestant Huguenots. From the most exotic of origins, silk was soon being churned out in not-so-exotic Macclesfield.

Historically silk has always been for the rich, with the exception of Genghis Khan's horde of Mongol warriors whose trashing of medieval China allowed them to rob silk storehouses and dress themselves in elite fabrics. This was rather handy in battle, because an arrow might pierce the flesh but it would not tear a silken shirt (silk is ridiculously strong), meaning arrow extraction was as simple as pulling one's clothes away from the body. These days, silk is considerably cheaper, but you don't see many fast-food workers draped in it. Instead, we commonly wear manmade fibres that simulate the silken sheen but can also be chucked in the laundry with our dirty socks. These are the fabrics of the modern world, the thermo-plastic nylon and the synthetic polyesters, both of which appeared around the time of the Second World War, which is no coincidence – a global war of such epic proportions was always going to need cheap, mass-producible materials for stuff like parachutes, ropes and uniforms – but now, of course, the demand for parachutes isn't quite what it once was, and synthetic fibres are now found in our drawers and wardrobes instead.

Oh, and speaking of which, it's time we chose some clothes for tonight. Where better to start than with our underwear?

THE PHARAOH'S PANTS

When Howard Carter thrilled the world with the discovery of King Tutankhamun's tomb in 1922, the headlines were taken up with the obvious stuff – gold, trinkets, that stunning sarcophagus, and the absurd curse more befitting an episode of *Scooby Doo*. However, what you didn't hear about were King Tut's undies. Yes, like a young boy waved off to Scout camp by an overanxious mother, his regal supplies included a gratuitous number of spare underpants: 145 pairs to be exact. Ancient under-crackers were the loincloth, or *shenti*, a triangular nappy that fastened at the hips. For some Egyptian peasants, toiling in the baking Saharan sunshine, these weren't merely underwear, they constituted the entire outfit.

In contrast, today most guys and gals wear fairly similar under-pants – a version of shorts or briefs – though many women also wear a bra. This is mostly to provide support to their bosom, although it's also because Western society greets the exposed lady-nipple with the binary opposites of 'phwoaaaaar' and/or pure righteous outrage. The bra and knickers combo is traditionally said to be a product of the mid-twentieth century, but the Romans sort of got there first. The *subligaculum* was a unisex leather garment, available as shorts or loincloth, worn by gladiators, actors and soldiers. While most male citizens likely went commando beneath togas and tunics, women probably wore underwear and accompanied it with a breast-band called a *strophium*. This tight-fitting bandeau provided support during exercise, protected their modesty and flattened large breasts to create the idealised silhouette of wide hips and a modest bust. Apparently, respectable ladies kept their *strophium* on during sex, as did many less respectable ladies depicted in Roman pornographic art, which seems to have been rather disappointing to their male partners.

Given the balmy climate, few Romans had the need for socks, apart from old dudes whose failing circulation saw them wrap insulating bandages around their legs, or those unlucky soldiers sent to defend the frosty fringes of the Empire. Archaeological excavations at Vindolanda Fort, the Roman military camp just south of Hadrian's Wall, has turned up hundreds of fascinating letters written on wooden tablets that detail the boring minutiae of daily life. Among the most famous is Tablet 346, in which some kind soul, perhaps a caring mother, has sent extra supplies to a soldier encountering the chilly northern wind: 'I have [sent] you ... pairs of socks from Sattua, two pairs of sandals and two pairs of underpants.' Well, at least it wasn't 145 pairs ...

To the Mediterranean ancients, leg coverings were typically a sign of either barbarism or failed masculinity, but that's easy to say when you're basking in the glorious sunshine. Further north, however, the weather could be bleaker than the plot of a Russian novel, so Celtic, Saxon and Viking chaps were all keen to slide long socks over their tootsies, and insulate their sensitive danglies with baggy linen breeches, or *braies*, though these weren't technically underwear because nothing was worn over them. Ladies, on the other hand, seem to have donned the long smock beneath their heavier dresses, but possibly didn't bother with knickers at all.

GETTING INTIMATE

We're well used to seeing patterned pants and bra: some sexy, some cute, some ridiculous – the fact they keep making those Christmas-themed novelty boxer shorts means someone keeps buying them – yet, for most of history, undergarments were just functional blank cloth. In ancient and medieval China, however, where fashion was carefully regulated by strict social mores, women's underwear could be highly ornamented as a secret expression of personal identity and desire, perhaps only glimpsed by those permitted to get close.

Such underwear, known as the *moxiong*, was often elaborate, featuring vividly colourful designs embroidered into diamond-shaped fabric that was then wrapped around the front of the torso and held in place by strong, stretchy cords. This was a tight-fitting top that covered breasts and belly but not necessarily the back, as, although a reverse panel could be added, the more risqué lady chose to leave her shoulders and the contours of her spine exposed under her long robes. Though such fashions evolved over many centuries, and the *moxiong* was just one of several popular styles, the ornamental beauty of such intimate lingerie remained right up until Mao's Cultural Revolution went and ruined the fun.

Back in twelfth-century medieval Europe, braies – those baggy outer shorts for chaps – started to shorten into underpants, being chased up the thighs by the lengthening of individual stockings which, by the fifteenth century, then evolved into two-legged pairs of thick hose. That said, it was also common for a gentleman to simply tuck his shirt under his goolies and not bother with pants at all, meaning we should probably refer to 'going commando' as 'going knight'. But when it comes to medieval women, the traditional history of underwear is now being rethought...

A MEDIEVAL WONDERBRA?

An angular, whitewashed structure with sloping grey roofing, Lengberg Castle in east Tyrol is a picturesque twelfth-century *schloss*, perched atop a defensive mound in the basin of a wooded valley. While pretty to photograph from outside, it's the hidden insides of this Austrian castle that have provoked surprise. Buried beneath fifteenth-century floorboards, a hidden vault was unmasked during restoration work in 2012 that contained long-forgotten fabrics which had survived the ravages of time and the nibbling of moths. These included four medieval bras with shoulder straps, things that might not enthuse those of us hoping for dead kings and Holy Grails, but costume historians reacted with a lot more jumping up and down. Until that point, bras were categorically a twentieth-century garment.

What separated bras from the aforementioned Roman boob-tube were not just the familiar straps, but that they were cupped to support each breast. Could this have been what Henri de Mondeville, a fourteenth-century surgeon, had meant when he wrote 'Some women... insert two bags in their dresses, adjusted to the breasts, fitting tight, and they put [the breasts] into [the bags] every morning and fasten them when possible with a matching band'? It seems, that the Wonderbra might be 600 years old, meaning its original slogan of 'Hello, Boys!' should probably have been 'Gooday, gentle syrs!'

But the revelations don't stop there. Historians are now wondering about medieval knickers (not in a pervy way, I hasten to add), because two pairs of underpants, with waist-strings, were also discovered. The big question is: were these worn by men or by women? It's more probable they were for gents, as there are scant references to knickers in this historical period, other than references to a woman's actual period. Rare translations of the Bible mention 'menstruous rags' in the Book of Isaiah, but is that a reference to medieval customs or ancient Judean ones? It's tricky to know. We do know that wealthy Italian women in the sixteenth century wore 'drawers', but they were the exception – in much of Europe, lady-pants were strictly off-limits.

Instead, most women continued with the long smock, (or *chemise* for the pretentious French-speakers at the English court), which remained fashionable well into the Victorian era. In fact, between the seventeenth and nineteenth centuries, a popular country sport in Britain, known as the 'smock race', saw young unmarried women racing against each other in just their delicates, while a huge crowd of onlookers cheered them on. The victor's prize, oddly enough, was another smock, presumably to replace the mud-stained one they'd just ruined. The logic was clearly flawed but many men gathered to watch regardless, delighted at the prospect of nubile ladies sweating in their underclothes. It was very much the wet T-shirt contest of its day.

But let's get back to today's choice of clothes. We're still umming and ahhing about whether to go with those tired-but-comfy grey underpants, or if we should cram our protesting flesh into those tight, bum-lifting ones that mask the gradual sag of our rear ends. While we weigh up the options, let's pick out some socks.

SOCK IT TO ME

In the mid-sixteenth century, stockings became the must-have accessory for European aristocracy and silk was immediately exalted over all other fabrics due to its price and softness. Queen

Picking an Outfit

Elizabeth I of England was gifted her first pair of silkies in the 1560s, and – after comparing them to woollen ones – immediately declared 'I like silk stockings so well, because they are pleasant, fine and delicate, that henceforth I will wear no more cloth stockings.' Soon after she started buying her own, spending a lavish £2 on each pair, which was roughly the annual wages of a junior servant. However, to show off her enormous wealth, she'd only wear them for a week before donating them to her ladies-in-waiting. Being given the Queen's intimate laundry was a tremendous honour, and perhaps it was like catching a rock star's sweaty T-shirt flung into the mosh-pit, but personally I'd be a little peeved if my boss gave me her used socks for Christmas (no offence, Caroline . . .).

Ironically, Elizabeth passed a law in 1571 demanding that most of her subjects wear woollen hats on a Sunday to support the English wool trade, a somewhat hypocritical move for a wool-renouncing silk lover. In truth, silk stockings were way beyond the budget of ordinary people and knitted woollen ones were much more common. Ladies' legwear stopped around the knee, while men's (called nether-stockings) carried on up to the nether-regions. For the male aristocracy, these were sewn into padded trunks decorated with the infamous codpiece – that projecting pouch of stiffened cloth that perched over a chap's package like a cricketer's protective box. However, at no point were any hard objects being hurled into their soft genitals by fellow athletes, so this was a purely aesthetic trend, a macho style to exaggerate a bloke's sexual potency. It was the Tudor equivalent of Derek Smalls from Spinal Tap stuffing a tinfoil-wrapped courgette down his pants, then waddling through airport security.

Anyway, having donned some slimming black socks, our mind must return to the underpants quandary.

LUCKY DRAWERS

So, when did modern underwear appear? Relying instead on layers of petticoats, most Western women only slipped into their drawers in the early 1800s, and these evolved into the risqué pantalettes – a feminine iteration of male drawers – that by the 1840s were frilling decoratively around the calves. These covered the full leg, but were usually crotchless for hygiene reasons. Men's undies, if worn at all, were essentially just long shorts and we know that in the late 1600s, King Charles II wore 13-inch-long silk boxers, tightened around his regal waist with ribbons, while the diminutive King William III – who booted Charles's Catholic brother James II off the throne – was said to go to bed in rough woollen drawers, green socks and a red vest, making him presumably resemble one of Santa's Christmas elves.

For the next 150 years, men's fashionable breeches became very tight, so long baggy underwear was sometimes eschewed in favour of tucking the shirt under one's bits. Gradually, shorter and snug boxer shorts gained popularity, most famously with the great philosopher Jeremy Bentham. When this brilliant, yet eccentric, man died aged 84 in 1832, his will demanded that he be turned into an auto-icon, or human scarecrow, and donated to University College London – the educational institution he'd helped to establish – so that he could eternally watch over its progress from beyond the grave, like some sort of benevolent pedagogy-zombie. Rather wonderfully, he's still there today, though his manky old head is now a wax replacement with some original hair stuck on top. But what was discovered during recent examinations into his state of decay was that Bentham's corpse sported some fetching woollen shorts beneath his breeches.

Bentham died during the reign of King George IV, Britain's joint-fattest monarch (he, Henry VIII and Queen Victoria all grew to have waistlines exceeding 50 inches), and it was plump King George who had famously worn a corset to suck in his bulging midriff. This, however, was not all that rare in the fashion-crazed Georgian era. Many a macaroni – the withering slang for the most outlandishly preening male fashionistas – had trussed himself up in whalebone stays to achieve the perfect silhouette, and even when these effete gents were replaced by the more masculine dandies, the corsetry remained trendy. But while the tummy was squeezed in, other bits of the anatomy, such as the calves and buttocks, were enhanced with padding, leaving one social commentator to snarkily observe that such fashion victims were entirely dependent on their 'shape merchants' and, when separated from their clothes and padding seemed to be 'quite a different species'.

WAIST NOT, WANT NOT

While macaronis were mocked, it was only their credibility and bank balance that was harmed. Women, on the other hand, could be physically damaged by the trend for tight-lacing, a form of stylistic corseting that dramatically altered the shape of the body. This reached its nadir in the nineteenth century when the idealised female form was for tiny waists but broad hips. Most fashionable ladies strived for a circumference of just 21 inches, but the French-Algerian actress Émilie Marie Bouchaud, who performed under the stage-name of Polaire, was famed for her pneumatic 38-inch bust and minuscule 16-inch waist.

This tight-lacing, inevitably, could cause irreparable harm to the body. For most, bruising was a daily occurrence, breathing was tricky and just climbing the stairs was enough to bring on dizzy spells – some ladies even wore corsets in pregnancy – but other common symptoms included muscular atrophy in the abdomen and back, reduced natural fertility and, in the worst cases, organ failure. It was rare, but not unheard of, for women – and even pre-pubescent girls – to lose their lives to this restrictive garment. Some contemporary doctors were aghast at such a practice, and the author of an 1837 book called *Female Beauty* was unambiguous in her concern:

> **women who wear very tight stays complain that they cannot sit upright without them, nay are compelled to wear night stays when in bed . . . the effect of stays is not only injurious on to the shape but is calculated to produce the most serious consequences.**

Eventually, by the early twentieth century, the fashion for boned-corseting did dwindle, leaving in its wake just the supportive fabric girdle around the waist that connected the brassiere to the hold-up stockings and short 'step in' knickerbockers. By the 1930s, the brassiere, pants and girdle were combined into a single garment called a corselette, but it too was abandoned by fashion-forward young women in the 1960s, who elected instead to expose their belly buttons and embrace the simplicity of just bras and knickers. But fashions are cyclical and the retro look is now back in style. Stockings, girdles, brassieres and suspenders have remained as intimate lingerie for bedroom seduction, or saucy glamour modelling, and the return of the belly-squishing corset, in the form of the flattering Spanx, shows we're not over the historical obsession with flat tummies. Hopefully, though, the fact they're elasticated, rather than rigidly boned, means no one will have to die this time.

Anyway, this morning, having pitted glamour pants against comfy undies, we've sensibly plumped for ordinary cotton briefs. These are descendants of men's Y-fronts launched in 1935, though their triangular cut is now considered a unisex design. With our underwear on, it's time to pick something to cover our bottom half.

ONCE MORE INTO THE BREECHES . . .

There's an oft-told story, much beloved by fashion historians, about a famous trouser incident (that's not a euphemism!) that occurred in Regency Era London. One night, possibly in 1814, the illustrious Duke of Wellington arrived at the door of the glamorous Almack's Assembly Rooms, a private club for the best-of-the-best in London high society. In just a matter of months, the Duke would heroically vanquish Napoleon Bonaparte at the Battle of Waterloo, and be lauded as a national icon of masculinity, but tonight not even he was getting into the party. Wellington, you see, had foolishly turned up wearing a pair of trousers, and the dress code was strictly breeches only. In fact, this story is a contested one, and he was possibly turned away for being a few minutes late, but it's true that loose trousers were, at this time, a shockingly modern garment. Wellington's own soldiers had only started wearing them in combat a few years before, and they'd slowly crept into daytime fashion, but knee-length breeches and tight pantaloons (with a strap under the shoe to keep them unruffled) were the only acceptable legwear for refined eveningwear.

We're so used to seeing trousers in our daily life that this might come as a bit of a surprise to us: are they really only 200 years old? Well, no. Outside of military wear, the Romans and Greeks found trousers (*braccae* in Latin) to be beneath them in more than just a literal sense, but it wasn't an opinion shared by their enemies and neighbours. Both the baggy *vajani* and the tight *churidar* pants were widespread in India, and the supposedly barbarian Persians – who, in truth, would have made even Christian Dior look like an unkempt lout – were enamoured of their brightly coloured trousers (*anaxyrides*), which were intricately patterned from dyed cotton or hemp and which could snugly follow the contours of the leg, or billow gently around ankle and knee like comfy pyjama bottoms.

Similarly, the later Arabs, who catapulted themselves from the desert to overwhelm the Persians and bring Islam to the world, were also trouser-wearers. The *sirwaal* was a pair of baggy, wide-legged pants worn to maintain hygienic freshness during sweltering Arabian temperatures. On the other hand, the Vikings and Saxons wore long trousers, or wrapped thin strips around their legs like bandaged Egyptian mummies to keep the heat in, as they lived in much colder climates. However, such legwear fell out of fashion in medieval Europe, despite remaining common in the East.

Why is this? It's been suggested that trousers predominated in horse-riding cultures, particularly those with a large citizen army. The reason for this is fairly obvious – they're just more practical for cavalry soldiers than skirts, and so it's no surprise that the horse-loving Scythians, Turks, Parthians, Persians and Mongols were all fond of a nice pair of slacks, with Middle-Eastern trousers being famously voluminous enough to shame even MC Hammer, hip-hop's premier doyen of enormous legwear. The Romans, Greeks, Chinese and Japanese, however, usually preferred to fight on their feet, but if they did begrudgingly take to the saddle – often in a desperate response to facing superior be-trousered horsemen – they too were pretty sharpish in swapping their kilts for kecks.

GOOD JEANS

As we gaze upon our shelves at the folded options for tonight's outfit, we're stuck with the eternal middle-class dilemma: casual or smart-casual? If it's the former, then we can get away with a fabric believed by some anthropologists to be so globally pervasive that around half of all the humans on the planet are wearing it right now. Yet, despite their ubiquity, jeans have a history that's difficult to discern. No one's quite sure where denim fabric originated, as the traditional story of it deriving from Nîmes in France (hence, *de Nîmes*) has been recently challenged by visual evidence of blue denim fabrics in seventeenth-century Italian paintings – indeed, there's a robust theory that the word 'jean' derives from Genoa – but what's certain is that strong, reliable denim was beloved by nineteenth-century American cowboys who spent months in the saddle, riding across inhospitable terrain and sleeping under the stars.

The chap who'd started making these durable clothes was a Bavarian immigrant named Loeb Strauss, who changed his name to the much cooler Levi Strauss when he opened a San Francisco dry goods store in 1850. His shop catered to the hordes of gold prospectors flooding into California, dreaming of plucking shiny mega-nuggets from the ground, and though many were probably disappointed, they were at least relieved to find that Levi's rugged jeans were up to the task, even if the fabric hadn't yet received its celebrated riveting. The honour of that invention fell to Levi's later business partner, Jacob Davis, a tailor who patented his riveting technique in 1873, thereby pinning the fabric together with a harder-wearing option than mere stitches.

Together, the pair clad the plucky pioneers of the Wild West, and when Hollywood started making westerns, the popular fashion for emulating the silver screen cowboys saw denim end up in the wardrobes of people who'd never even seen a cow in real life, let alone wrangled one. Of course, fashions come and go – who among us isn't mortified by embarrassing photos of our teenage outfits? – and the cowboy look might have started to become old hat were it not for the arrival in the 1950s of rock 'n' roll. When this youth culture exploded with greased-up, hip-swivelling verve, it was those rugged Levis, built to withstand punishment, that the bikers picked up off the shelves, giving jeans an edgy, hip new cache as the uniform of sexy rebellion.

Today, of course, they're the uniform of tired, middle-aged people whose knees creak when they stand up, but oddly they haven't been abandoned by young'uns either. Somehow, jeans have achieved a quantum superposition of being both cool and the exact opposite of cool – not so much Schrödinger's cat as Schrödinger's catwalk.

REVOLUTIONARY TROUSERS

Given that breeches dominated until the early 1800s, how did trousers become fashionable again in the modern West? Perhaps the most famous early adopters were the *sans-culottes*, the French Revolutionaries of 1789, who wore eye-catching, ankle-skimming stripy trousers.

Surprisingly, stripes have a controversial history. In medieval fashion they were vilified, probably due to a proscription in the Book of Leviticus banning the wearing of two types of cloth. Consequently, stripes had only been worn by lepers, illegitimate bastards, executioners and other social outsiders – it's no coincidence that modern prisoners have often been trussed up in stripy pyjamas, as the German word *strafen* (to punish) is fascinatingly similar to *streifen* (to stripe). Gradually, however, the meaning of stripes softened, becoming redolent more of servile status, and then transforming completely into a positive symbol for radicalism in the Age of Enlightenment, culminating in the proudly stripy flag of the newly independent USA.

Though loose-legged trousers were vulgar and modern in the 1790s, once the French stripes were removed, and the Duke of Wellington had shown them off a bit, they quickly superseded breeches to become the approved legwear of all men by the 1820s, and they've remained the standard gentlemanly dress ever since. But what about women's trousers? In modern history, the first major campaign to see women don pants came from America in 1851. Amelia Bloomer was a Quaker, temperance campaigner and suffragist, and she found the clothes allotted to women to be restrictive in both a physical and symbolic sense. Her answer was to champion huge Turkish trousers, nicknamed bloomers in her honour, but it says a fair amount about the attitudes to women at the time that the response was an outcry of moralistic fury. *Punch* magazine claimed it would lead to a society in which ladies literally wore the trousers in the relationship, writing: 'he will have to wear a gown; if he does not quickly make her put her Bloomer short-coats down'.

In the end, the hostile opposition was just too strong and it took another three decades for bloomers to be adopted, not as day-to-day wear, but as sporting attire. Just as horse-riding soldiers had switched to trousers, the late-nineteenth-century arrival of the bicycle, and the increasing popularity of female-friendly sports, saw women abandoning impractical skirts in favour of 'rational dress'. Bloomers and pantaloons allowed safer movement without the risk of snagging one's billowing petticoats in the bike spokes and being flung headfirst into a tree. This, and the fact that bicycles also allowed women to travel unchaperoned, meant that trousers played an important role in women's liberation.

The first designer to make women's trousers suitable for an evening out was the French queen of elegance Coco Chanel. Her wide sailor pants, worn with such elan in the 1920s, were symbolic of a new era in which feminine fashion played cheekily with masculine traditions. After all, women had only just clocked off from their factory shifts, having stepped into men's roles during the First World War, so now high-status ladies cropped their hair short and stepped out with the deliberately androgynous look. But society parties in the Hamptons were one thing, a high street in Bolton, Lancashire was quite another. Inevitably, Coco Chanel's reach barely penetrated the customs of the working classes, and though the Pit-Brow ladies of Wigan's collieries had been wearing trousers under their skirts since the mid-1800s, it wasn't until the Second World War that a woman could wear slacks on the average high street without attracting filthy looks. In fact, it was technically still against the law in Paris, until 2011, for women to wear trousers for anything other than cycling or horse-riding.

SKIRTS FOR HIM AND HER

But maybe trousers aren't our thing? Perhaps today is a good day for a skirt or dress? After all, there's a long history of both being worn by either gender. Traditionally, the British Army's Highland regiments were well deserving of their fearsome reputation for bravery and ferocity, no matter the fact they fought in short kilts and, in the First World War, even rolled on a pair of tights as well, to protect the skin from the blistering effects of gas attacks. Frankly, they could have charged the enemy lines dressed as Barbra Streisand, singing Broadway ballads in a shrill falsetto, and they still would've been super-butch.

In India, male labourers and farmers have long worn the *lungi,* a calf-length tubular skirt, or the ancient *dhoti* of the Harappans, a long loincloth tucked in at the front in the same way as you might fasten a bath-towel around your waist, after a shower. Skirts were also a garment of male nobility and ancient Babylonian and Egyptian kings often strutted about in just an ankle-skimming sarong, occasionally ruffled in the famous *kaunake* style to imitate the tufty texture of animal wool. Rather than skirts, wealthy ancient Egyptian women wore floor-length dresses that hugged the figure, tapering in around the hips, thighs and calves but often leaving the breasts exposed to the eye through the transparent mesh of fine fabric, which probably explains how Queen

Cleopatra managed to wrap two powerful Roman statesmen around her little finger.

Such liberal attitudes to nudity were also seen elsewhere in the Bronze Age. On the Mediterranean island of Crete, the ancient Minoans wore a distinctive look. Though most ordinary people wore simple tunics, artistic evidence shows high-status males seem to have taken their fashion advice from the children's cartoon, *He-Man*, as they leapt about the place in little more than a loincloth and metal girdle. The posh women, on the other hand, wore startlingly modern bell-shaped skirts that were almost redolent of Parisian fashion in the 1870s. These were intricately woven with extravagant patterns, and sometimes strips of differing colour were sewn together to create a banding effect. Much like an upturned shuttlecock, this allowed the long A-shaped flounces of fabric to float widely around the ankles but nip in tightly at the waist where short demi-corsets squeezed in the midriff but stopped short of the bosom, leaving the wearer's uncovered breasts to be propped up like two melons displayed on a greengrocer's shelf.

So, to attend a high-status party in Minoan Crete was to perhaps see men running about in their pants and women showcasing their boobs – it sounds like an 18–30 holiday and, sadly for the inhabitants of modern Crete, it's probably what they have to witness when the hedonistic youth of Britain invades every summer.

DRESSING UP, DRESSING DOWN

In many parts of the world, including Crete, Mongolia, Scandinavia, Greece and Rome, it was the dress – or tunic – that was the most common garment for both genders. For the Greeks, the two basic varieties were the *chiton* (unisex) and *peplos* (female only), and they looked similar at first blush. The simplest was the *chiton*, a tubular dress made by stitching a front and back panel together at the side-seams, like a long T-shirt, and then rucking up the middle to flop over the belt. Ladies almost always wore theirs long, while young chaps seem to have preferred it at knee length. Perhaps it was in response to constant tripping incidents because their mothers never told them not to run with swords? Who knows?

By contrast, the long feminine *peplos* was a single wrap of oblong cloth folded around the body, like one of those slankets you see advertised on TV shopping channels, and it usually draped down over one shoulder. The *peplos* could sometimes leave one side of the body naughtily exposed to the eye, a thrilling peepshow of leg and hip, so, as well as being pinned at the shoulder, it was occasionally closed up with a brooch (*fibula*) to stop the unwanted leering from passing sex-pests. It's for similar reasons of personal modesty that many Muslim women wear the *burqa* – a loose single garment draped from the head down, with a hole cut out for the eyes, that covers almost every scrap of flesh to the ankles – or the dark-coloured *abaya* robe that stops at the neck and can be accessorised with the *niqab* veil and/or *hijab* headscarf.

Muslim men also traditionally wear modest coverings, most notably the cotton *thawb*. This long tunic-dress with full-length sleeves is much older than the Islamic faith and was originally designed not to preserve modesty, but to protect the skin from the burning glare of the Arabian sun and regulate body temperature through internal convection of a gentle breeze. With Islam having expanded enormously from its desert roots, the *thawb* is now seen across the world, though with some regional variations – in Morocco, for example, the sleeves tend to be shorter and in other parts of the Gulf region it has picked up other names, such as the *dishdasha*. Crucially, however, it's worn by every class, from the lowliest goat-herder to the skyscraper-building, football-club-owning oil billionaire. In fact, it's so generic that the word *thawb* literally just means 'clothing'.

THAT'S A WRAP!

As we rummage in our cupboard, desperately looking for that favourite garment, we might accidentally discover that bed-sheet we wore a couple of years ago as fancy dress. It was an emergency costume for a hastily arranged toga-party, and wrapping our torso in an awkward amount of fabric made us curse the stupid Romans and their stupid fashion sense. But we can't be angry at all of them, as it was only citizens who were permitted to wear it and, even then, it was only the elite classes of the Late Republic and Early Empire who did so in practice, leaving most Romans to make do with knee-length tunics just like the Greeks. But that's not to say tunics were a lowly garment, as even senators and emperors wore them beneath the toga, no doubt because the huge swathe of wraparound fabric was only held in place by the wearer keeping their left arm outstretched at waist height, as if they were balancing an imaginary tea tray over the arm. Given that it took two slaves to put the blasted thing on, it possibly required only the slightest stumble for one's toga to slide off again and crumple embarrassingly around one's ankles.

The Romans pretty much nicked the idea for the toga from the Etruscans, but, in truth, ensnaring the body in wraps has been fashionable throughout place and time; it was carried off with aplomb by both genders of Babylonian and Assyrian aristocracy, and today we might think of such a style as a distinctly Indian custom where the traditional *sari* – a long, elegant cloth wrapped over one shoulder and around the torso and legs – is still worn by women over a tight, cropped blouse called a *choli*. Remarkably, there are something like 100 different ways to wrap a *sari*, making the marketing for my 'versatile, reversible rain jacket' seem woefully over-egged in the use of the word '*versatile*'.

CRIMES AGAINST FASHION

In 1681, during the Edo period of Japanese history when Tokyo (Edo) was established as the new capital city, a fleeting moment of excruciating social embarrassment caused a sizable ripple in the still waters of fashion history. The new ruler of Japan, the fifth Shogun Tokugawa Tsunayoshi, found himself nattering with a luxuriously dressed woman, having assumed she was legitimate nobility. It was all seemingly going fine, except he'd blundered his way neck-deep into a class-based equivalent of when straight men in the 1970s accidentally chatted up other straight blokes, having been flummoxed by the new trend for long, flowing hair. So, was this lady a prostitute? A criminal? An assassin? No, it was far worse than any of those – she was a merchant's wife.

Since the late nineteenth century, Western aristocracy have dressed in much the same clothes as the middle classes, though with better tailoring – the outward difference between a modern duke and a banker is not so obvious – but fashions had previously been symbolic labels of status. Across the world, so-called sumptuary laws were introduced to prohibit the lower classes from dressing like their superiors, even if they could afford to do so. For example, medieval England's King Edward III demanded that purple, gold and silver fabrics should be restricted to royalty only, and one had to be of knightly class to get away with velvet. On the other hand, in the 1570s Pope Pius V thought the colour blue, which had become popular with the lowly artisan classes, wasn't prestigious enough a dye to be included in Catholic liturgical use, as it would diminish the religious power to see such a common colour at the altar.

But sumptuary laws didn't just apply in Europe. A golden tsunami of cash was flooding into seventeenth-century Japan, creating a bourgeois class of nouveau riche to challenge the traditional order and imitate the styles of the land-owning *samurai*. Such was Shogun Tokugawa Tsunayoshi's irritation at accidentally making small talk with a commoner that he passed the first of many laws to restrict the opulence of middle-class fashion. This targeted several aspects of social display but, in particular, sought to squash the sudden popularity of gorgeous silken *kosode* (what we now call *kimono*), short-sleeved open robes belted around the waist with a sash. It wasn't so much the garment that was the problem but the way it was being decorated – mercantile show-offs were having theirs strewn with incredibly vivid and detailed imagery drawn from mythology and the natural world. It was like us seeing a gaggle of estate agents, normally bedecked in bland black and grey, suddenly strutting around in haute couture gowns made of reflective silver foil.

But the Shogun's edicts were weak and became dubbed the 'three-day laws', as people immediately began to flout them by sneakily wearing prohibited red fabrics as hidden underwear beneath their newly muted and unpretentious *iki*-style *kosode* – a more restrained version better in keeping with the rules. Others appear to have flaunted their more garish robes in private, or derived a secretive thrill by donning them during sex sessions with prostitutes – a double-whammy on the naughty scale – but it also seems that many of the outlawed patterns were merely copied from the silk of *kosode* onto the skin of the wearer, later creating a tattooing craze called *Irezumi* in which the entire body could be permanently inked with these mesmerising designs.

Fascinatingly, this trend is still highly regarded in certain quarters of modern Japan, and I've even heard of a Tokyo museum that paid living people a cash advance so that, when they died, their tattooed skins could be flayed from the body and hung on display like a Botticelli painting. Prohibition laws often result in unusual consequences, but I doubt any of the Shogun's advisors could have predicted art galleries filled with hollowed-out humans becoming an actual thing...

BIGGER IS BETTER

Somewhere in our cupboard there might be a massive dress: some sort of unnaturally inflated, Disney princess, puff-ball gown, or even a wedding dress – something reserved for special occasions, anyway. These, however, didn't use to be one-off attire for glitzy events; they were everyday clothing, worn even by relatively lowly women, though that doesn't mean they were practical. Though European medieval gowns were long, and covered the arms and legs, they weren't wilfully luxurious in their deployment of extra fabric. Yes, they flowed elegantly down the back, and they could feature those wizardly sleeves which dangled from the wrist like folded wings, but most followed the lines of the body and then gently fanned out around the ankles.

This began to change in the fashion-conscious fifteenth century when tastes radically shifted towards luxurious excess. Now, aristocratic ladies instead wore long *houppelands* with trains that dragged behind them and amassed around their feet like shimmering puddles of sunlit rainwater. Yet even this was nothing compared with what was looming on the horizon. By the time of Elizabeth I of England, in the late sixteenth century, high-status fashion had gone padding crazy. Though the waist was sucked in with a laced-up bodice, thus compressing the torso, the hooped farthingale skirt – the equivalent of wearing a cartwheel around one's midriff, and then suspending fabric over it like a tent – gave noble ladies a puffed-up bottom half, as if their legs had been replaced with beautifully tailored hovercrafts. Obviously, exaggeration was the intention and further cushioning was also attached under the rear of the dress to give women: 'a bummbe like a barrel' that 'make[s] their buttocks most monstrously round', or at least that's what the critics thought.

This bum-inflation was a fashion which continued to pop up over the next three centuries, and in the late seventeenth and mid-eighteenth centuries, the taste for maximum drapery saw aristocratic women swishing around as mobile clothes horses, bedecked in floating layers of drapes, capes, shawls and skirts. But the most ostentatious style was surely the colossal Mantua dresses worn at the royal courts. These were beautiful gowns suspended over hidden scaffolding that projected sideways out from the hips, similar to those shopping paniers you can clip to the sides of a bicycle, and the result made ladies appear very strange indeed. The *Weekly Journal* of 1718 reported 'I have seen many fine ladies of a low stature who, when they sail in their hoops about the apartment, look like children in go-carts'.

By the 1740s, these court dresses were so wide that ladies had to shuffle crablike through open doors, one at a time, or else they'd become stuck in them like jack-knifing lorries wedged in a narrow tunnel. One can only imagine the difficulty they had in trying to clamber into a raised carriage, given that they were also wearing huge, elaborate, heavy wigs and sported no knickers under their petticoats, meaning the potential for embarrassment must have been immense. Such elaborate gowns required considerable assistance to don, with the wearer standing stock still while a team of assistants buzzed around, fitting her out piece by piece as if she were an F1 car being serviced by a well drilled pit crew.

Perhaps inevitably, this outlandish fashion swiftly vanished in the wake of the bloody French Revolution, which saw nervous aristocrats hastily jettisoning the grandiose tiers of fabric and wiggery, so redolent of the deposed monarchy, in favour of naturalistic hairstyles and the slender gowns familiar to us from the movie adaptations of Jane Austen novels. Ironically, however, this simpler style had actually originated with none other than the doyen of massive dresses herself, Queen Marie Antoinette, whose curious hobby was to role-play as a mere shepherdess in a purpose-built theme park of rustic fiction called the Hameau de la Reine, erected near the Palace of Versailles. Here she pretended to be a lowly farm girl, far away from the trappings of royal splendour, and milked cows as a sort of bucolic life-swap fantasy. As peasants and farmers milled around her, she and her kids swished about in simple muslin dresses, unaware of the revolutionary horror that would soon befall them.

DRESS TO KILL

And yet, despite the Jane Austen simplicity, in the mid-nineteenth century the Victorians reintroduced the Big Dress, harking back to those Elizabethan farthingales with newly improved caged crinolines – rigid under-petticoats built like cross-braces of the Eiffel Tower. This visually emphasised the womanly fertility of a small waist and broad hips, by contrasting the dainty midriff with a vast ocean of soft fabric wafting out from the body, as if the wearer had poked her head through the top of a deflated hot air balloon and then yanked it down around her hips.

Crinolines were undoubtedly elegant but they had their downsides. Due to their parachute-like construction, a decent gust of wind would easily flip the skirts over the wearer's head. You can probably understand why the pantalette – those frilly ankle-length drawers – suddenly lurched into fashion, as revealing one's bum and naughty bits was pretty much the most embarrassing disaster a woman could suffer in a society that was shocked by the merest glance of an ankle. But accidental flashing was not the only peril. Crinolines could also be a tremendous safety hazard, as many were made from the ferociously flammable celluloid, an early thermoplastic better known for its use in cinematic film, and the smallest spark from a cigar or unguarded fireplace could cause a fashionable lady to erupt into a human fireball, tragically rendering some women literal fashion victims.

Thankfully, hooped skirts were more commonly a source of clumsy slapstick than terrifying horror. Having become enormously popular with even working-class women, crinolines were a cumbersome threat to economic productivity. In 1863, the female staff at an English pottery factory accidentally caused £200 worth of damage just by knocking stuff over with their massive dresses – proof that you don't need a bull to cause chaos in a china shop.

HISTORY REPEATING

The end of the Edwardian era witnessed a landmark sea-change in the cut of women's dresses. From the over-draped, über-inflated proportions of the mid-eighteenth and nineteenth centuries, which had emphasised a woman's natural curves with artificial corsetry and padding, the 1920s delivered the complete opposite: the nascent Hollywood glamour suddenly made the hipless, boobless flapper girls the epitome of style, and all that stuffy, stiff rigidity was chucked out for sleeveless knee-length dresses that hung from bony shoulders and shimmered under the dancehall lights.

The fashion of the 1750s and 1850s had been big, brazen and exaggerated but the counterpunches of the 1820s and 1920s had stripped that all away. It's an interesting reminder that the history of fashion is a rapidly changing story of reactionary trends that reject, as much as embrace, what went before.

GETTING SHIRTY

If we're plumping for jeans or a skirt, then we're going to need a top to accessorise the look, otherwise our friends are going to feel really uncomfortable at dinner. We've already discovered that the reliable, ever-present tunic was the mainstay of the past, a versatile garment sported by men, women and children for millennia. By the sixteenth century in Europe, the male version had shortened in length into the doublet, a hip-length fitted jacket with buttons down the front, and this upper layer was then connected to the breeches, or hose, with suspenders. It was an entirely sensible idea, but not ideal for those with runny tummies or nervous bladders, as it did mean a certain amount of dextrous fiddling was required before a chap would drop his kecks.

In the aristocratic style, the sixteenth-century Tudor doublet was heavily padded in the chest to bulk up the wearer, giving them the posture of an obese pigeon that's feasted on too many discarded chips. For everyone else, it was a warm over-layer beneath which a waistcoat might be worn, and then under that was the linen shirt with the billowing sleeves – the filth-preventing underwear – though peasants mostly stuck with a coarse woollen smock and jerkin. Neither the shirt nor smock was buttoned down the middle, but the shirt featured a small turn-down collar which, for the nobility, famously morphed into the detachable and concertinaed ruff of starched linen that radiated 360 degrees around the neck. The odd result of this was to make the head appear to float unattached from the body, as if it'd been severed by a deranged psychopath and presented as a gift in an ornamental doily.

Picking an Outfit

In fact, these ruffs grew so wide by the end of the sixteenth century that some people allegedly had to use elongated spoons to feed themselves, as they couldn't get their hand close enough to their face. Queen Elizabeth I herself, always something of a trend-setter, preferred to cut out the front section and have the rear rise upwards behind her head, like the neck frill of a triceratops dinosaur, as this allowed her to showcase much, if not all, of her regal bosom, which she continued to do even in her old age, much to the distaste of foreign ambassadors who weren't prepared for the sight of geriatric boobs.

The ruff fell out of fashion in the 1620s and the more modest collar returned, but by the 1700s the shirt began to ruffle at the neck, the frill being known as a jabot, and became increasingly decorous and flouncy. The notorious trendsetter of Regency Britain, George 'Beau' Brummell, was an obsessive perfectionist who changed his shirt three times per day, wore his collar high and accessorised it with a cravat, though even this simple fashion seems to have been an almost insurmountable daily challenge for him. One famous story saw a friend enter Brummell's room to see a heap of cravats discarded on the floor, and Brummell's valet diligently smoothing out a new one. Bemused, the friend pointed at the pile and enquired what was going on, to which the fashionable dandy declared 'Sir, those are our failures.' You won't be surprised to learn that Britain's premier clothes horse was so fastidious he cleaned his shoes with champagne, and famously dumped a woman because he'd seen her eating cabbage.

Yet, despite Brummell's enormous attention to detail when it came to his shirt, it wasn't meant to be seen by anyone else. For anything other than the frill or collar to be visible was wholly indecent as, let's not forget, a shirt remained underwear until the early twentieth century, by which time it had acquired buttons. But those who couldn't wear a shirt, such as soldiers and sailors, were issued with a tight-fitting, buttonless version instead.

A T-SHIRT NAMED DESIRE

Cropped at the biceps, and scalloped at the neck, the T-shirt had first evolved from the white flannel undershirts worn by nineteenth-century American sailors, and – though its origins are debated – we know that it became regulation wear in the US Navy in 1913. It was also adopted in the 1930s as practical running gear by athletes, but for everyone else it was just underwear. That's not to say you wouldn't have seen guys stripped to their tees on a hot summer's day, but these were working-class labourers and none would have flaunted their cotton-quilted chests in a bar that evening. In order for the T-shirt to become an outer garment in its own right, a dollop of Hollywood glamour was required, and in 1951 that moment arrived in iconic style.

In the classic adaptation of the Tennessee Williams play *A Streetcar Named Desire*, Marlon Brando scorched the silver screen as a white-hot beacon of potent masculinity. His Stanley Kowalski was a primal, muscular, über-man who emitted an erotic charge so compelling he could probably have powered a small town. Crucial to his magnetism was the look – the tight-fitting T-shirt, straining at the seams to contain his impassioned frustration – and though he was sweaty, furious and psychologically damaged, audiences could not take their eyes off the anti-hero. Almost overnight, the youth of America knew where the future of fashion lay... and it most definitely wasn't with the frilly ruff.

Right, so having finally chosen an outfit, and done a quick pirouette in the mirror, it's time we start preparing for our guests' arrival. We prepped the food in advance last night, so all that needs to be done is to open the bottle of bubbly, and lay the dinner table. Thank goodness for forethought.

7 p.m.

A CHAMPAGNE APERITIF

Tonight we're hosting a little party to celebrate the birthday of a good friend, and as our guests arrive, looking glam and chipper as they come through to the dining room, we proffer a glass of champagne to each of them. After all, champers is the default drink of the celebratory gathering – but it wasn't always so.

THE DEVIL'S WINE

Here's a lovely story for you. On 4 August 1693, an aged Benedictine monk by the name of Dom Pierre Perignon was standing in the winery at the Abbey of Hautvillers with a grin plastered across his face. Shouting excitedly for his monastic brothers to gather around him, he declared 'come quickly! I am drinking the stars!' He had every right to be thrilled. After years of experimentation, he had finally cracked the secret to producing fizzy champagne. Alas, this charming anecdote is mostly bollocks. The idea that Dom Perignon set out to invent fizzy white wine is a nineteenth-century marketing myth, and the origins of the world's most luxurious drink derive from a combination of accidental discovery, and – to my French mother's undoubted horror – the ingenuity of the English.

Champagne is not a specific type of wine, it's actually a French wine-producing region – Spanish Cava and Italian Prosecco are fairly similar drinks – and medieval champagnes were still in nature and greyish in colour, rather than lightly sparkling whites. Though well respected at the time, they didn't match the exalted reputation of Bordeaux's superior offerings, but because they were grown in close proximity to the king-crowning cathedral of Reims, Champagne's winegrowers could at least rely on royal patronage. Okay, so champagne's origins were decent but not spectacular, but can we assume it became the first ever sparkling wine? Nope, that honour went to the Blanquette de Limoux produced in 1531 by the Benedictine monks of St Hilaire, not far from the southern fortress city of Carcassonne. And no, Dom Perignon didn't learn his craft there either, that's just one of the several mini-myths compacted into the 'drinking the stars' propaganda campaign. *Pardonne-moi, maman*!

In truth, the bubbles currently effervescing in our glass were actually the bane of Dom Perignon's life, and the reason he hated them was because they were a symptom of failure in the manufacturing process. Sparkling champagne was an infuriating anomaly – to him, it was *le vin du diable* (the Devil's wine) – but we now know that it wasn't Satanic meddling to blame, but instead a quirk of organic chemistry. The northerly Champagne region succumbs to chilly winters, and the yearly frosts were temporarily pausing the yeast-based chemical reaction that turns sugar into alcohol, meaning the fermentation process, thought to be finished by autumn, was actually biding its time. When the new vintage was bottled in March, the summer sunshine reactivated the dormant yeasts, producing a sudden surge of carbon dioxide inside the bottle, and therefore bubbles.

But, it gets worse. Due to the poor quality of French

glass-making, this internal pressure caused some of the bottles
to explode, which was a costly and embarrassing disaster for
Dom Perignon, and also forced those entering the cellars to wear
protective padding and an iron face-mask, to stop them being
blinded. Those bottles that didn't shatter – perhaps because the
oiled hemp rag, or wood stopper, placed in the top wasn't airtight
– were hurriedly shipped off to customers in France, but, more
importantly, also found their way into England. When it arrived
off the boat, the champagne was often re-bottled by the English
to ensure its longer lifespan, but their bottles were produced in
hotter furnaces that burned sea-coal instead of wood, resulting in
tougher glass. Crucially, they also preferred airtight cork stoppers
instead of rags, meaning something novel soon occurred – the
gently effervescent wine became increasingly fizzy, as the gas
pushed against the tougher walls of its glass and cork prison.

With bubbles being a symptom of poor quality control, you
might think the English would have reacted stroppily to being
sold dodgy goods by their on/off enemies, but the sparkles were
greeted as a thrilling novelty in King Charles II's party-mad
Blighty. Dom Perignon was certainly dedicated to improving the
quality of wine production, and had successfully produced a still
white wine from red grapes, and was experimenting with blended
grape varieties, but at no point was he expecting overseas orders
to flood in for the Devil's wine. However, before long, his refined
French clientele also began requesting bubbly champers, and the
puzzled monk was forced to adapt.

ROYAL FIZZ

By the time Dom Perignon died in 1715, his vineyards were
producing both still and sparkling wines, but it was the latter
which was poured into the Duc D'Orleans' cup when he became

Regent of France in that same year. This was the launch-point, the moment when champagne first won celebrity acclaim, and soon upwardly mobile merchants began sniffing out business opportunities in the sparkle trade. Nicolas Ruinart, the nephew of Dom Perignon's close friend, Dom Thierry Ruinart, established the first champagne marque in 1729, and was followed in 1743 by an enterprising wool-dealer called Claude Moët who somehow snared King Louis XV's mistress Madame de Pompadour as a loyal customer. Her proclamation that: 'champagne is the only wine that leaves a woman looking beautiful after drinking it' was the kind of incredible PR that you just couldn't buy in the eighteenth century. As other merchants eagerly leapt into the bubble-biz, it became clear that a small aristocratic market would not support all these new wineries. Champagne would have to broaden its customer demographic.

Having finally discovered the secret of toughened glass and corks, champagne growers could ship their wine to far-flung places without the bottles spontaneously exploding like badly wired grenades. By the end of the century, champagne was gliding down the elegant gullets of Tsar Peter the Great and America's own republican superhero George Washington. It was suddenly the drink of power, elegance and luxury, but people didn't have to be a monarch to slurp it. Indeed, nineteenth-century advertising campaigns cunningly traded on the perceived opulence, yet carefully aimed their product at the rising middle classes. That said, some marques were forever out of reach – Cristal, produced by Louis Roederer, was bottled exclusively for the Tsars of Russia, and remained unavailable to the hoi polloi until the end of the Second World War.

Tonight, we are not enjoying Cristal – it's still affordable only to rappers and footballers – but when we sauntered down the supermarket alcohol isle, hunting for a bottle, we were able to choose from a broad range. The once sweet grey wine of medieval

France is now available as the saccharine *doux* and *demi-sec*, or the dry *sec* and *brut*, or even the über-dry *extra-brut*. And, of course, there are those made from white grapes (*blancs de blancs*), those from red (*blancs de noirs*), the alluringly pink *rosés*, and the esteemed *cuvée de prestige* made predominantly from a single year's vintage. But one unchangeable thing that clearly defines champers is its fizziness. Bubbles are to champagne what headbands are to 1980s stadium rock – the defining, thrilling essence without which the experience becomes immediately disappointing.

So, with glasses charged, let's drink to the birthday girl and get the evening underway.

DINNER

The party is underway and everyone is chatting freely, but the excitable chirp of the oven timer tells us that dinner is pretty much ready. If truth be told, it's not exactly a culinary masterpiece that we're about to serve up, but no one's insulted when we reveal the menu. After all, it's not really the food that's brought people out tonight – no, we're here for each other's company. We're here to share.

BETTER TOGETHER?

The Ice Age was a rather chilly time to be a human. We're not talking Antarctic extremes, exactly, but at night the inhabitants of central Europe had to contend with sub-zero temperatures as well as the constant menace of marauding predators. In the swooping glacial valleys of Moravia, in what is now the Czech Republic, 30,000 years ago the wind must have whipped through with bitter ruthlessness. It's hardly a surprise, then, that archaeologists excavating at the village of Dolní Věstonice have found ample evidence of burnt hearths. Not only does fire warm the body, but cooking chemically unlocks the extra calories in meat to boost the body's resistance to the chill, and speeds up digestion – for Ice Age people, a hot dinner was a no brainer, even when they were eating animal brains.

But these hunter-gatherers weren't just huddled by the fire, ignoring each other. The hearth was probably also the focus of social bonding. In fact, *focus* is the Latin word for hearth – the fireplace has been the pulsing organ of commonality for many millennia. What's more, cooking the food didn't just make it tastier, and more nutritious, it also softened the tough fibres that were beyond the jaw-strength of gummy infants or the toothless elderly. We know from prehistoric skeletal remains that people with physical disabilities were not abandoned to starvation, but were cared for by others. To barbecue dinner, then, was also to provide sustenance for the most vulnerable, and gathering around the flames brought everyone into the fold. We use the word 'companion' to mean a life partner, but the word is intimately tied up with food – it's Latin for someone with whom we gladly break our bread.

I'LL HAVE WHAT SHE'S HAVING

Feasting together has been a widespread custom for as far back as the evidence can carry us, and sometimes the necessity of calorific intake had nothing to do with it. The Iron Age hill-fort at Hambledon Hill, in the English county of Dorset, was an impressive ancient earthwork, erected atop a 200-metre-high slope and designed to fend off rival tribes. But it's not the Celtic defenders that interest us here; instead it's the Neolithic people, and those of the later Bronze Age, who had previously utilised the hill as an intermittent meeting station. They didn't live on it, but instead turned it into a ceremonial party-venue-cum-ancestral-cemetery, and then appear to have invited others from far and wide to unite there, as summer's long days faded, to feast upon cow, deer and whatever else looked vaguely delicious in the nearby fields.

It was, by the looks of it, a bit like the Glastonbury music festival – people arrived, had a great time, left a whopping great mess and then went home again – though one hopes the toilets were more civilised. Why they did this is a mystery. Perhaps it was a religious festival? Maybe it was simply an annual knees-up for the in-laws? Or maybe it functioned as an inter-tribe dating service, culminating with uplifting weddings for the newly matched lovebirds? Frankly, we're stumped, but the absence of domestic houses on the site tells us that this was clearly the place to be seen in late July, but that the only things still there by December were the carefully buried bones of the eaten animals and mourned-for human ancestors.

Feasting, then, could be fun, and not simply a matter of dogged survival. But it also played an important sociological role of lubricating the revolving cogs of society. In Bronze Age Mesopotamia, a shared meal was a contractual signature to approve a Babylonian business deal, with ancient legal documents often mentioning that 'bread was eaten, beer was drunk, and bodies were anointed in oil', which sounds way kinkier than it actually was. In particular, salt and wine were demonstrably shared between the partners as a symbol of new-found fraternity, and to refuse the offer wasn't just impoliteness, it could be a deal-breaker. A Mesopotamian feast was like a modern handshake for the cameras when footballers join new teams – not strictly essential, but unsettling if absent.

This moment of union, whether in business or marriage, might sound like a trivial gesture, but the ancients took a dinner vow incredibly seriously, to the point that it could skip the generations. In Homer's celebrated poem *The Iliad*, the warriors Glaukos and Diomedes come face to face on the battlefield and are about to start stabbing each other, when one of them recognises the other's name and immediately offers up his armour as a gift. Charmed, his intended victim puts down his sword and returns the favour, and both agree to maim some other unlucky sod instead. Had they once made a vow over a decent glass of vino? No, but their grandfathers had, many years ago. Such a gesture of *xenia*, or guest-friendship, was as hereditary as male-pattern baldness to the Greeks, and could endure as long as living memory perpetuated it.

As you can probably gather, the Romans and Greeks believed eating together – or what we might call conviviality – was the deepest social bond, a way of communicating with others, and though ruffian barbarians and feral animals were rumoured to eat in vague proximity, to the Romans they lacked all the rules and etiquette that made sharing food a civilising presence. As the writer Plutarch elegantly put it: 'we do not sit at the table only to eat, but to eat together.' And so, every day, wealthy Romans feasted on a meaty meal called a *cena*, in groups of up to about 12 people, though a truly epic feast was known as a *convivium*, and a special religious banquet was an *epulum*.

Of course, like us, their tummies gurgled before and after this grand repast and so they often partook of cold snacks dubbed *a prandium*, but this was purely nourishment to keep them from keeling over in a hypoglycaemic crash, whereas *cena* was a sacred meal elevated to the role of social glue. Whether the poorer Roman underclass mirrored their superiors in this way is tricky to gauge, but they found some measure of communal dining in *popinae* – take-away food shops – and the larger, rowdier *tabernae* where drink, food, gambling and prostitution were all handily located for the less discerning client.

WHERE TO SIT?

As respectful hosts, the imminence of our meal means we start to gesture to our guests, gently wafting them away from the sofas in the direction of the dining table. But, having not laid out name cards, we notice a moment of hesitation as our friends weigh up which seat to claim. We see the married couple fleetingly ponder if they should sit side by side, or face each other so they can silently communicate with the subtle eye rolls and facial twitches honed over years of cohabitation. Others ask whether we're doing a boy/girl/boy/girl alternating set-up, while the svelte vegetarian with the slender waist politely volunteers to perch in the cramped corner, seeing as she's dinkier than the rest of us.

It's a light-hearted moment of group indecision, and one that generates knowingly embarrassed grins, but this tiny theatre of social awkwardness reveals why most cultures in history had rules about whose bum got parked on which seat, and whose bums weren't welcome at all. Plutarch, in his work the *Symposiacs*, pondered whether it was the host's responsibility to seat his guests or let them work it out for themselves, but other Roman hosts mostly elected to meddle, and used their banqueting space as a mirror image of social stratification. In such scenarios, where there was no shared dinner table and people reclined on couches, the host would often sit at the head of the room with the favoured guests close by, while the desperate hangers-on, embarrassing uncles and boring dullards who worked in admin were banished to the furthest ends of the sofas, safely out of A-lister earshot.

To make it even clearer that their presence wasn't much desired, these lesser guests might be served inferior food and cheaper wine, and they knew it all too well because the good stuff was paraded in front of them, mockingly out of reach.

High-status Greek men dined together in a room called the *andron*, or 'man-room', and did so without their overly serious wives, though that didn't stop them inviting courtesans, dancers and flute-playing totty to entertain, flirt and possibly offer up more explicit services of the naked jiggling variety. But the Romans seem to have been less restrictive than their Aegean neighbours and wives were often permitted to sit upright in more formal chairs while their hubbies slouched on the couches. Being invited to drape one's self horizontally was probably a rare treat for most ordinary ladies.

Outside of the 'civilised' world, the writer Athenaeus described the Celts – whom classical sources variously described as Caesar-bothering, weirdo barbarians with blue-dyed skin and handlebar taches – as a martial people that praised macho violence above all else. Accordingly, their dinner arrangements elevated the generous host and the strongest warrior to the centre of the feast, while lesser men, and the gathered women, orbited around them like ale-quaffing satellites, munching boiled meats and vegetables from ceramic plates and wicker baskets. Yet if we jump forward a few centuries to the Middle Ages, paintings of grand feasts in majestic halls show that women were sometimes absent entirely – dining together elsewhere, as was also the case for aristocratic Chinese women who dined behind concealing screens – or were grouped together on the far end of a bench, banished to the edges of the party as if their invitation had been a hasty afterthought.

Much like the Roman snob who condemned his unwanted acquaintances to the fringes, the English medieval banquet was usually structured so that the host and his closest guests sat at a permanent table *(table dormant)* that was raised up on a dais and which was positioned horizontally at the far end of the hall. It's a layout still commonly seen at British weddings. From here, the host could gaze upon his guests arrayed before him at trestle tables arranged lengthways up the hall. These people were welcome to his food, but were considered 'below the salt', meaning they were not worthy of the lord's raised table upon which perched a beautiful salt cellar, often crafted from silver and perhaps encrusted with shining jewels, that glistened at his right hand. Sometimes this cellar came in the form of a stunning ship called a *nef*, and by the sixteenth century these even featured mechanical working parts and little wheels so the salt could be rolled up the table like a gilded Tonka Truck crafted for a billionaire's infant son.

But elsewhere in Europe, it was equally common for the host to abandon the dais and continue the Celtic tradition of claiming the centre for himself, sitting proudly in the middle of a long table, with the guests radiating outwards in order of their importance. One wonders if the unwanted people at the far extremes of the table, who might well be ladies, grumpily harrumphed about their humiliating position or, like unpaid interns permitted access to the company Christmas dinner, were simply delighted that they'd be invited at all? But this clear division in the room went through various nuanced transitions, and then, in the seventeenth century, aristocrats ceased this mass extravaganza entirely, instead dining more selectively with small groups of noble equals. But, even then, a duke would still be served his grub before a mere viscount.

Yet, such preferential treatment didn't always apply outside of the rarefied world of the elite. If we were currently sitting in a lovely restaurant, rather than our home, none of us would feel obliged to get up and move seats when someone with a higher-paying job walked in. In England, at least, this informality began in the coffee houses of the seventeenth century which, as we've already discovered, became meeting places for male poets, writers, scientists and merchants. Accordingly, in a sub-culture that prized new ideas over all else, the old customs of bowing and scraping to one's superiors were abandoned, and in 1674 a new guide to coffee shop manners explained in clear terms:

First, Gentry, Tradesmen, all are welcomed hither,
And may without Affront sit down Together
Pre-eminence of Place, none here should Mind,
But take the next fit Seat that he find,
Nor need any, if any Finer persons come,
Rise up for to assigne to them his room.

Another surprise to European travellers was that English men were happy to let respectable women dine with them in taverns, and Samuel Pepys' diary entries reveal that he regularly invited his wife along for a group meal in London's tasty establishments, though it's unlikely that they opted for the boy/girl alternating seating plan, as – even a century later – John Trusler's *Honours of the Table* reported it as a novelty in 1788, saying: 'a new promiscuous mode of seating [has begun with] a gentlemen and lady sitting alternatively around the table, and this for the better convenience of the lady being attended to, and served by the gentlemen next to her.' Similarly, in mid-eighteenth-century Paris the restaurant was a new venue for dining, and these newly established eateries were just beginning to serve women alongside men, rather than shooing them into their own private booths. Slowly, some of the old rules were eroding away.

But not all of them . . .

AFTER YOU, NO, AFTER YOU . . .

With our guests having now picked a seat, we allow them to sit at the same time. But Trusler's report from 1788 was clear that, for the upper classes, the traditions of rank remained: 'the ladies, whether above or below, are to be served in order, according to their rank or age, and after, the gentleman in the same order.' This sounds simple enough until one examines the baffling complexity of the British social hierarchy, in which there were lords, ladies, earls, dukes, barons, knights, countesses, princes and princesses – all with variously titled offspring waiting to step into their hereditary shoes – and that whenever someone got married, or was widowed, they might be bumped up or down the dinner table's order of precedence, forcing the host to play a secret game of mental Top Trumps in which the guests were pitted against each other in various battles of merit and prestige until a clear hierarchy had been discerned.

Intriguingly, the opposite applied in traditional Chinese etiquette, where the guests would quite literally try to shove each other through the dining room doorway first, with all involved desperate to let the next person be seated before them. To outsiders, this surely sounds like a bizarre Monty Python sketch in which competitive politeness escalates into physical violence, but no one was trying to hurt the other. It was a charade in which everyone knew their role, and once the ritual had clocked up enough awkward seconds, someone – usually an older guest – would pipe up with the lovely phrase 'better obedience than deference' and the guests would respond immediately to the host's invitation to take their places.

But back in the West, another minefield of manners was hosting a soirée in which the guests outranked the host; it left the latter open to accusations of pretentious social climbing, or it threatened the possibility that the cookery, cutlery and conversation would fall beneath the standard demanded by the superior guests, or that the servants simply wouldn't be well drilled enough to pull off a flawless dinner without accidentally flinging hot soup over a dowager countess. The hosting of a Victorian dinner party was fraught with all the dramatic terror of a tightrope walker juggling chainsaws – at any moment the slightest slip might be catastrophic and could have ramifications that endured for years.

Finally, there was also the curious superstition about how many people could gather around the table. Christians have seemingly worried about it for centuries, on account of Christ and his 12 disciples munching mournfully at the ill-fated Last Supper. With this in mind, in nineteenth-century France, if you invited 13 others to join you for a dinner party, and one of them dropped out at the last minute, then you could hire an emergency guest known as a *quatorzieme* (the 14th) to make sure no bad luck befell your feast. This chap would lurk in his apartment from 5 p.m. onwards, already dressed in a dinner jacket, awaiting his heroic callout as if he were some debonair middleclass superhero, scanning the sky for a distress signal.

So prevalent was this religious triskaidekaphobia – the fear of 13 – that in the 1880s a certain Captain William Fowler, a military veteran of the US Civil War, established New York's Thirteen Club with the noble intention of disproving the superstition. He and his 12 guests, who later included five American Presidents, planned their events to begin at 7.13 p.m. on 13 January, and then served 13 dishes and gave 13 toasts, while members rejoiced in their rationalism by deliberately doing unlucky things, such as walking under ladders, spilling salt, smashing mirrors, opening umbrellas indoors, decorating the room with skeletons, skulls and cross-bones, and hanging banners that proclaimed 'we who are about to die salute you'. In short, they didn't just tempt fate, they poked it relentlessly in the eye, safe in the knowledge that their eventual death wouldn't be the result of some supernatural scything by an undead hitman, but more likely the result of a heart attack caused by overindulgence.

SITTING AT THE TABLE

After much toing and froing, we're at last all seated into a neatly aligned perimeter of bodies flanking a long rectangular table. This is, for most of us in the West, the standard layout for any feast – we share the same eating surface, upon which we might find place mats, candles and cutlery, and we all sit upright in our high-backed chairs. But it wasn't always this way.

In the very early days of dynastic Egypt, until around 4,000 years ago, the upper classes reclined on mats of woven rushes or plumped-up cushions, with their drinks resting on the floor and their dinner perched on a low table in front of them. If we'd stuck a television in front of them, and put them in a hoodie, they'd have looked much like me when my wife isn't home and I'm feeling lazy. Yet, by the time of King Tut and Ramesses the Great, the high-backed chair was making inroads into the dining room, so clearly tastes had matured, even if mine haven't.

The Greeks and Romans, on the contrary, didn't opt for either of these things – at least, not the affluent ones, anyway. Instead, as we've already touched upon, they preferred the reclining couch, (*kline* in Greek), upon which the dinner guest would lean sideways on the left elbow, propped up on pillows, with their knees bent and the waist twisted to create a stable posture. From this coquettish pose, they remained static but could lean forward and pluck food with the fingers and thumb of the right hand, as low tables and passing slaves brought the delicious nibbles within their limited reach.

Dinner

Whereas we're gathering around a large central table, the Romans didn't adopt the same layout. Their dining room was known as the *triclinium*, so called because it traditionally featured three large *klines* (or *lecti* in Latin), arranged into a U-shape, allowing Romans to feast together while servants scurried back and forth with copious amounts of booze and snacks. Of course, if someone was hosting an epic shindig, then a larger room could hold many more couches, each of which seated between two or three languorously horizontal guests, but Plutarch cautioned against cramming too many tables and chairs into one massive space, as it would inevitably lead to an obnoxiously noisy ruckus.

When we talk about famous meals in history, there's one that instantly springs into the mind of anyone raised in a Christian culture. Our imagining of the Last Supper – with Christ and his disciples sat at a long trestle table, munching bread while Jesus does that swooping wide-armed gesture that resembles a goose coming into land – is actually a facsimile of medieval Italian dining customs. In fact, it's much more likely that ancient Palestinian Jews ate on the floor, and if they had attended a banquet, then they'd have been down on their elbow like Plutarch and his pals. We know this because the Gospel of St John tells us so:

> **Now there was leaning on Jesus' bosom one of his disciples, whom Jesus loved. Simon Peter therefore beckoned to him, that he should ask who it should be of whom he spake. He then lying on Jesus' breast saith unto him, Lord, who is it?**

In case it's not clear from the seventeenth-century prose, Jesus was sharing a couch with another man who was lying in front of him with his head resting on Christ's chest, so that to talk to his saviour this disciple had to crane his neck and rotate his body. It's a surprisingly intimate arrangement – the Messiah platonically spooning another chap.

Centuries later, in the great medieval halls, the noble host and his most illustrious guests had the honour of having their backs turned to the roaring fire, so they might enjoy its heat while they supped, while everyone else was perched on backless benches and merely hoped for any residual warmth to gently waft their way. For more rustic types, for whom hall feasts were a reverie never to be realised, tables were a domestic rarity – as were expensive candles and lamps – meaning food was probably eaten near the front door, or before the lit hearth, so people could see what they were chewing in the dark. If no table were present, then they sat on a small bench (*buffet*), with the food laid out in front of them, and sometimes there was only one chair for the master of the house, leaving the rest of his family to squat on little stools or straw mattresses.

Our bums, of course, are not perched on dried hay stuffed into sacks, but that's a fairly recent change: dining chairs for the masses only started to appear regularly in the 1500s, being acquired by wealthy Renaissance families to surround their new, elegant dining tables that featured extendable leaves for extra space. These tables were frequently protected by thick, intricately patterned rugs called Turkey carpets, named after the country of their origin rather than the large gobbly bird soon to arrive from Mexico. Ironically, some such rugs were actually Islamic prayer mats, but in the early days of the fashion no one had realised, and so there arose the curious oddity of European Christians – who for much of the century were frequently locked in a bitter war with the Ottoman Turks – eating their dinners on a holy cloth sacred to Muslims.

Table beautification didn't end there, though. Tonight we're ac-companied by a couple of candles and a small bouquet of flowers, but in the eighteenth century it became immensely fashionable in plush European dining rooms to focus the attention with ornate and memorable centrepieces. These might be a massive bouquet of fresh flowers or, better yet, fake ones sewn from silk, but other gorgeous objects, designed to lure the eye and prompt a witty conversation, could include sculptures of precious metal and glass, miniaturised fake gardens sprawled across flat silver plates, artistic drawings in trays of sand, and – most exotically of all – a lone pineapple: a fruit of such mysterious rarity that people didn't dare eat it, they just mounted it on the dinner table for others to coo at in bemused wonderment.

PERUSING THE MENU

One day, possibly in 1810, the magnificently dressed elite of Napoleonic Paris assembled in the grand abode of the Russian Ambassador Prince Alexander Borisovich Kurakin for what promised to be an outlandish feast. He was, after all, known as the Diamond Prince of Russia, on account of his exquisitely expensive taste in clothes, and so all were expecting spectacular luxury. None, however, were expecting to enter a dining room devoid of food. The decorations were there, the cutlery too, but dinner was conspicuously absent.

The table in front of us now is much the same – well, it's not carved from elegant mahogany, but you know what I mean. Tonight, we will be serving each course pre-plated, as is the fashion in most restaurants, but Kurakin's shocked guests were expecting many courses spread in a uniform pattern across the whole expanse of the table, from which they would sample a bit of everything. This customary *service à la française* created a majestic scene for the diners, in which the hors d'oeuvres – which weren't initially appetisers, but side dishes, (*hors d'oeuvres* meaning 'outside the works') – flanked the perimeter edges while the various main dishes were placed in the table's centre. The rubric varied, but really lavish feasts aimed to serve 12 times as many dishes as there were guests, meaning the larger table could groan beneath the gargantuan array of hundreds of individual bowls, though not all were served at exactly the same time.

The first course was usually soups in tureens; the second featured meats, fishes, vegetables and sweet desserts – essentially, all the things we'd consider worthy of a complete meal today – and then the tablecloth was lifted off to reveal a fresh one underneath, before the third and final course of cheeses, fruits and yet more desserts was brought out (*dessert* derives from 'de-served', meaning the table was cleared first). To plough through this vast ocean of grub took literally hours, swelled the belly, wasted a bin-load of ingredients and inevitably led the food to swiftly turn cold, but it was a theatrical style of banqueting that trumpeted the host's enormous generosity.

Yet Kurakin's *service à la russe* – in which the cutlery was pre-laid and each course came out separately – caught on quickly in high society, and was accepted custom by the 1880s. How so? Well, the practicalities helped: food was now served hot rather than lukewarm, and the meal was done in a mere 90 minutes, rather than being a gruelling four-hour endurance event. Furthermore, the constant table service required many more footmen to ferry all the plates back and forth, meaning the reduction in dishes was compensated for by the increase in employees. Much as with modern celebrities, the size of the host's entourage became the new symbol of wealth.

BLESS THIS FOOD

Having served the starter to everyone at the table, we sit down and begin to start eating. But if we were devoutly religious, then no morsel would reach our mouth until a blessing had been uttered over this bounteous gift of food. Many Christians (though traditionally not the English) say grace before a meal – a short, simple prayer of thanks to the Almighty – and Hindus do something similar, whereas Jews utter the Birkat Hamazon after a meal in which bread has been eaten, while Muslims cover their bases with a bookending duo of *Bismillah* ('in Allah's Name') beforehand and *Alhamdulillah* ('praise be to Allah') afterwards. It's worth noting medieval Muslims had to wait until the food was all gone before proclaiming Alhamdulillah, as to say it in the midst of the munching was to sound like one wished it was over already, and had other more important stuff to be getting on with.

But pre-dinner rituals have not always been religious in nature. In Bronze Age Mesopotamia we know that the banquet couldn't begin until all the guests had been anointed with oil seasoned with myrtle, ginger and cedar, making their hands smell as delicious as the dinner on offer, if not more so. The Egyptians, Romans and Greeks preferred to purify their hands in water instead – as did later medieval diners – though the elite class of the Nile Valley also turned up for dinner wearing a garland of flowers and a scented wax cone on their head. This, strangely enough, proceeded to melt over the course of the meal, releasing a pleasant aroma from their fashionable wigs as if they were human Febreze dispensers.

The Greeks didn't adopt that fragrant curio, but they did carry on with the ceremonial garlands to remind themselves of Prometheus, the mythical Titan who had crafted humans from clay and then stolen fire from his fellow gods to bestow upon us. For this altruistic thievery he had paid the ultimate price, a neverending torture of having his regenerating liver pecked out every day by a really annoying eagle. In any case, thanks to the myth of Prometheus it was believed the gods could eat the sizzling fat of a sacrificed animal, provided it was slaughtered in their sacred name, which is why a major feast in the Classical Mediterranean began with a religious burning of animal fat and a ritual song to accompany the filling of a wide-brimmed wine cup. This, apparently, was enough to appease the notoriously moody gods, which was splendid because it left all the meat and booze for the Greeks to guzzle.

Hand washing has been pretty standard for millennia – it was an obvious solution to the minimal use of cutlery – but those in power didn't just fear dirt in their food. In medieval France, a horn was blown at noble houses shortly before the feast, so people knew to scrub their fingers in the water jugs stood on a nearby table; but, while they did this, the official food-taster assayed the courses with vaguely magical or alchemical techniques, using shark teeth, bits of frog or shiny crystals to search for poisons in the grub. If the substances bled, or changed colour, then poison was present and an assassin was probably lurking in the room! For the most prestigious guests, the food was then tasted, sometimes by a pet dog called a *chien goûter*, but that still didn't reassure the completely paranoid. King Louis XIV mostly ate alone, or joined solely by the Queen, and his dinner was delivered to him in locked containers escorted from the kitchens by armed musketeers, ensuring it arrived safe to eat. Alas, when we visit a restaurant, there are no gun-wielding commandos to prevent the waiter spitting in our soups, and more's the pity.

WHAT THE FORK?

Philoxenos was a curious oddity of a man, a poet and philosopher by day, but a wandering stomach in search of a meal by night. He was a gourmand – a gluttonous foodie – and, in order to further his addiction, he developed a strange technique to ensure that he would have primary access to the food at his own parties. Apparently, he would sit in the Greek baths and deliberately scald his hands and tongue in the hot water so that they became desensitised to the heat, and then he instructed his slaves to cook the food to extreme temperatures and serve it while it steamed with the ferocity of an Icelandic geyser. The guests would reach out from their couches, burn their fingertips and recoil in confused pain; but cunning Philoxenos, with his asbestos hands and flame-retardant face, would hungrily snatch up the best food and wolf it down without a problem. Such was his greed, he was willing to suffer nerve damage for just a few extra seconds of unchallenged dining dominance.

Tonight, we have not mirrored Philoxenos for several reasons – one of those being that he was clearly a bit of a weirdo – but the most obvious distinction is that we are using cutlery, whereas many ancient societies, such as the Romans, Babylonians, Greeks, Jews and Egyptians, predominantly ate with their fingers. And even if they did use cutlery, it was likely to be spoons for liquids and knives for cutting, rather than forks to prong the morsels in the direction of their gaping maws. Of course, they used crockery to serve the food, and the famous Tivoli Hoard is a beautiful example of upper-class Roman silverware designed for elaborate feasting and drinking sessions. In fact, the era of the emperors saw a great fashion erupt for elegantly decorated glass bowls too, though the Roman poor made do with drab terracotta.

By the first century CE – when Caligula, Nero and the other notorious emperors were busily earning reputations as deranged deviants – the Roman spoon came in two forms: the wide *ligula* used for soup and soft solids, and the *cochlea* which consisted of a small bowl on the end of a slim handle, a bit like a tobacco pipe, and which was best suited to shellfish, eggs and other dainty treats. Interestingly, *cochlea* is Latin for snail shell and it's quite possible that the history of spoons began way back in the Stone Age with our ancestors scooping up stuff in hollowed-out oyster shells, like kids playing at the beach. This isn't so far-fetched an idea, and it's thought that bone 'spatulas' found at Paviland, in south Wales, might be utensils dating back 26,000 years.

Roman cutlery designers were nothing if not inventive, and New York's Metropolitan Museum of Art has a collection of ancient cutlery that includes a reversible spoon–fork hybrid – with three prongs on one end and a scalloped bowl on the other – and a spoon that had once included a foldout blade secreted under the handle. Was this actually a cunning trick by some devious assassin plotting to spoon his way into his victim's party, and then stab him in the guts with the hidden knife? No, clearly not. But it's fun to imagine a spoon assassin, isn't it? Imagine seeing that on the evening news!

But let's get back to forks. In Roman times they were likely to be serving implements only, and in the Middle Ages they vanished from the dinner tables of western Europe, with only one famous exception. In 972 CE, the heir to the Holy Roman Empire, Prince Otto, welcomed his newly imported Byzantine bride to the Rhineland. Princess Theophano was the Rolls Royce of political spouses – elegant, sophisticated and bloody expensive to acquire – and while Prince Otto was hardly some two-bit princeling, this inter-dynastic mega-marriage was a prestigious coup for the Germans. The Byzantine Empire was enjoying its second Golden Age, and Theophano's glamorous arrival was like that moment in 2008 when a newly moneyed Manchester City signed the Brazilian superstar Robinho, and every football fan in England simultaneously choked on their cornflakes.

Theophano's expansive entourage and dress collection came as no surprise, but it was at the dinner table that she shocked the gathered court when she refused to eat with her fingers, and instead 'used a golden double prong to bring food to her mouth'. The reaction to such extravagance wasn't pretty, and the fork's European reputation was instantly tarnished along with hers, but gradually the pasta-loving Italians began to realise that the fork was a marvellous antidote to the inevitable splatter of hand-scooped linguine, and by the 1400s it was welcome at their table. Indeed, it was in Italy, in around 1608, that the English traveller Thomas Coryat encountered the fork, and when he returned home to publish his adventures he brought it back with him. The response, however, wasn't positive.

The English immediately ridiculed these continental utensils as being effeminate and unnecessary: 'Why should a person need a fork when God had given him hands?', wrote one sceptic, and even Coryat's literary friends John Donne and Ben Jonson cheerfully mocked him. But the much-maligned traveller noted that the Italians had adopted forks as a hygienic solution, as: 'all men's fingers are not alike cleane,' and that was a strong argument in an era of portable chamber pots being welcome in the dining room. Slowly, then, Coryat's logic gained traction and forks came to be adopted by the wealthy, becoming beautiful prized possessions. Initially they were small, slender-handled devices which usually featured two straight prongs. Generally, they were deployed for sweet, sticky foods or stuff that might stain the fingers, though there's some suggestion people speared their food with the fork and then plucked it from the fork with the fingers to pop into the mouth, which somewhat defies the point.

If we look at our fork currently clutched in our hand, we'll see it has four prongs, which is probably the perfect number, but this took a little while to develop. By the 1700s they'd acquired a third prong and began to curve, so the scooping action of the spoon was no longer needed, and the fourth prong arrived in the 1800s, or at least it did in Europe. When Charles Dickens visited the USA in the 1840s, he was surprised to find American forks remained an uncommon rarity and, if used at all, were still two-pronged and straight. More worryingly, he reported these fearsome implements being forced deep into the gullet, making his fellow diners appear to him like sword-swallowing clowns. It took another few decades for Americans to join the four-prong fork club, and neither were they fooled by the dubious merits of the failed five-prong fork, an unnecessary upgrade reminiscent of Gillette constantly trying to flog us increasingly massive multi-blade razors.

But during the fork's long metamorphosis from random stabby thing to essential table implement, another utensil had been steadily enjoying all the praise. Sharpened stone blades, used by *Homo heidelbergensis* for slicing meat, are traceable as far back as 1.6 million years ago, and the knife has stayed in fashion ever since. Throughout the Middle Ages it was king, so much so that guests even brought their own to other people's dinner table. Yes, much like the cast of *West Side Story,* everyone was packing a blade – including peasants and monks – and the celebrated founder of the Benedictine monastic order, St Benedict, even went as far as to remind his monks not to go to sleep with their knives at their sides, in case they rolled over and accidentally severed their goolies.

Because we haven't laid out steak knives, the blade in our hand is disappointingly blunt; if we chucked it at the wall, it wouldn't thump into the plaster and stick there with a pleasing twang, like a thrilling scene in *The Mask of Zorro*! But medieval knives were sharp; in fact, they were all-purpose daggers with a razor tip, designed for self-defence, hunting and practical chores, which is why it's always been bad manners to point with one's knife at fellow guests, or grasp it in the fist as if it were a weapon. In the medieval world, stabbings were the crime *du jour*, and for everyone in the room to have access to a sharp blade and copious quantities of booze wasn't always the smartest idea.

Given the menacing possibility of cutlery – and let's not forget our terrifying spoon assassin! – it's not surprising that Cardinal Richelieu, who was part-time scourge of the imaginary Musketeers and full-time advisor to the not-so-imaginary King Louis

XIII, banned all pointy knives at the dinner table in 1637. This resulted in the inwardly curved broad blade, attached to a pistol-grip handle that curled in the opposite direction, giving the knife a gently undulating S-shape, like a meandering river. This design wasn't just a safety feature, it also helped the wrist comfortably articulate the hand up to the mouth and thereby lift food such as peas and cake into one's gob on the flat blade, rather than having them sit in the curve of a spoon or dangle from a fork prong.

CHOP AND CHANGE

Tonight we're using pasta-twirling forks like medieval Venetians, but a similar dinner party in east Asia would instead feature chopsticks, probably the modern world's most commonly used eating utensil, after fingers. In China, this simple technology was once called *Zhu*, but is now known as *Kuaizi*, meaning 'quick sticks' or 'fast fellows' – both fantastic names for hockey teams, just in case you're thinking of setting one up. Anyway, chopsticks appear to have originated in China, perhaps as far back as 5,000 years ago when people cooked their food in large insulated pots and probably used snapped-off twigs to fish it out while the grub was piping hot.

Annoyingly for historians, this archaic era suffers from being murkier than the politics of an Italian election, so it's hard to be exact. An early manual on etiquette known as *The Book of Rites (Lǐ jì)*, mentions that the last king of the Shang Dynasty (1600–1046 BCE) used fancy ivory chopsticks, but this text was composed many centuries after his death, so its reliability is questionable. Thankfully, archaeology has leapt to our rescue and excavations at the Ruins of Yin – the ancient capital of the Shang, now found a couple of miles outside Anyang City in

Henan province – revealed a lovely set of brass chopsticks dating to more than 3,000 years ago.

Later on in history, other materials were permitted. The poor have always stuck with wood and bamboo, but the rich have been able to pick from gold, agate, lacquer, brass, jade and silver, the latter of which was thought to change colour in the presence of cyanide poison – a useful gimmick for the powerfully paranoid – but is unfortunately virtually frictionless when wet, so the food would just squirm out of the user's grip becoming not so much chopsticks as dropsticks... which is the tagline for my new diet book, the catchily titled *Frustrated and Thin! The Silver Chopstick Revolution.*

By the sixth century CE, chopsticks had spread into other parts of Asia, and, though they were initially reserved for religious feasts, in Japan they took on their own style, becoming mostly wooden, sometimes beautifully lacquered, often rounded instead of rectangular, and sharpened to a point at the tip. They also tended to be a couple of inches shorter than China's nine-inch offerings, with women's dinkier than those of men, and by the late 1800s the Japanese had even developed disposable ones, split into two sticks, to be the Asian equivalent of the floppy plastic cutlery we cheerfully chuck in the bin after munching a cheap takeaway dinner.

MAKING A MESS

Our starters of dainty bruschetta and cured meats have been relatively easy to eat, but as we bring out the main course of Spanish chicken served in a rich tomato sauce, everyone suddenly becomes aware that our clean clothes are soon to be imperilled by splatter. Almost en masse, we anxiously unfold our napkins and jokily ask if it's embarrassingly childish to tuck them into our collars. But for how long have these protective shields been part of the dining experience?

The napkin seems to date back to the Romans, who shared a communal towel for drying their hands, but were also given an individual small cloth called a *mappa* to wipe their mouth and fingers. Allegedly, Emperor Nero once started a chariot race in the Circus by chucking his napkin out of a window. Romans probably used tablecloths sometimes, but it was in the Middle Ages that this became more prevalent, in order to absorb the stains from one's greasy mitts. This didn't go down terribly well with the hosts, as such cloths were often hand-woven heirlooms passed down from mother to daughter as part of the marriage contract, and having them ruined by pig juice and wine wasn't exactly what they'd imagined on their romantic day. But, nor could people justify hoarding them in cupboards, as the tablecloth (*longerie*) acquired a powerful symbolism as something to connect all the people at the same table, no matter their rank. Therefore, it was a tremendous humiliation for the host to order a nearby guard to unsheathe his sword and slash the cloth to a guest's right and left, as this metaphorically ostracised them from the convivial sharing. It was the medieval equivalent of making the naughty school kid eat their lunch all alone while the others stare and point.

The inevitable dirt from greasy fingers and dirty cuffs meant many a medieval lord invested in table runners, or *sur-nappes* (*nappe* having evolved from Latin *mappa*) to cover the two edges of the tablecloth where most accidents were likely to happen. In fact, this smearing of grime wasn't always an accident. The brilliant sixteenth-century humanist Erasmus found time in his busy schedule to write an etiquette manual in which he suggested 'It is equally impolite to lick greasy fingers or wipe them on one's cloths. You should wipe them with the napkin or tablecloth.' The equally famous French essayist Michel de Montaigne admitted he too spent his days ruining mouth-cloths as he made 'little use of spoon or fork'. These were some of the most sophisticated scholars in Europe, and such apparent slovenliness was deemed good manners. That said, the Portuguese missionary Father João Rodrigues noted the Japanese tastemakers of the same century were 'much amazed at our eating with the hands and wiping them on napkins, which then remained covered with food stains, and this causes them both nausea and disgust.' By the sounds of it, even the cultured Montaigne would have seemed as boorish to them as Monty Python's explosively crude restaurant diner, Mr Creosote.

Montaigne and Erasmus were writing in the 1500s, when each guest now received their own wiping cloth called a diaper or serviette, though these might be a metre in width and length, making them fairly unwieldy. By the end of the century, the ruff – that starched radiating collar – had come into fashion, forcing posh diners to tuck their napkins around their neck, to stop any lingering grease dripping from chin to fashionable frill, and this custom survived the abandonment of ruffs so as to defend the frilly shirt of the seventeenth and eighteenth centuries. In fact, it was only in the 1800s, when cutlery more reliably delivered food to the mouth, that the much-shrunken napkin became a familiar fixture in the lap, instead.

TABLE TALK

Though everyone's cheerfully chewing their way through the meal, the birthday atmosphere is providing plenty of good cheer and chat. This would have impressed the Roman writer Plutarch, who was keen to ensure that his guests enjoyed themselves. He didn't want to sit there listening to jealous rivals bickering, and believed that the meal should be a democratic affair to unite everyone. Accordingly, he suggested useful conversation topics, including the classic paradox, 'what came first, the chicken or the egg?', and also recommended quizzing any passing sailors for exciting travel anecdotes which could be deployed if the table talk got a bit dull.

Another famed writer, Marcus Terentius Varro, thought: 'conversation . . . ought not to be about anxious and perplexing affairs, but [should be] diverting and cheerful.' A Greek character in Xenophon's *Symposium* tells us he used to get dinner invites all the time, because he was a quick-witted jester – the life and soul of the party – and people wanted to laugh together. But woe betide the guest who tried to crack a joke and got it horribly wrong, managing to dig themselves into a shallow grave of excruciating social embarrassment like a toga-clad Larry David. Clearly having witnessed some spectacular gaffes himself, Plutarch also advised caution on breaking out the funnies: 'the man who cannot engage in joking at a suitable time, discreetly and skillfully, must avoid jokes altogether'. What's more, those gags had to be: 'casual and spontaneous, not . . . previously prepared entertainment.' Put simply, Plutarch wanted to be in the company of wits, not sub-par Seinfelds trotting out hackneyed routines: 'so, what's the deal with chariots . . . ?'

In China it was more common to get the chatting done before the meal, and then eat very quickly, whereas traditional Japanese banquets began rather quietly, but gradually gathered pace as everyone relaxed. Across time and geography, it was also the custom to enjoy entertainments during a banquet – whether jugglers, musicians, singers, or even gladiators trying to mangle each other – but it's unlikely anyone's going to start wrestling in the living room, so tonight it's up to us to entertain each other. But we should be careful about the topics of conversation we muster, as we don't want to seem crass or dull, even if we're among good friends.

After all, though Montaigne was a brilliant philosopher, he was also a humane, down-to-earth man who found it frustrating when people relentlessly pursued highbrow discussions at dinner: 'What? Would they try to square the circle while also shagging their wives? I hate that we should be enjoined to have our head in the clouds while our bodies are at the table.'

On the other hand, the eighteenth-century aristocrat Lord Chesterfield advised his son to never be seen laughing in public, as gentlemen merely smiled in appreciation of good humour. Given that Chesterfield was missing most of his teeth, I'm not sure smiling did him any favours, either. In his day, young people were supposed to stay quiet – and ladies were usually well drilled in behaving demurely – so much of the dining advice was aimed at boorish men. They were variously counselled not to be self-obsessed narcissists, mention embarrassing things, insult fellow diners, make smutty jokes, launch into boring classical quotations in extinct languages or chuck around increasingly dogmatic opinions about politics and morality. In short, the advice was simple: don't be a snooty-nosed arsehole.

By the late 1800s – at least in Britain – etiquette handbooks were becoming tremendously popular as the middle classes began to imitate the customs of the aristocracy, and many guides were written by women, meaning the advice suddenly came with a witty redress to casual sexists:

> **a gentleman should pay [women] the compliment of seeming to consider them capable of an equal understanding with gentlemen ... when you 'come down' to commonplace or small talk with an intelligent lady ... she either recognises the condescension and despises you, or else she accepts it as the highest intellectual effort of which you are capable, and rates you accordingly.**

Ouch.

MIND YOUR MANNERS

The food is going down nicely, and the wine is vanishing even quicker; everyone is relaxing into a tipsy giddiness and the hubbub is growing noisier. However, we must be careful not to slip too far into slummy rudeness – these might be forgiving friends but there's no justification for burping, or scratching our itchy bums in their presence. Table manners are one of those things that anthropologists find absolutely fascinating because they vary from culture to culture, but typically bond the group by censoring the individual. Put simply, etiquette is a form of socialised self-control designed to avoid upsetting those around us. We make sacrifices so they don't shun us at work, or disinvite us to their wedding, and in return we get the continued pleasure of their company or – if it's our boss – another pay cheque.

A fine example of this might come from China, where the ancient *Book of Rites* suggested never touching food with the left hand, because it's been historically associated with profane acts such as bum wiping. The word for 'left' in Latin, *sinister*, tells us quite a lot about the inherent negativity formerly associated with left-handedness, and the same applied in the medieval Islamic world. Here, though, the rules were slightly slacker and it was permitted to hold bread, or anything not plucked from a communal plate, in the left hand. The rationale was presumably that, if people wanted to take their own chances with pooey fingers, so be it, but just don't go smearing faeces all over everyone else's dinner too.

On a familiar note, Chinese and Japanese chopstick etiquette demanded that one didn't fish around looking for the best morsels, thus contaminating the bowl with saliva-soaked sticks, but instead claimed the first thing one touched. It was also rude to eat straight from the serving dishes, a polite guest first transported food into an eating bowl, and one also had to be aware of other people's chopsticks crossing paths with your own. Etiquette on this last matter was fairly relaxed, suggesting accidental contact was a regular blunder that everyone learned to politely laugh off, rather than being a justification for a punch-up in the car park.

Some historical etiquette was entirely familiar to our own preferences. The Greek writer Hesiod calmly explained that cutting fingernails at the dinner table was gross, and Erasmus pointed out that fidgeting in one's seat was likely to make people think you were discreetly farting, so it was best to stay still. In contrast to the Hollywood vision of the raucous medieval feast, the twelfth-century etiquette book *The Fifty Rules of the Table* by the Milanese poet Bonvesin da la Riva advised the reader not to speak with their mouth full, discuss upsetting subjects, ask questions when someone was trying to drink, make annoying noises or chatter endlessly about trivial gossip. In summary, the aim was to: 'behave correctly at table – courteous, elegant, cheerful and light-hearted.' Other authors chimed in with yet more sensible suggestions – don't sneeze on people, don't pet animals at dinner, don't shout, or be boastful, or chew with your mouth open, or grab food, or slouch; don't cross legs, or raise elbows, or pick one's teeth with fingers or knife, or lick the plate, or your lips, or the cutlery. And definitely don't fart!

Yet Erasmus was more forgiving than these earlier writers. He thought it okay to belch, cough, sneeze and hiccup, provided these were involuntary reflexes of the body, as: 'to suppress a sound brought on by nature is characteristic of silly people who set more store by good manners than good health.' In this, he was following the Roman Emperor Claudius's edict that men could trump in his presence if medically necessary, a judgement he'd declared after he'd heard of a man who'd stoically elected to die rather than let out a botty-burp in front of his glorious ruler. But less familiar to our modern mores was the freedom to spit.

Only the ancient Persians have been said to withhold from this commonplace custom, and the Greeks and Romans had decided that it was fine to gob if it was done with a certain amount of subtlety. Erasmus agreed, saying that as long as people weren't hocking a loogie over great distances, like some sort of overly competitive llama, he was okay with it. It didn't even have to go in a receptacle, either, as the floor was perfectly acceptable.

Spitting grew to new levels of popularity in nineteenth-century America, where tobacco was a national pastime, and even President Andrew Jackson requested brass spittoons be installed in the White House so he could stomp around the halls while constantly chewing. Surprisingly, it was only in the 1900s that health concerns, spurred on by the fear of communicable diseases, saw spitting become a taboo frowned upon by nice middle-class types, and none of us at this table would even contemplate catapulting a globule of saliva from our mouths. In fact, like the Victorians, we still apologise for mannerly failures even when it's not our fault, such as when we have to elegantly flop a lump of chewy gristle into our napkin, then quietly mouth 'sorry...' to everyone in the vicinity.

Another thing we all agree upon is that this isn't a food-scoffing race. We're here to enjoy our food, but also to interact as a group, and none of us would dare clear away the plates the moment the first of us finished our food. Oddly, though, that was exactly how things were done when Queen Victoria dined. Royal etiquette demanded that she be served first, and the moment the grub hit her plate she began scooping it hurriedly into her mouth. While everyone else was still being served, Victoria would polish off her plate in record time, which perhaps explains her later weight gain.

Unfortunately, protocol dictated that once she had finished, all plates were to be removed from the table, despite the fact most guests had barely even touched their dinners. On one memorable occasion, the eccentric Lord Hartington saw his half-eaten saddle of mutton suddenly vanish from his view and exploded with rage, demanding, 'Here! Give that back!' Everyone's face surely drained to a deathly white at this rude outburst, but Victoria was amused at his clear frustration, and generously beckoned for the wandering plate to be returned to its hungry owner. Even a reigning monarch knew that a good host put the wishes of one's dinner guests first.

With the main course suitably dispatched, it's time to turn out the lights, bring through the chocolate cake, and serenade our friend as she blows out the candles. It's been a lovely evening so far, and we're all very merry, but there's no need to stop now. We're all adults here, and it's a Saturday night, so it's time to break open the booze cabinet.

9.30 p.m.

DRINKS

As our guests move from the dinner table back to the comfy sofas, it's incumbent upon us as hosts to offer them a drink. Surveying the room, we realise they all have quite different tastes – there are wine connoisseurs, beer lovers and spirit slurpers among us – so we rummage through the drinks cabinet and list the various options, to see who wants what. Visibly displaying a range of available drinks is a very recent custom in Britain, being a middle-class trend that emerged in the 1970s. Previously most people simply went down the pub. But it would be utterly wrong to assume that humans haven't been enjoying alcohol for millennia. In fact, it may even have pre-dated the emergence of our species.

PARTY ANIMALS

Type 'drunk elk' into Google and you will be rewarded with a hilarious photograph taken in Sweden of an inebriated moose that, after guzzling a bellyful of fermenting apples, drunkenly clambered into the tree to reach the higher ones, and managed to get its body stuck between the branches. As complex as we

242

like to make it with our varied list of boozy beverages, alcohol is basically just fermented sugar, meaning even wild animals get to enjoy the sensation of being giddily shit-faced. In which case, it seems a fair hypothesis to presume that throughout the Stone Age humans also delighted in getting sozzled on rotten fruit, not only because it's fun, but because there are more calories in a gram of ethanol than in a gram of protein or carbohydrate, and it sounds like a much more enjoyable way to consume your five a day.

But when did we deliberately start manufacturing alcohol, and why is there such a variety of drinks?

FARMERS OR FERMENTERS?

The earliest evidence for manmade hooch comes from about 9,000 years ago, during the Neolithic Era. At Jiahu, in the Henan province of China, chemical analysis of ancient pottery has detected traces of fermented drinks made of rice, honey and fruit. As was the case with Sweden's celebrated boss-eyed elk, the honey and fruit were left to ferment naturally on their own, but the rice was different – it had to be chewed, its molecular structure broken down by human saliva, before it could be spat back into the pot and drunk. This doesn't sound entirely appetising, and the frothy soup that resulted wasn't exactly easy on the eye, either. But the drink – which had to be slurped through a straw – delivered a sweetened, calorific high with an alcohol content of about 10 per cent, which after a couple of bowls was probably enough to make people forget how the stuff was made in the first place.

But what's most fascinating is how quickly farming and boozing became synonymous. In an era that predated the invention of the wheel, people were falling off the wagon long before they even knew what a wagon was. Some archaeologists don't even think this was a coincidence. According to one theory, fermentation was the whole reason the Neolithic Agricultural Revolution took off in the first place. Alcohol wasn't a fun by-product of growing crops; crops were a handy offshoot of making alcohol!

FOR GOODNESS, SAKE

Rice remained the principal alcoholic ingredient in such places as India, China, Korea and, of course, Japan where rice wine is now known as *sake*. Traditional recipes could be as simple as adding human saliva to boiled rice and leaving it for a week, but others involved complex procedures that would test the patience of a saint. Here's a how-to guide, just in case you fancy making up a batch at home:

---

1. Cleanse the rice of impurities by washing it several times.
2. Steep it in hops for a week.
3. Steam it for an hour, then pour cool water over it.
4. Lay it out on bamboo mats to dry, and then add it to a big pan of water.
5. Tip in natural yeasts and enzymes, adding different varieties of rice that have also been washed.
6. Ferment the mixture in a warm jar for 70 days.
7. Pasteurise the batch by adding 'Two pieces of beeswax, five slices of bamboo leaves, and half a pill of serrated arum'.
8. Boil and then leave to cool slowly.
9. Drink!
10. Fall over!
11. Complain about headache!
12. Repeat!

This bacteria-busting pasteurisation allowed the wine to be stored in jars for up to ten years, and right now we're discovering our drinks cabinet has been hiding some equally aged bottles of weird liqueurs, the ones optimistically acquired on foreign holidays. Alas, the room falls into awkward silence when we shout 'who wants some Croatian plum brandy from 2003?' Defeated, we try a more popular suggestion – 'okay, who's having beer?'

MINE'S A PINT

In western Iran, in the south-eastern corner of the Kangavar river valley, there sat a whopping great mound of earth, behind which the Zagros Mountains loomed cinematically in the distance. This unnatural lump was a tantalising invitation to archaeologists, and in the 1960s it became the focus for excavations by a North American team who quickly discovered the buried remains of an ancient village, Godin Tepe, founded 7,000 years ago. The dig continued on and off for three decades until, one day in 1992, the researchers uncovered clay storage vessels, dating to around 3500 BCE, and closer examination revealed they were the earliest evidence ever found of one of history's most significant drinks – ale.

Godin Tepe was a tiny node in the sprawling trade network that connected up the earliest Sumerian cities, such as Uruk, but its modest size didn't mean it was importing ale from afar. The inhabitants were making it themselves; and it wasn't a simple process, either. The grains had to be moistened and then dried until they sprouted, before being dried again in a warm kiln and then coarsely powdered by smashing them with a basalt stone. Water was then added to create a mushy paste, and then heat was required – probably with boiling water – to commence the fermentation process where the malt sugars began to caramelise. Sounds tricky, doesn't it? Well, we're not done yet . . .

A natural by-product of brewing is a brownish crystalline substance called calcium oxalate, sometimes dubbed 'beerstone'. These days we carefully dispose of it, as it can make the drinker nauseous for all the wrong reasons and none of the fun ones, but 5,500 years ago there was no industrial process to extract it, so Neolithic brewers plumped for a simpler solution – they scratched grooves into the bottom of wide-spouted ceramic jars, allowing the 'beerstone' to settle into these pits while the rest of the ale remained unpolluted. Eventually, the batch could be flavoured with other ingredients to produce a wide range of nutritious lagers and sweet ales.

Obviously, this was a lot more effort than dribbling on some rice and leaving an apple in the sunshine, but the pioneering brewers of the Zagros Mountains clearly shared Homer Simpson's philosophy that beer is like a woman: 'They smell good, they look good, and you'd step over your own mother just to get one!'

LIQUID BREAD

Once ale had been discovered, there was little chance of it being forgotten again thanks to the invention of writing. It says a tremendous amount about the importance of alcohol that among the first things ever recorded by humanity were administrative records for ale production. But this wasn't simply because our ancestors were drunken louts, stumbling around ancient cities grabbing strangers and slurring 'you're my besssht friend, you arrrree...'. No, the translation for Sumerian ale was 'liquid bread' and it was perceived as a daily ration for labourers throughout Mesopotamia and Egypt. Again, like the Jiahu rice wine, it was slurped through a straw like a savoury milkshake, and there were probably 19 varieties on tap – eight of barley, eight of wheat and three of mixed grains. That's considerably more than you'll find in a modern pub, even a pretentious one where all the bar staff are called Clarence.

It was human experimental zeal which gave the world this marvellous beverage, but it's understandable why all credit was duly plonked in the lap of the goddess Ninkasi, recipient of the oldest drinking song in the world – the 'Hymn to Ninkasi', which is a decent effort but not nearly as catchy as Thin Lizzy's 'Whiskey in the Jar'. Still, I'm willing to be kind as it was written 3,800 years before the twin-guitar solo was invented, and it's useful to beer-archaeologists (yes, there really is such a thing!) because it alludes to the ale-brewing process, although it's frustratingly vague in the detail, meaning modern experiments with Sumerian homebrew have been like the recent *Star Wars* prequels – so disappointing that you start to question the quality of the originals.

Despite its noble reputation in Egypt, ale acquired a bad reputation in the ancient Mediterranean world, as it was the preferred drink of those trouser-wearing, forest-dwelling barbarians lurking menacingly on the edge of civilisation. Having never been conquered by the Romans, the Germanic tribes of the North remained resolute ale quaffers, but they were also tremendously fond of a honeyed drink called mead, and these two beverages played an enormous part in the political and social culture of the people who later became known as the Vikings and Anglo-Saxons. In fact, such was the importance of mead that the feasting hall – the focus of political power – might be named in its honour. It's a shame we haven't continued the tradition, but it seems no one wants to sign my petition to rename the British Houses of Parliament as the National Gin and Tonic Lounge.

So, what went on in the Saxon mead-hall?

MEAD MEN

You're standing in a field, a mead-field to be precise, and before you is a large wooden hall from which riotous sound escapes through the rafters. You march forwards, enter through the door and are immediately confronted by rows of bearded men sat on their mead-benches (*medubenc*) guzzling greedily from their mead-cup (*meduscenc*) and laughing boisterously from their honey high (*medugál*). You hang around, and after a few hours some food gets munched and a more aggressive atmosphere descends. Soon, a loose-tongued mead-fool (*meduwanhoga*) accidentally insults a mead-crazed (*meduhátheort*) warrior, and is lucky to escape being the victim of mead-manslaughter (*medumanslieht*). With crisis averted, everyone returns to their drinking and singing, but eventually the mead runs out and the communal despair of mead-deprival (*meduscerwen*) sets in.

As you can probably tell, the Anglo-Saxons really rather liked intense boozing sessions – the fact their language was so crammed with mead-related idioms is a bit of a giveaway – so when the Christian Church set out to try to convert them, the binge-drinking was non-negotiable. Instead, the Church somewhat begrudgingly began endorsing ale too, even though wine – the miraculous blood of Christ – was the official libation. Indeed, whereas Christ had turned water into wine, by the fifth century the Irish miracle-worker St Brigit of Kildare was said to be turning water into ale. Soon, medieval Irish kings were even doling out the ale at Easter, the holiest time of the year. Inevitably, therefore, it wasn't long before the Church was doing more than just permitting the drinking of ale; it began manufacturing it too.

ALE MARY, FULL OF GRACE

Monastic booze production might sound a bit unexpected – it's almost akin to the Dalai Lama launching his own cigarette brand called Holy Smokes – but small beer, a weak ale made from the second boiling of barley mash, was glugged throughout Christendom in huge quantities, even by those who had taken sacred vows of fun-renouncing abstinence. You'll see plenty of history books argue this was because water was unsafe to drink, but that's a modern myth – there are many ancient and medieval sources describing everyday water consumption. If ale was preferred, it was probably because it enriched the body with nutrients, added calories to the diet and, crucially, it tasted delicious. And boy did they drink it! Some monastic rules allowed each monk as much as five litres of small beer per day which, even in weak concentration, must surely have been enough to induce a case of the wobbles. This ration was in addition to wine as well, and St Benedict of Aniane declared that his brethren could drink twice as much ale as they did wine, which, given the generosity of the ale-allowance, would surely have put his monks into the Ernest Hemingway category of high-functioning alcoholism. But we should be grateful to medieval monks, as it was they who first thought to add hops to ale and thereby invented the much-celebrated beer.

A couple of friends have accepted our offer of beer, but there are still several people with empty glasses. Perhaps this crowd is more amenable to grape than grain?

AN EXCELLENT VINTAGE

We pull out a bottle of merlot from the wine rack, and read out the label. Apparently it's fruity and well suited to red meat, but how do we know if it's any good? After all, it was only £5 in a supermarket, and might taste like sink unblocker. Of course, the French have a classification system for this exact reason – there's the bog-standard *vin de table*, then *vin de pays*, then there's *appellation d'origine vin de qualité supérieure*, and, at the top, there's the best stuff: the *appellation d'origine contrôlée*. Yes, there are far too many unpronounceable syllables lurking there, particularly if you're already a bit sloshed anyway, but the system seems to work.

But what about the ancients? Were they equally rigorous in their distinctions, or was it all just indistinguishable plonk to them? Well, Egyptian wine snobs employed a three-tiered system. If a wine was good it was an *nfr*. If it was very good it was an *nfr-nfr*, and if it was exceptional it was a ... well, you can probably guess (yes, an *nfr-nfr-nfr*) – it's nice to know drunk people have always repeated themselves. Such a sophisticated ancient palate might surprise us, but the Egyptian upper classes took their wine very seriously, investing huge sums in both locally manufacturing their favourite drop and shipping it in from nearby Israel. In their religion, wine was the gift of the great god Osiris, and the wealthy barely touched anything else. Accordingly, archaeologists frequently find ancient wine amphorae inscribed with the details of the content's vintage and provenance, meaning it isn't just modern wine buffs who read the label before they pop the cork.

But jumping forward a couple of millennia, in Rome the undoubted champion of wines was Falernian, which was harvested in the cold frost from the vineyards of Mt Massico. This was a powerful, sweet drink of such booziness (16 per cent alcohol) that Pliny the Elder claimed it was flammable, but more importantly it was the Cristal of the Roman world, the stuff Emperor Nero served at his imperial shindigs. It came in three varieties: 'the rough, the sweet, and the thin,' and the all-time best vintage had been harvested in 121 BCE, a century before the Empire had even superseded the Republic. So, can we presume that Nero never got to enjoy this premium vintage?

Well, no, because Falernian had a reputation for maturing beautifully, so those who could pay the ludicrous prices still drank it many decades after it was produced. Julius Caesar probably had a lovely time sipping it in 60 BCE – it might have been the ancient equivalent of us enjoying a '55 Chateau Lafite Rothschild – but, a century later, Pliny was disappointed to taste what was over-priced vinegar, 180 years in the making. He wasn't the only one to fall for the hype, either. The satirical writer Petronius, who was the author of the scabrous *Satyricon*, made sure that his boorish character, an ex-slave done good called Trimalchio, served the same Falernian 'of Opimius' vintage' to impress his guests. This was a way of informing the audience that Trimalchio was a world-class berk, but a berk with deep pockets.

Falernian's fame inevitably led to knock-off imitations, with one tavern in Pompeii claiming to offer it for the equivalent of a single *sestertius* coin – a suspiciously good deal on a par with a Rolex watch being hawked for 50 quid by a bloke named Honest Trev. But, Pompeii is an excellent example of the broader Roman pub-lic's love for wine. In this town of around 20,000 people over one hundred bars (*popinae*) and inns (*cauponae*) have been discovered by archaeologists, and though quite a few may also have doubled up as brothels, it's likely that the majority sold alcohol to paying customers. That's hardly surprising, really, because Pompeii was something of a wine-producing town, so the local produce would have been cheaply available. When Vesuvius erupted, many Pom-peians were likely to have been cheerfully sloshed.

So, were the Egyptians and Romans the first to plant vineyards? No, to get to the bottom of that puzzle, we'll have to head back to Iran again...

DRINK WITHIN A YEAR?

The mud-brick village of Hajji Firuz Tepe isn't all that far from Godin Tepe, and there's not much to outwardly distinguish between them. But what makes Hajji Firuz Tepe fascinating is that here evidence of wine predates the manufacture of beer by 1,500 years, with wine-stained storage jars dating to around 5000 BCE having been recovered. It's the oldest known wine in history, but it's the sheer scale of the operation that impresses most.

Demonstrating forward planning typical of the Neolithic era, the villagers stored their wine in 9-litre ceramic jars sealed with a clay stopper. Six of these carafes were discovered in a single kitchen, suggesting deliberate mass production occurred on site. While it's tempting to wonder if these 54 litres were intended to be knocked back all at once, perhaps at the prehistoric equivalent of an office Christmas party, scientific analysis of the pots has found traces of resin from pistachio trees, which was probably added to preserve the wine for a longer lifespan. This resin would undoubtedly have seeped into the fermenting grapes, and it's charming to imagine Neolithic wine snobs wafting the drinking vessel before their noses and enthusing about nutty, woody aromas while their long-suffering spouses rolled their eyes in unison.

It was a technique which caught on. The Greeks also made efforts to preserve their wine and if you were to hand a glass of Athens' finest vintage to a modern connoisseur, they'd probably spit it all over their own shoes and then stare at you in affronted confusion, because not only was tree sap added to the grapes, but also spices, herbs, bits of plant, or honey. To top it all off, the wine would then be diluted with mountain snow – a refreshing coolant on a scorching summer's day – or, less appealingly, with briny sea-water. For the Greeks, only barbarians and fools drank their wine neat, mostly because it had a potent effect on the brain...

IN VINO VERITAS

Having already enjoyed wine with the meal, our guests are in the golden window of tipsy wittiness, when the loosening of inhibitions sees us become more playful and confident. For the ancient Greeks, wine (*oinos*, from where our word derives) was the stimulus of human creativity – a drink worthy of warriors, kings, philosophers and poets – but it was prohibited to women, slaves and youths because they didn't want these troublesome sorts getting any bright ideas about upturning the social hierarchy. Wine was the crucial libation for religious ceremonies and powerful oaths between allies and enemies, and was even prescribed by physicians to perk up many an ailing patient, but – most of all – to drink it was a mark of cultural distinction.

Still, caution was advised as to how much could be necked in a single session. Alcohol's properties were considered vaguely magical, as they could induce a person to blurt out hidden secrets, giving rise to the Roman aphorism *in vino veritas* – 'in wine, there is the truth'. The Greek writer Athenaeus put it even more elegantly, dubbing wine a 'mirror to the mind'. For pretty cynical reasons, therefore, it was expected that Athenian political orators should be a bit drunk when delivering their speeches, so they couldn't mask any dastardly intentions from the gathered crowd. Those politicians who refused to comply – such as the great Demosthenes – were popularly mocked for being 'water-drinkers', though debate raged over whether it was wise to encourage drunkenness among those making key decisions. The comic poet Amphis wrote 'There is, I take it, often sense in wine, And those are stupid who on water dine' but Eubulus cautioned that 'wine obscures and clouds the mind'. That said, everyone agreed that getting utterly trollied, and developing a pot belly, wasn't very statesmanlike. The Athenians would not have voted for Boris Yeltsin.

Drinks

Between the upright Demosthenes and the horizontal alcoholic lay the Goldilocks zone of optimum inebriation. A *philopotes* was the word for a 'drink-lover', yet it wasn't a euphemistic insult for a problem alcoholic, but a positive endorsement of a person's attitude to life. Male drinking parties, called *symposia*, were cheerfully boozy but they weren't raucous orgies – the focus was on philosophical discussion and, much like modern middle-class dinner parties, these wine-lubricated gatherings were fraught with perilous etiquette traps. Even the drinking vessel (*kylix*), a wide-brimmed bowl with two handles, was unnervingly tricky to bring to the lips without sploshing wine down one's chin, forcing the holder to drink slowly. It could also be decorated with a glaring human eye, as a reminder that society was watching very closely, just in case anyone got a bit tipsy and thought it would be funny to piss on any sacred statues or hotwire a battleship...

THE WATER OF LIFE

Alcohol gets its name from *al-kohl,* an Arabic word for a black powder produced by the chemical sublimation of antimony. That, on first glance, is a bit of a weird etymology because booze isn't made of heavy metals, and most Muslims don't drink alcohol anyway. What's more, the word 'alcohol' didn't even refer to a recreational drink until the 1700s. So, what's going on there, then?

It all stems from the alluringly strange story of alchemy, a medieval intellectual movement that blended science, religion and philosophy in the pursuit of higher knowledge and vaguely magical powers. Most alchemists were hunting the elixir of eternal youth, or the philosopher's stone, and – despite their doubtless intellect – their experiments might seem ludicrous to modern eyes. Take, for example, the Italian aristocrat Bernardo de Treviso who wasted his fortune, and much of his life, trying to transform lead into gold by smearing it in a disgusting mixture of vinegar, chicken eggs and horse dung. Yet, despite such inevitable failures, alchemical research wasn't entirely pointless – it gave the world alcoholic spirits.

It wasn't technically a medieval discovery. The ancient Greeks had already been distilling liquid two thousand years beforehand, and more recently medieval Arab scholars had done it with wine, but when these European amateur wizards first witnessed such experiments, they were immediately spellbound and dubbed it *aqua ardens* (burning water), because it would ignite under a naked flame. But that wasn't its only baffling characteristic, as it also evaporated in sunlight, had a profoundly powerful effect on body and mind, and stopped food from rotting. Across Europe, rumours soon spread among learned chin-strokers of this newly found quintessence – the fifth element – to join water, air, fire and earth. If this miracle substance could preserve food, then perhaps it preserved life too?

The thirteenth-century Spanish alchemist and physician Arnaldus de Villa Nova was one of the first to distil wine into brandy and snappily named it *aqua vitae* – the 'water of life'. With such a catchy hook, it's understandable how spirits were soon adopted by the medical community as a hard-hitting panacea, particularly when the Black Death's merciless ravaging of Europe revealed most medicine to be as useless as an umbrella in a hurricane. Alas, *aqua vitae* doesn't appear to have been much more effective either, and a third of Europe succumbed to an agonising death made all the worse, in some cases, by a brandy-induced headache. But that didn't mean distilled alcohol was going to lose its place in the pharmaceutical cabinet just yet.

NOT WHAT THE DOCTOR ORDERED

It's a little early in the evening for a whiskey nightcap, but perhaps our guests will take a dram or two later on. If they do, they'll hopefully not follow in the fatal footsteps of medieval Irishman Risderd Mag Ragnaill who, according to *The Annals of Connacht* for the year 1405, hubristically discovered that the 'water of life' could have the opposite result, if drunk in excess. It's probable that he'd got his greedy hands on the medical-grade *aqua vitae*, but it's also plausible that he might have been one of history's first whiskey drinkers, as we know that by the end of the fifteenth century malt barley was being distilled into what the Irish later called *uisce beatha* (whiskey). To be honest, it's remarkable Mag Ragnaill was able to drink enough to kill himself in the first place, as early whiskey wasn't aged in barrels and probably tasted like paint-stripper, so let's give the fella some kudos for his persistent, suicidal stoicism in the face of such unappetising hooch.

While whiskey spread north to Scotland (where it's been called whisky since the 1800s), other nations caught the distillation bug and, in the sixteenth century, began producing their own regional tipples. The French made brandies from wine and cider, the Danish created aquavit from grain mash flavoured with spices, and the Dutch added juniper berries to grain to produce gin. But by the 1600s, if you were a pirate, or a sailor in the British navy, there was only one true drink. So, do any of our guests fancy a rum and coke?

YO HO HO, AND A BOTTLE OF RUM

Rum's origins are unclear, but the roots of its modern popularity lay in the Caribbean sugar industry where a sticky by-product called molasses was the subject of experimentation by the slave-owning plantation bosses. Looking to monetise their waste, they began adding it to the remnants of boiled sugar, and then drenched it with recycled water used to clean the sugar-boiling pans, to produce a concoction known as wash. This was then left to ferment in the tropical humidity, while coal ash and citrus fruit were added to balance the acidity levels, and extra flavouring might come from dead animals, or human urine, tipped into the bubbling pot. I should add that these weren't key ingredients (don't worry, tonight's rum and coke isn't made of dead badgers and drained bladders), in fact they were means of dissuading the thirsty slaves from drinking the stuff before it was bottled. Once the bubbling had stopped, the wash was then heated so the boozy essence evaporated and passed through tubes into a cooler container, where it condensed into a strong alcoholic liquid. This, in short, was rum.

In Barbados, rum's nickname was kill-devil, which was a less-than-subtle indicator of its fiery potency, and it was drunk in unbelievable excess by a horde of bewildered and sunburned immigrants who'd come to the Caribbean to seek their fortune, only to find disease and disappointment. According to Thomas Verney, a despairing eyewitness, it was common to see young men stumble drunkenly out of taverns and pass out face first into the sand, where they'd be immediately harassed by the island's indigenous army of beach-dwelling crustaceans. In seventeenth-century Barbados drunks could catch a nasty dose of crabs without even taking their breeches off.

While kill-devil was a nickname, rum may have got its formal name from a longer word – 'rumbullion', meaning riotous uproar. The fact is, it really didn't taste very nice, but it was incredibly cheap and thought to be good for curing tropical diseases, so an entire island population would guzzle it as if it were mere mineral water. The result was inevitable violence and discord, hence 'rumbullion'. With such a reputation it's easy to see how the drink ended up being the preferred choice of infamous hell-raising pirates such as Edward 'Blackbeard' Teach, Henry Morgan and the deranged psychopath Ned Lowe (who apparently rejoiced in forcing his captives to eat their own body parts).

OLD GROGRAM

Famously, the scourge of Caribbean piracy – the British Royal Navy – also elected to allow its crewmen to drink rum, as it was safer than water and it didn't spoil as quickly as beer. Obviously, there were risks associated with having seamen shuffling clumsily around the decks of gunpowder-crammed warships, so Vice-Admiral Edward Vernon diluted the ration in 1740. This weaker grog was so called in honour of Old Grogram, the affectionate nickname Vernon had acquired due to the material of his trusty waterproof cloak. When ascorbic acid's ability to combat scurvy was medically proven in 1755, naval regulations required lime also be added to grog and wine, thereby inspiring the 'limeys' nickname given to Brits in America and Australia.

Back on dry land, rum wasn't all that popular in Europe, but in the urban towns of the Eastern Seaboard, the average American was probably drinking five tots per day – and when I say average, I mean anyone over the age of 14. Strict licensing laws meant bar owners were soon looking for ways to circumvent the rules and one such method was mixing rum with other stuff, such as limes, blueberries, junipers, cloves, cinnamon, mint and nutmeg. From here, it seems, our modern cocktails began, and the most popular drink was rum punch, served in a bowl with sliced citrus fruit.

It seems everyone at the party now has a drink in their hand, so we can sit back down and relax. But, while it's a Saturday night and a special occasion, we don't want to overindulge and find ourselves in a police station or hospital...

DRUNK AND DISORDERLY

Spare a little sympathy for Noah. He's just built a mighty ark and rescued breeding pairs of every animal from the damnation of God's apocalyptic flood. Yet, as the Old Testament points out, he follows this success by getting plastered on home-grown wine, throwing off his clothes and stumbling naked around his tent in a drunken stupor. To make things worse, the following morning, Noah's son, Ham, finds his comatose dad sprawled naked on the floor and runs off to tell his brother. Now, Noah isn't considered the bad guy, here – it's Ham who comes off as ungrateful for grassing up his awesome dad – but this story reveals how even the godliest can succumb to the indignities of drunkenness, so what hope was there for the rest of us?

The Greek playwright Eubulus stated that three cups of wine was the perfect amount for the wise fellow to imbibe before toddling home to his bed, but for each cup thereafter the results become increasingly dramatic: a fourth cup induced hubris, a fifth caused shouting, a sixth incited quarrelling, and a seventh led to punch-ups. On the eighth cup, furniture was smashed and the police were called, by the ninth deranged madness set in, and the tenth cup saw the drinker pass out. Presumably the anecdote recounted by Timaeus of Tauromenium qualifies as a 'nine-cup tale'. He relates how a gaggle of young men got so utterly smashed that they convinced themselves they were sailing in a trireme warship, in the middle of a howling storm, and needed to lighten their load to avoid sinking. Imagine the bemusement of passing strangers when chairs and beds were hurled out of nearby windows by a staggering gaggle of confused inebriates.

As we've already seen, the standards of drinking in Anglo-Saxon society were beyond epic and, even after the arrival of the Christian faith, ordinary folk continued to drink each other's health (a toast known as a *wassail*) before then drinking each other under the table. But it wasn't just the ordinary populace getting hammered, as the exasperated canon decrees of Church bureaucrats also attest to monks and priests having been found carousing in bawdy alehouses. Even when they were dragged out, it seems some carried on the party back at their gaff, leading the tenth-century Archbishop of Canterbury Aelfric to moan that: 'men often behave so absurdly as to sit up all night and drink to the point of madness within God's house, and defile it with scandalous games and lewd talk'. Getting pie-eyed in a pub was bad enough, but drunkenness in a sacred building was essentially flipping a middle finger to the Heavenly Father.

One of our guests is enquiring whether we might have any gin and tonic stashed away somewhere? Luckily, we do – but we're careful to pour out the measures correctly. Too much gin tends to bring out the worst in people...

MOTHER'S RUIN

In 1751, the campaigning artist William Hogarth published his celebrated engraving 'Gin Lane'. It depicts a mother pouring gin down her infant's throat, while another booze-addled addict barely notices as her child tumbles headfirst off a flight of stone stairs. In the foreground, a skeletal corpse sits propped up with glass in hand, and on the left a dog shares a bone with its master, the pair gnawing away like savage beasts. What could have inspired such a terrible vision?

In the 1680s, Britain's love affair with brandy had become problematic. The nation was frequently warring with its export-ers, the French and Dutch, and so, in order to compensate with a home-grown spirit, the government drastically deregulated the production of gin, enabling the sprouting up of many new distilleries. Even by 1726, records show London was straining at the seams with 8,659 'brandy houses' catering for a population of only 700,000 Londoners – that's a ratio of one gin shop for every 80 people – on top of the pre-existing 5,975 alehouses already selling beer and wine.

The result of this unprecedented gintoxication was human misery, and gin became known as 'Mother's Ruin'. Between 1749 and 1751 alone, the population of London was said to have plummeted by more than 9,000, as a direct result of negligence by alcoholic parents. It was even claimed that when Mother's Ruin was drunk in sufficient quantities, maternal breast milk became laced with gin. To walk around London was to literally stumble over the bodies of men, women and even children lying unconscious on the floor of drinking establishments, or even in the street, in huge heaps of intertwined limbs. Like heroin addicts, they had become trapped in a vicious cycle of wild highs and comatose lows, and gaining access to their fix was as easy as breathing – 8,000,000 gallons was being declared to the authorities each year, but the black market likely produced the same amount again.

Having caused the whole nightmare, the government attempted several times to shut the proverbial stable door by making it costlier to own a distiller's licence, but the horse had already bolted, galloped out of the stables, nicked a Porsche and sped off into the sunset. The laws were unenforceable, the patterns of behaviour deeply established, and gin ruled the streets. Over its 60 years, until the Gin Act of 1751 successfully targeted both consumers and wholesale producers, the Gin Crisis inflicted immeasurable damage. Yet the moral panic which accompanied it was not an attack on alcohol itself. The opinion formers in the middle and upper classes blamed gin, and only gin, for the disaster. Indeed, Hogarth's 'Gin Lane' engraving was accompanied by a virtuous sibling called 'Beer Street', in which the Londoners are robust, healthy and cheerful. Like any self-deluded addict, Britain blamed a scapegoat for a wider problem. It was gin – that cheap, foreign muck – that was the cause of all this chaos, but there was nothing wrong with regular helpings of good old nutritious beer.

Yet this attitude would come to be challenged by the end of the nineteenth century.

A NOBLE EXPERIMENT

A century ago, in America – a nation of committed drinkers – a total prohibition on the sale of alcohol was enacted into law in one of the most remarkable events in modern history. So, how did it happen? And why did it fail so spectacularly? Well, the truth is that no alcoholic regulation has ever properly succeeded. Beginning around 2100 BCE, when the legendary Emperor Yu the Great was said to have forbidden the manufacture of alcohol, China enacted prohibition numerous times, but each of these bans were later repealed. In 650 BCE the author of the *Shujing* (Book of History) stated 'the people will not do without beer. To prohibit and secure total abstinence from it is beyond even the power of sages.' The great Mongol conqueror, Genghis Khan, was similarly pragmatic: 'A soldier must not get drunk more often than once a week. It would, of course, be better if he did not get drunk at all, but one should not expect the impossible.' Genghis achieved military feats so vast, and killed so many people, that the forests regrew on all the abandoned farmland and CO_2 levels dropped by 700 million tonnes – yet even a man who could reverse global warming couldn't stop his soldiers getting tipsy.

So, throughout history there have always been moralists despairing at the state of the nation, and gesticulating with accusatory venom towards the drunks littering the floors of taverns, but doing something about it has often been difficult, or has caused unforeseen consequences. Back in tenth-century England, King

Edgar the Peaceful tried to restrict the number of alehouses and standardise the size of drinking vessels. His idea was to create eight pegged notches in each mug, and the law stipulated a man could only drink a single peg's worth of ale in a single sitting before the 'pottle' was given to the next customer. Ingeniously, the English – being both unwilling to have their liberties curtailed, and also showcasing their notorious obsession with politeness – realised that if they accidentally drank more than a peg, then the person after them would receive less ale, which was clearly unfair.

So, it became customary to drink to the next peg instead, in order to even things up again. But then they might accidentally overshoot this peg too, which was quite easy to do if the peg was hidden under thick, soupy ale. So then they'd try again, but all the while they were getting drunker and drunker, and their judgement was becoming more impaired, meaning they probably overshot the... well, you get the picture. As is so often the case in prohibitive acts of censorship, King Edgar's law conversely resulted in more drunkenness than ever. So why, given the extensive failing of past attempts, did American prohibitionists think it was a good idea to close down the bars?

THE BENIGHTED STATES OF AMERICA

In 1829, President Andrew Jackson was hosting his inauguration ball at the White House when things got a little out of hand. As the drink flowed and the atmosphere became more boisterous, the building was overrun by thousands of drunken well-wishers whose political enthusiasm swiftly turned into a frat-house rampage. Having gleefully trashed government property, including some rather pricey crockery, the rowdy mob had to be lured out onto the front lawn, like a horde of drunken rats pursuing the Pied Piper of Hamelin, by bowls of rum punch and liquor. The new President, meanwhile, had to escape through a window and sleep in a nearby hotel. Never has Donald Rumsfeld's observation that 'democracy is messy' seemed more apt.

As you can see, it wasn't just Britain that had succumbed to alcohol's heady charms. Drinking culture was endemic in America – beer, wine, rum, porter, whiskey, madeira and brandy were all drunk to excess. In the early nineteenth century, farmers had discovered their unused grain and corn surplus could be redirected to whiskey distilleries for a tidy profit, meaning that by 1830 the average American knocked back seven gallons of alcohol per year, while heavy boozers were easily reaching ten gallons: the equivalent of a bottle of Jack Daniel's every week. If not even the President could escape the plate-smashing hullaballoo of drunken citizens, then clearly things were bad.

A moral backlash was inevitable, and it came initially from the recently founded American Temperance Society. This instantly popular group of progressive reformers initially promoted individual restraint, but this led to internal squabbles about how much a person could justifiably claim was 'moderation', so tougher guidelines had to be set. The Society's message spread rapidly across Sweden, Denmark, Norway, Germany and the Netherlands, where like-minded Christians formed their own organisations. Ireland's Father Theobald Mathew emerged as a superstar preacher with something like seven million converts to his no-booze pledge, but pan-European support plummeted after the failed Revolutions of 1848 – there's nothing like having your political optimism crushed to make you crave a pint. This left only the Church of England Temperance Society and the Irish Temperance League as heavy hitters by the 1870s.

But while Europe's affair with abstinence was fleeting, in America the famous Carribbean 'kill-devil' was now being rebranded as 'demon rum'. Personal abstinence was no longer enough of a sop to temperance campaigners; the religious organisations would fight all the way to Capitol Hill to ensure that nobody was going to get a drink.

BAN THIS FILTH!

In 1874, the Women's Christian Temperance Union was founded with the explicit goal of enforcing the total outlawing of alcohol. They argued that drunkenness had a damaging impact particularly on females, many of whom were unable to support themselves, had few legal rights and were in abusive relationships with violent alcoholics. Further to that, they took the religious view that alcohol was a moral sin in the eyes of God, and one which caused irredeemable social harm; as did tobacco, prostitution, urban poverty, anti-immigration bigotry and various other societal ills. Clearly, these women weren't frothing fundamentalists – they just wanted a better, more humane America – but they were elbowed aside by a gang of political sharks more willing to play dirty.

Beginning in rural Ohio, The Anti-Saloon League went national in 1895 and, for these guys, all means justified the end. Their spin-off movement, the Scientific Temperance Federation, felt no shame in (mis)educating the public with pseudoscientific anti-alcohol propaganda, and their unofficial heavies – the Ku Klux Klan – used violence and intimidation to drive drink from the rural South. But the League itself was a political organisation devoted to harassing politicians with an aggressive strategy now known as the pressure group. The brilliant architect of this relentless campaign was Wayne B. Wheeler, the League's top lawyer and a man who caused outrage in his own movement by negotiating with whiskey-drinking senators and congressmen. But Wheeler didn't care if they drank, provided he could induce them to hypocritically support national prohibition. And if he couldn't bring them to heel, then that's when he revealed his teeth . . .

Central to pressure politics was the kind of burning retaliatory vengeance more akin to Glenn Close's spurned lover in *Fatal Attraction*. If a politician turned down the League, then the League would go beyond mere bunny-boiling; they would not rest until that political career had been utterly destroyed. Thanks to the bipartisan system in America, Wheeler's outfit didn't even need a majority to wield enormous power; it was a kingmaker and could essentially evict whoever it wanted and then replace them with a loyal puppet who knew not to bite the hand that fed. Wheeler was described as a man who could 'make the American Senate sit up and beg', as if it were an obedient hound hoping for a biscuit, but one that was still fearful of the rolled-up newspaper.

Despite success in the rural areas, where the Ku Klux Klan had no qualms in burning down drinking saloons, the League and its associates failed to influence attitudes in the big cities. So, to win the public round, Purley Baker – a Methodist minister – instead launched a vitriolic campaign against America's easiest targets: Catholics, Jews and Germans, the latter being labelled 'gluttonous eaters' who drank 'like swine'. Such anti-German propaganda went down a storm in the run-up to the First World War, and by the time the US Army started shipping out to the battlefields of Europe, 23 American states had outlawed alcohol. The Anti-Saloon League's multi-pronged assault was a phenomenal success. When America's soldiers returned victorious in 1919, they found that the 18th Amendment had banned the manufacture or transportation of alcohol for non-medicinal purposes. America would be drier than the Gobi Desert. Or that was the theory.

AL CAPONE'S AMERICAN DR(E)AM

We might logically expect that outlawing booze production would reduce the amount of societal damage inflicted by alcohol. After all, wasn't the Gin Crisis the result of lax licensing laws and too many economic incentives towards mass production? Well, some people really subscribed to this naïve philosophy . . . and I mean *really* subscribed. Allegedly, some were so convinced that a teetotal society would renounce crime that they imagined selling off their jailhouses, but these incurable optimists had neglected one crucial factor – Americans loved booze!

As soon as Prohibition came in, upheld by the infamous Volstead Act, people began hunting for ways around the law. Because it was not illegal to own alcohol (only to manufacture and transport it), the wealthy acquired excess stock from panicking beer, wine and liquor producers, who now needed to diversify into making other products, and moved it all into their wine cellars for personal consumption. Those without mansions swiftly discovered that whiskey could be sold for medicinal purposes from pharmacies, and that wine was also available for religious rituals – indeed, while the Coors Brewing Company switched to making soft drinks, porcelain and ice cream, Californian wine-growers soon made a fortune. Most charming of all, ordinary people could buy concentrated bricks of grape juice which came with wonderfully faux-innocent instructions that said: 'After dissolving brick in a gallon of water, do not place the liquid in a jug away in the cupboard for twenty days, because then it would turn into wine.' Well, they wouldn't have wanted that to happen, would they . . . ?

But these were just the legal loopholes – far more serious was the emerging black market. Secret distilleries sprang up all over the country, producing the famous 'bathtub gin', so named either because it was fermented in bathtubs, or because the glycerine-flavoured concoction was mixed with water in large vats under a bath tap. Such were the profits available that even respectable figures took to the illicit hobby, including several police officers who spent the 1920s running their own elaborate liquor cartels.

The poorly manufactured hooch – also known as moonshine – was shipped into the cities in high-powered cars designed to outpace the cops (this was the origin of modern NASCAR racing), or it was carried by the tide in floating crates from an Atlantic offshore rig called Rum Row. Other quality stuff had to be smuggled in from Canada, Mexico and the coastlines, but that meant it was pricier.

Wherever the alcohol came from, it found its way into the illegal speakeasy bars and backroom parties made so famous by Hollywood movies. But the glamour ended there. Bathtub gin was bloody awful, sometimes lethal, to drink – 4,154 people were killed by it in 1925 alone. Even on a good day it could still cause brain-warping headaches, or even partial blindness, but the worst stories are surely those of the desperate people who believed that filtering antifreeze through a loaf of bread would render it safe to drink, which, needless to say, was as an idea even more dangerous than smearing yourself in blood and jumping into a shark tank.

Across America, people suffered hangovers so debilitating they would crash their cars or just fall asleep drunk in the road. Those who couldn't get their regular fix, and wouldn't do without it, turned to cocaine, cannabis and opiates. The economy stagnated, tax revenues dropped, police spending increased, the legal system was stretched to breaking point and – worst of all – organised crime, racketeering, bribery and corruption all grew, as mobsters like Al Capone exploited the situation.

NO BOOZE IS TOO MUCH BOOZE

Despite the widespread availability of booze in speakeasies and pharmacies, and the fact Maryland and New York put minimal effort into enforcing the law, recent historical research has shown that the 18th Amendment reduced nationwide consumption of alcohol by about 70 per cent, bringing about a huge drop in cases of alcohol-related diseases. In terms of public health, this was ostensibly good news – but by trying to banish the harm, the law inadvertently unleashed many other destabilising forces into American society. Prohibition was a dangerously drastic course of action, the equivalent of heating your house on a chilly winter's day by pouring gasoline over the carpet and lighting a match. This would have been no surprise to Abraham Lincoln – himself a temperate drinker – who'd allegedly argued as much in 1840, stating:

Prohibition will work great injury to the cause of temperance. It is a species of intemperance within itself, for it goes beyond the bounds of reason in that it attempts to control a man's appetite by legislation, and makes a crime out of things that are not crimes . . .

Although this speech seems to have been a posthumous invention, never uttered by the man himself, it still makes a valid point. Outlawing something that patently seemed a basic right inflamed a form of protest drinking among the outraged ordinary, and produced deadly consequences. Inevitably, Prohibition was scrapped in 1933, though President Roosevelt's celebrated quote, 'what America needs now is a drink', was somewhat redundant given that the nation had just spent the past 13 years getting shit-faced on homemade gut-rot.

What America really needed was normality, with all the problems that brings, because at least those problems didn't transfer terrifying amounts of power to the Mob. After all, while only 42 per cent of the global population are drinkers, to many of us it's a natural part of daily life. And to the British, at least, the pub is the focal point of all that is good in society. It may seem like we are a nation of tea-drinkers, but if anyone tried to ban pubs then even the reigning monarch would march on 10 Downing Street, a pint of ale in one hand and a cricket bat in the other, ready to smash some windows.

But I digress. We've had plenty to drink tonight, and one by one our friends are saying their farewells. It's late, and our eyelids are becoming droopy. Drunkenly surveying the dirty plates and glasses, we decide to ignore them – well, at least until the morning. Right now, we should probably go to bed.

11.45 p.m.

BRUSHING OUR TEETH

Dragging our leaden feet up the staircase, we look longingly at our bedroom door. But, before we can clamber gratefully under the duvet, a nagging voice in the back of our head demands that we complete one crucial daily ritual, the one our parents always made us do, no matter our protestations. It's time we brush our teeth.

WHITE TEETH

We've reached the point where celebrities' teeth are eerily radiant slabs of alabaster showcased in perfectly carved symmetro-jaws. Teeth have been elevated beyond their biological purpose of food mashing to become aesthetic fashion statements. But for virtually all of human history, they were primarily functional chewers without which our ancestors would have starved to death. And starving was sometimes a genuine possibility, as the challenge wasn't to maintain the blinding radiance of a kilowatt grin, but simply to keep one's teeth vaguely proximal to the lower half of one's face. Teeth are sturdy little blighters but over time they're naturally susceptible to bacterial infection, gradual wear and tear, blunt-force damage and acidic decay. In short, they can fall out.

So, given the necessity of tooth-care, it's not that surprising that the story of dentistry begins in the Stone Age.

NEOLITHIC GNASHERS

The pain was sharp, a fierce buzz that ricocheted down through his body all the way to his toes. He kicked his heels against the floor in frustrated protest, angry at having to endure this torment, but remained flat on his back – the last thing he wanted was for the drill to slip from its user's grasp and plunge into the soft tissue of his tongue. The dentist loomed over him, sawing back and forth like a lumberjack, with an expression of intense concentration. The sound of the drill grinding against the decayed molar reverberated through the patient's skull, a quiet whittling to accompany his muted winces of pain. The patient closed his eyes, and thought of something else. It would all be over soon. And within a minute, it was.

Nine thousand years ago, at a place called Mehrgarh in modern Pakistan, possibly the world's first dentist was plying his or her trade thousands of years before the blueprints for Stonehenge were even being drawn up. This seems one hell of a claim, but the evidence is visible in the teeth of skeletons found in the remains of this Neolithic town. To the ordinary eye, tiny holes of 0.5–3.5 mm depth aren't terribly impressive, and we probably wouldn't even notice them at first glance, but to archaeologists their uniform shape is unmistakably proof of dental drilling. More than 5,000 years before anyone was wielding malleable metal tools, this dentist used a flint-tipped bow-drill to quickly burrow through enamel into the pain-causing caries. Typically used to puncture eyelets in jewellery beads, the sharpened flint would have been fixed into a wooden shaft which was then looped with string and attached to what looks like an archer's bow, so that by dragging the bow back and forth – as if sawing a piece of wood – the shaft would rotate clockwise and counter-clockwise on its axis, gouging a tiny hole in the tooth.

But how do we know this was therapeutic dentistry, rather than some religious ritual or an ill-advised fashion statement? Of the 11 drilled teeth discovered at the site, at least four were afflicted by inflamed caries, and the fact that only rear molars – lurking in the hidden recesses of the cheeks – were operated on probably quashes any notion of this being some sort of snazzy smile modification. If you're gonna spruce up your grin, surely you want the design to be front-facing? Given that caries cause sharp pain, it's much more likely that this procedure aimed to alleviate chronic toothache. Intriguingly, drilling wasn't the limit of a prehistoric dentist's powers. An Italian team of boffins has recently proven that a skeleton found in Slovenia, the remains of a young man who died about 6,500 years ago, boasted what seems to be the world's first filling – a beeswax resin poured into a cracked tooth. Whereas the drilling in Mehrgarh had presumably been to scoop out an infected cavity, this was apparently designed to encase an exposed nerve.

So, despite modern dentistry being a high-tech business with X-rays, lasers and electronic gadgets, what remain our most common treatments – fillings and drillings – date back thousands of years. What's more, our dentist will tell us that sugary foods are enemy number one, and this too was a familiar issue for our prehistoric ancestors. The Neolithic farming revolution led to greater consumption of starchy foods, such as bread and porridge, increasing the level of natural sugars in the mouth and thereby inviting cavities and acid erosion to do their worst. But the chief destroyer of ancient dentine was the abrasive coarseness of grit lurking in the loaves, an unfortunate by-product from grinding flour on quern stones.

Perhaps the most famous early victim of this dental attrition was our long-dead pal Ötzi the Iceman, the Neolithic murder victim from Tyrol. His teeth were in a terrible state: discoloured, smashed up in places, worn down in others. He'd lost a cusp on one molar, probably from enthusiastically chomping on a stony loaf, and serious damage to one of his front teeth suggests someone, or something, had smacked him violently in the face. The fact that he later wound up with an arrow in his back suggests he wasn't one of those lovable Tom Hanks types. While Ötzi was perhaps particularly unlucky, his mouth was broadly representative of normal dentition in prehistory. Teeth aren't invulnerable, and by the end of a Neolithic person's life, even in their forties, their attempt at a Tom Cruise grin would have more likely resembled the aftermath of detonating a tiny grenade in the movie star's mouth – there would still be teeth, but it sure wouldn't be pretty...

THE TROUBLE WITH TOOTH WORMS

Miniature rocks and natural sugars may have been the true culprits, but the scapegoats who took the blame were far more sinister. As the Bronze Age arrived, both Babylonians and Egyptians developed a strongly held belief in monstrous little creatures called 'tooth worms', thought to spontaneously generate in the mouth like the respawning ghosts in *Pac-Man*. It was a theory perpetuated by the Romans and still in vogue during the eighteenth century, which meant dentists spent millennia conjuring up treatments for critters that didn't actually exist.

Accordingly, the Bronze Age response to toothache often involved superstitious incantation: the Babylonians donned protective magical amulets and, if the dastardly worms showed up, implored the great god Ea/Enki to destroy them. If that failed, a dentist might smoke them out. By 2250 BCE, oral fumigation – burning henbane seeds, kneaded into beeswax, near the mouth – was the established treatment and once the wriggly enemy had been slain the cavity was filled with gum mastic and more henbane. Yet, despite the early promise of Neolithic drill technicians, the Babylonians weren't ones for surgery or fillings. Their dentistry was surprisingly low-tech.

TEETH IN THE LAND OF KING TUT

The funerary complex of Saqqara is a vast man-made landscape dedicated to death, though it hasn't served as a cemetery for a very long time. It was once the official necropolis of the Bronze Age capital of Memphis, and so boasts the oldest of the Egyptian pyramids, the step-pyramid of Djoser, which still stands as symbolic testament to the power of ancient kings. Yet, so much of Saqqara is a mystery to us; some optimistic Egyptologists believe only 30 per cent of its secrets have been found, and jokingly claim that if you bung a spade into the ground at random then you'll probably strike lucky.

One recent discovery to emerge from the ocean of sand was a tomb initially found by thieves in 2006. This was a high-status monument, built of limestone and mud-brick around 4,000 years ago, with beautifully decorated interiors and a trove of grave goods stored for the afterlife. But this mausoleum hadn't belonged to a princess or noble; instead it was the final resting place of a trio of unrelated men named Iy Mry, Kem Msw and Sekhem Ka. Though their mummies are mysteriously absent, the hieroglyphs on the wall make their identities clear – these guys were dentists to the Pharaoh, a title which had been first held

600 years beforehand by Hesi-Re – the earliest named dentist in history, and official tooth-wrangler to Pharaoh Djoser himself.

Despite their grandiose name badges, these Doctors of the Tooth shared the Babylonian reticence for surgical intervention. Hesi-Re and his subsequent accomplices would have relied on masticatory chews, mouthwashes and plasters made from a range of deliciously aromatic ingredients: frankincense, myrrh, onion, cumin, yellow ochre and honey – frankly, it sounds less like medicine and more like an overly ambitious stir fry – but not everything was quite so appetising; one particularly weird treatment saw the warm body of a dead mouse being sliced in half and rubbed on the afflicted tooth.

The Egyptians were a vain bunch who took enormous pride in their appearance, so it's surprising that there's minimal evidence for any kind of cosmetic treatments on those with gappy grins. The only clues we have for prosthetic dental work are artificial bridges of errant teeth, strung together using gold wire, plonked back in a mummy's jaw. This seems to have been a funerary touch-up to 'complete' the corpse, rather than a daily worn implant – the ancient equivalent of painting mortuary make-up onto a person lying in an open coffin.

We tend to combat the threat of dental infections with mouth-wash, dental floss, toothpaste and regular visits to the dentist. The Egyptians had it much harder. We know, for example, that Mutnodjmed – the Queen consort of Pharaoh Horemheb, who himself had formerly served as military advisor to Tutankhamun – had lost all her teeth by the time she died in her forties, making her a gummy mummy (sorry...). It's rather sobering to discover she wasn't alone in her suffering; a recent scientific analysis of 3,000 mummies has revealed that 18 per cent of them had struggled with serious dental disease, with a few infections being lethal. Just as with Neolithic sufferers, it's likely that food was a major cause of tooth problems, even for the rich and powerful. As P.J.

O'Rourke quipped about the lure of nostalgia, 'when you think of the good old days, think one word: dentistry.'

It's not known why surgery was off the cards in Egypt. Anaesthetic in the form of opium seems to have been available for the mollification of severe pain, and occasionally holes were drilled into the jawbone to drain abscesses, but deliberate extraction of infected teeth, which might have saved the lives of many a patient, was almost never practised. Instead, those with inflamed gnashers relied upon nature taking its course, a maxim espoused in a book of wisdom known as the *Instruction of Ankhsheshonq*: 'There is no tooth that rots yet stays in place.' Poor Mutnodjmed knew that only too well, and perhaps it explains why the Egyptians had no equivalent of the Tooth Fairy – the poor thing would have been almost instantly bankrupted by the ceaseless stockpile of missing teeth hidden under all those pillows ...

By contrast, the ancient Greeks were enthusiastic interventionists and it was the father of medicine himself, good old Hippocrates of Kos, who came up with the idea for dental forceps (*odontagogon*). Hippocrates was the great rationalist of the ancient world and mostly rejected divine superstition in favour of empirical diagnosis based on visible symptoms. This courageously led him to seek clues to his patients' maladies by tasting their urine, sweat, earwax and nasal mucus. In truth, he wasn't always entirely on the money when it came to being scientifically rigorous, and both he and Aristotle believed men had more teeth than women. You'd think such geniuses might have thought to peer into a mouth or two for proof, but they were probably far too busy dissecting camels and quaffing piss.

GOLDEN GRINS

If we lost a tooth, perhaps by accidentally walking into a glass door, we might expect our dentist to fit us with a dental bridge. This is an idea first utilised around 700 BCE by the Etruscans – an agricultural people from northern Italy – who ingeniously developed a working technique for both replacing and stabilising missing or wobbly pearly whites. Using flattened gold strips as orthodontic brackets, any vulnerable tooth could be supported by its strong, healthy neighbours – the dental equivalent of tightly tethering a weakling like me to the front row of a rugby team.

If a tooth had already been lost then a false one might be plucked from an ox, bored through the centre with a drill, pinned to the metal bracket, and then dropped neatly into the available space to continue the vital work of its absent predecessor. While a metallic grin is more famously linked to James Bond's cable-munching adversary, Jaws, perhaps what is most impressive is how these ancient dental prostheses were not merely aesthetic attempts to cram empty mouths for the sake of it. They were likely to have been working dentures that allowed their users to chew food and live lives unimpeded by the monotony of endless bowls of soup.

A couple of centuries later, in the eastern Mediterranean during the fifth century BCE, the alphabet-wrangling, seafaring Phoe-nicians were using gold wire, rather than flat brackets, to truss wobbly teeth together like fence posts in a farmyard. Remarkably, an example of a golden-lassoed lower jaw survives in the Archaeo-logical Museum of the American University of Beirut. Known as the Ford Mandible – which sounds more like the model of car driven by a photocopier salesman – the bone shows evidence of pyrea, a nasty disease which would have made the teeth fall out under normal circumstances. But in this case the gold thread held them in place for the remainder of the patient's life. It's quite astonishing that ancient dentists were able to not only practise restorative prosthetic dentistry, but also preserve nature's intended design in the face of stubborn opposition from nature itself.

By the time the Romans showed up, having first crushed the Etruscans and then subsumed the Greeks into their ballooning empire, cosmetic dentistry was pretty nifty. As well as falsies made of wood or ivory, gold-capped teeth became so common that the legal system had to intervene to assert that such precious metals were to be buried or cremated with their dead owner, and not covetously squabbled over by money-grabbing relatives eager to monetise granny's funeral. Having metal dentures wasn't always a question of necessity, though. At the turn of the fourteenth century, the enigmatic Italian traveller Marco Polo reported that he'd encountered a mysterious Chinese tribe called the Zar-Dandan ('The Golden-Teeth' in the Persian language) who'd emulated the Etruscans by slotting gold plates over their teeth, but that this was a purely aesthetic choice, making the Zar-Dandan pioneers of the metal grill long before Lil Wayne was flaunting golden gnashers in hip hop videos.

On a similar theme, earlier Vikings appear to have filed grooves into their teeth, perhaps as some kind of scare tactic to terrify the enemy, while – on the other side of the world – high-status Aztecs and Maya went further by drilling cavities into their incisors and canines and then plugging them with beautiful inlays of quartz, gold, jade or turquoise, resulting in the ultimate bling grin.

SCRUB, GARGLE, SPIT

Drunkenly we stumble into our bathroom and recoil in alarm at our bleary-eyed reflection in the mirror. Hopefully we didn't look like that all night! Reaching out, we grab our toothbrush in one hand and the mangled tube of toothpaste in another. We flip open the cap, squint in concentration, and attempt to squeeze a pea-sized blob of minty paste onto the bristles, a task of childlike simplicity on most days, but a fiendishly tricky test of hand-to-eye co-ordination with boozy double-vision.

Would a Roman have done something similar? Well, yes. A 2015 project using CT scans on the victims at Pompeii revealed that these people had surprisingly healthy teeth. This may have been due to naturally high levels of fluorine in the local water supply, but it's also likely that Romans practised good oral hygiene. The brilliant polymath Aulus Cornelius Celsus recommended regular cleaning of the teeth, particularly for those aristocratic sorts who guzzled vast quantities of refined foods, which – he rightly suspected – might accelerate tooth decay. However, even though fulsome white smiles were keenly prized in Roman high society, the rich were not about to forego their lavish dinners; they literally wanted to have their cake and eat it. So, how did a Roman aristocrat keep their gob in good order? The answer, perhaps not surprisingly, was regular brushing – but they weren't going to do it themselves. In order to avoid the need for dentures, an indentured slave would wield the soft twig, onto which polishing powders were applied, and then they would gently scrub their master's teeth and gums to clean away food stains.

The choice of toothpaste was varied but the allegedly sex-crazed Messalina, wife of Emperor Claudius, chose to whiten her smile with powdered stag antlers which was also believed to be a powerful aphrodisiac – horn apparently produced horniness – and, like us, Romans had a version of our medicated mouth-washes to freshen their breath, only it wasn't very minty. Or very nice. Yes, perhaps to our horror, they chose to gargle undiluted human urine, preferably the super-strength stuff shipped in all the way from Portugal where piss was believed to contain more ammonia. Knowing that, it's a wonder Messalina managed to find any lovers at all . . .

In southern Asia, the sacred Vedic writings were also dishing out sage dental advice. The big kahuna of Indian Ayurveda medicine was Suśruta, commonly known as a scholar from the sixth century BCE, but it's possible that he was a legendary aggregation of many anonymous physicians. In any case, his orthodontic recommendation was to use a frayed twig of aromatic tree bark as a toothbrush (*dantakashtha*), and he suggested regular brushing in conjunction with an application of paste made from honey, powder and oil. Other than this delicious-sounding toothpaste, one's breath might also be improved by chewing betel leaves, which have a mild stimulant effect and are also said to be an aphrodisiac, perhaps explaining why they crop up in the *Kama Sutra* – it seems popping a little betel was the Indian equivalent of chewing some minty-fresh Viagra.

Betel is still popular across South and South-East Asia today, particularly when combined with areca nut, and this combo is known in India as *paan*. However, sustained use turns the teeth a ghoulish hue of blackish red, and it's also likely to cause mouth cancer. Yet, despite the warnings, neither of those things seems to have hurt its popularity in Vietnam, India and Pakistan.

AND IN CHINA . . .

Brushing of the teeth with sticks and rags was common across various parts of the world, but the first people to invent a brush for this purpose were the Chinese, who stitched pig bristles into bone handles during the medieval Tang Dynasty – around the time when the Anglo-Saxons and Vikings were squabbling for control of England – though it's possible that it may have been used even earlier.

Chinese medical philosophy was a bit different from the Greek Four Humours and Babylonian superstition, though the Chinese too believed in the dreaded tooth worm (3,500 years ago the written Chinese symbol for dental caries was a smug worm perched triumphantly on top of a vanquished tooth as if it were a mountaineer stood atop Mt Everest). In any case, Traditional Chinese Medicine (TCM) was founded on the mystical writings attributed to the legendary Yellow Emperor Huang-Ti and the Emperor of the Five Grains Shen-Nung, who supposedly ruled between 4,500 and 5,000 years ago. They were the ones who first set out the Five Phases (*Wu Xing*) of Earth, Wood, Metal, Fire and Water – the vital elemental interactions of the cosmos, not to be confused with Earth, Wind & Fire, the American soul band who wrote the funktastic *Boogie Wonderland*.

The two emperors also wrote of the cosmological constant of yin-yang, a recursive feedback system of mutually mingled opposites, by which there could be no man without woman, dark without light, or good without evil. So, in short, TCM preached a harmonic balance in the body, and any disturbance to that even distribution of elements caused illness. Indeed, due to the holistic perception of the body, Chinese dentistry didn't involve poking the teeth but mostly focused on acupuncture, massage or herbal medicines. If these didn't work, the dentist might have ventured closer to the mouth by preparing medicinal pills made from garlic, horseradish, human milk and saltpetre, but then, instead of dropping them into the mouth, he'd cram them up the patient's nostrils instead. And, if that also failed, or if a dastardly tooth worm was spotted, then dentists were not morally opposed to dangling an arsenic pill near the offending tooth. This was particularly dangerous, as accidental arsenic ingestion can be fatal. Suddenly our modern phobia of dentists is starting to seem childishly trivial, isn't it?

THE PATRON SAINT OF TOOTHACHE

Back in the medieval West and Middle East, dentistry had failed to progress beyond the energetic strut of its ancient adolescence and – much like The Rolling Stones – was stuck on a perpetual nostalgia tour, playing the same old hits: Tooth Worms, the Four Humours and Blood Letting. Though oral hygiene is tremendously important in the Islamic faith, and the Prophet Muhammad used a stick (*miswak*) cut from a *Salvatora Persica* tree to brush his teeth – even the eleventh-century genius Ibn Sina stuck confidently to the Roman habit of oral fumigation when treating toothache, though a religious aversion to bloodshed probably prompted many Arab surgeons to emulate the Chinese practice of slowly killing a tooth with arsenic rather than yanking it out.

But in western Europe it was ancient Roman wisdom, filtered through Catholic doctrine, that was passed down through the generations, leaving most dentists to continue the traditions of powdering, boiling, pulping and smearing an assortment of odd ingredients – including newts, lizards, frogs, ravens' dung, herbs and even human excrement – as part of the eternal struggle against tooth decay. If potions and poultices didn't work then people could always pop along to their neighbourhood blood-letter for a quick draining session or, if knives weren't really their thing, they might have visited a holy shrine dedicated to the famous St Apollonia, a Christian martyr whose tortured execution had involved her teeth being systematically extracted and/ or smashed before she was burned alive. A prayer to her might wangle a bit of divine mercy from the Big Man upstairs, though if I were St Apollonia I would have written back saying 'you think *you*'ve got toothache?'

Waiting for divine intervention was the optimist's choice, and undoubtedly many pious Christians could point to examples of known miracles to reinforce their faith, but the more pragmatic sufferer may have found better long-term relief in the short-term horror of surgery, despite the fact that the medieval dentist wasn't someone with particularly inspiring credentials...

BARBERS AND BARBARISM

The noisy crowd throngs around the stage, laughing and shouting in gathered fascination at the scene unveiling before their eyes. A clown in a harlequin costume is juggling apples while a man clutching a pair of pliers addresses the crowd. 'Who amongst you has toothache?' he asks, jabbing his finger at the curious faces of the front row. The audience murmurs nervously, but nobody steps forward. The man asks again, louder this time. There is a voice from inside the huddled mob: 'I am suffering. Can you help me?' The man smiles and beckons the suffering patient onto the stage, laying him down on his back. The juggling clown puts down his apples and clambers onto the patient's chest, pinning him down. Now the crowd surges forward to watch, sucking in its breath as the pliers reach into the young man's mouth and wrench out a rotten, yellowed tooth. There are gasps of anguished shock, and yet... there is no blood. Instead, the patient waves cheerfully, 'I am cured! It's a miracle!' The crowd bursts into joyous cheering, and the many sufferers of toothache begin to queue with their coins at the ready, eager to enjoy their own pain-free surgery...

This was probably a fairly common scene in the cities of medieval Europe. The man on the stage was one of many tooth-wrangling charlatans proclaiming themselves toothers or tooth-drawers. If they were really trying to milk it, they might even call themselves kind-hearts, but the Germans who'd suffered at their hands weren't fooled by such saccharine self-promotion and dubbed them tooth-breakers *(zahnbrechers)*. In fact, their

reputation across Europe was beyond notorious – these mounte-
banks were a class of disreputable fraudsters for whom no insult
was too good. And yet the agony of a rotten tooth induced gullible optimists to queue up, regardless, having been seduced by
the tooth-drawer's charisma and the stagecraft of his clowning
assistant, the Merrie Andrew or Zany. What's more, like at Las
Vegas magic shows, stooges hid in the crowd waiting to enjoy a
pain-free, faked extraction to boost the crowd's confidence. By
the time the real teeth were being prised out of reluctant jaws,
and warm blood was spraying across the front rows, the excitable roars of the audience probably drowned out the sound of
screaming. Or maybe not.

While we cheerfully brush our teeth, with minty dribble running down our chin, we might suddenly discover a painful abscess
in our jaw, or a wonky tooth, and – though slightly anxious about
it – we'd probably phone the dentist in the morning, confident
in their framed certificates hanging on the wall as evidence that
they probably won't maim us. But if medieval people had opted
against the tooth-drawers, their other choice was to visit a man
whose shop-front featured a pole wrapped in bloody sheets, and
whose windows and walls were decorated with buckets slopping
over with human blood and a rack of fearsome instruments. These
bloodied props were supposed to reassure the patient by showing
them how experienced the dentist was, though we'd now take
them as proof of his being a demented psychopath flaunting his
trophies. Least encouraging of all, the guy primed to poke a pair
of pincers into the patient's mouth was also likely to be their
hairdresser, because when it came to seeking dental expertise one
had options... but all of them were dreadful.

At the bottom of the heap there were plain old barbers,
essentially fringe-trimmers with a sideline in tooth extraction;
then there were the better-trained barber-surgeons, whose basic
medical knowledge allowed them to conduct the most simple of

operations. These two rival classes were then looked down upon by the university-educated physicians, who pretty much shunned surgery entirely and were much more interested in medical theory. At various stages over the centuries, governments had set out the boundaries between these tiers of professionals, yet only medicine was officially regulated, meaning dental patients could legally be pinned to the ground, with their limbs flailing like a felled wrestler resisting a three count, by a knife-wielding hairdresser.

It's fairly obvious then why all efforts towards avoiding surgery, and maintaining healthy teeth and gums, were highly advisable.

THE QUEEN'S TEETH

So, what were the top tips for a healthy medieval mouth? Oooh, it's time for another list!

1. Use wooden or feather toothpicks as early forms of dental floss.
2. Scrub the teeth regularly with tooth-sticks (similar to *miswak*) or mouth cloths.
3. Apply an abrasive paste or powdered cuttlefish to chase away tooth stains.
4. Regularly gargle an acidic mouthwash – commonly wine, vinegar or even aluminium sulphate.
5. Freshen the breath with mint, cloves, cinnamon, sage, rosemary, musk or rose water.

There's little reason to believe that medieval mouths were particularly obnoxious to the eye or nose. You may not have wanted to snog any of them, but few people's grin would have had you recoiling in horror or holding your nose in disgust. Yet, as larger quantities of sugar were shipped in from the New World and exotic East, elaborate sugar work desserts – essentially large, edible sculptures – began dominating wealthy dinner tables, resulting in an aristocratic dental crisis. Elizabeth I of England, a lover of such eye-wateringly sweet delicacies, unsurprisingly struggled with shockingly bad tooth decay and endured terrible, sleep-bothering toothache. Yet her considerable pain wasn't quite severe enough to force her into the dentist's clutches, and she only had a rotten tooth plucked in 1578 after the Bishop of London had bravely volunteered his mouth to the dentist, as a human guinea pig, to prove it wasn't so bad.

By the end of Elizabeth's life, she had almost constant toothache and possessed little more than a blackened jumble of sparsely populated chompers, causing her to wander around her palace with her fingers in her mouth, and padded cloth stuffed in her cheeks to reflate her sunken maw. England's illustrious queen wasn't the only European ruler in need of a good flossing. Across the Channel, half a century later on, the stench of King Louis XIV's bad breath was so overpowering that his mistress, Madame de Montespan, was forced to douse herself in powerful perfumes just so she could stand near him without retching.

A SUGARY SMILE

By the time Louis died in the early 1700s, a novel trend for strong, healthy teeth was starting to take hold among the fashionable and the wealthy. Having an adequately stocked mouth also assisted the clarity of one's speech, and eighteenth-century Britain was witnessing the emergence of Received Pronunciation – that mannered style of English pronunciation you hear quite a lot on the Death Star because, apparently, Darth Vader recruits his officers solely from Hertfordshire. So, teeth were now needed to sound classy, but, with more sugar in the diet than ever, keeping them in one's mouth was getting increasingly challenging.

In our modern bathroom, with the tap gently sprinkling, we are careful not to brush too forcefully, or else we'll destroy our gums. This was a lesson learned the hard way by eighteenth-century aristocrats who got carried away with their rigorous tooth-care program, and did more harm than good. For example, Lord Chesterfield (whose toilet-related advice we've already encountered) regretted the energetic brushing of his youth, complaining to his son about his use of: 'sticks, irons etc, which totally destroyed them [his teeth], so that I have not now six or seven of them left...'. Indeed, the pursuit of white smiles had seen people abrading their teeth with abrasive powders, including chalk, salt, soda and ashes, while overeager barber-surgeons applied nitric acid to the enamel, thereby unwittingly dissolving nature's only barrier against dental decay.

But clumsy dentistry wasn't the only problem. Following the global rise of the British Empire, sugar was no longer the preserve of wealthy monarchs and bewigged dandies. Now it was increasingly available to the masses, and the simple rags and toothsticks of yesteryear were ill equipped to deal with the sucrose onslaught. To add further complication, the medical profession's obsession with therapeutic vomits, which regularly coerced the stomach into heaving up strong stomach acid, blasted beleaguered teeth with nature's finest corrosive agent. It was becoming clear that dentistry needed to throw off the amateurish shackles of barber-surgery to counteract this rising threat. What the eighteenth-century profession needed was a hero, not in a spandex onesie, but with a better quality of medical training.

THE FATHER OF DENTISTRY

Pierre Fauchard had learned his trade in the French Navy, fixing up all manner of smashed jaws and wonky teeth, but it was back in Paris where he earned the honorary soubriquet of 'the Father of Dentistry'. His first major achievement was to use the microscope to rubbish the myth of tooth worms – this alone was enough to make him a revolutionary, obliterating 5,000 years of ardent belief – but his radicalism didn't stop there. If you've ever worn orthodontic braces, then you have Pierre Fauchard to thank, though if you hated being called 'metal-mouth' as much I did, perhaps 'thank' isn't the right word?

In fact, several of the treatments we expect from our modern dentist derived from his inquiring mind. Did you have your teeth straightened when younger? That was Fauchard's idea. Did you have fillings made of gold or lead? Him again. Know anyone with false teeth? Yup, it was the illustrious Frenchman who emulated the ancient techniques of dental prosthesis, carving new teeth from ivory and fixing them into the jaw with gold wire. He also designed better forceps (known as the pelican), a more accurate drill (after studying the nimble-fingered exertions of watch-makers), and chose to sit his patients in upright armchairs, ending the practice of people being forced to lie on the floor while the barber-surgeon loomed over them like a torturer in a video nasty.

In many ways, Fauchard was a brilliant early scientist, who doggedly hounded the charlatans and quacks he encountered, chastising them with his empirical genius and publishing accounts of their incompetent malpractice for the world to hear. That said, all his innovations didn't stop him exalting human piss as a peer-less hygienic mouthwash or persisting with the medieval belief in therapeutic blood letting, but nobody's perfect.

WATERLOO TEETH

Fauchard also dabbled with tooth transplants – a subject of dental experimentation for the preceding couple of centuries, already – but this eighteenth-century practice was more commonly attributed to the contemporaneous English surgeon John Hunter. Though some people were opposed on moral grounds, and the practice could also spread syphilis, the only major obstacle for dentists was where to locate sufficient donor teeth. In some instances, impoverished children could be bribed into surrendering theirs for implantation into the mouth of some cash-laden toff, but corpses were a much likelier source. Executed criminals, victims of disease and even soldiers found on battlefields had their gnashers recycled, the practice consequently acquiring the nickname 'Waterloo Teeth', in honour of the battle of 1815.

So, thanks to orthodontic imagination, the 1700s witnessed the return of the toothy smile, best personified by 1787's controversial self-portrait by Marie-Louise-Elisabeth Vigée Le Brun which broke with centuries of convention by depicting the pretty artist with a Cheshire Cat grin on her face. Full-frontal nudity the art world could live with, but visible teeth in a painting was nothing short of scandalous, as was noted by one journalist: '[it is] an affectation... artists, connoisseurs and people of good taste are unanimous in condemning.'

THE JAWS OF VICTORY

George Washington and Paul Revere were two of America's revolutionary heroes, both famed for their involvement in the War of Independence (1775–83), but the pair were also connected by something less illustrious: dentistry. Revere – a gifted silversmith and the son of a French immigrant – followed in Fauchard's wake by dabbling with his own dental treatments and recommending a toothpaste made from butter, sugar, breadcrumbs and gunpowder, which really makes one hope none of his clients were tobacco smokers. Given that they were literally rubbing sugar and high explosives onto their teeth, it's perhaps understandable why there was also a thriving market for false dentures, and Revere was a noted provider of these too. I can't help but applaud his opportunistic pragmatism.

And what of Washington? Was he an amateur dentist, whiling away the hours between revolutionary battles with a spot of impromptu descaling? No, quite the opposite. Having lost all but one of his teeth by the time he became president, Washington was forced to wear various sets of clunky dentures that made his jaw jut outwards and his lips bulge. These artificial replacements were composites of animal ivory, his own extracted teeth, other human teeth, gold and lead, and though they allowed the great soldier the opportunity to chew and speak – pretty vital for a guy in charge of a nation's destiny – they also gave him enormous discomfort, forcing the first President of the United States to frequently rely upon the relief of laudanum, an opiate similar to heroin. It slightly changes one's perspective on the revolutionary hero to imagine him either suffering debilitating toothache, or being off his face on Class A drugs, but given that he had begun losing his teeth in his twenties, it's perhaps even more impressive that Washington didn't succumb to a more ordinary fate.

GIMME SOMETHING FOR THE PAIN

Of course, if we needed dental surgery, we too could expect some pharmacological pain relief. Yet, the history of dental anaesthetic is a strange one, because it took longer to arrive than it should have done, condemning many a poor patient to little more than a swig of gin and an eye-bulging grimace. After all, the eighteenth century was the era when experimentation with narcotic gases first began, so you might expect the history of pain relief to originate here, yet the story doesn't quite fit that logic.

During Washington's lifetime, nitrous oxide – or laughing gas, as it's sometimes known – had already been discovered by the English chemist Joseph Priestley, who snappily dubbed it dephlogisticated nitrous air. Priestley's research was picked up soon after by the young Humphrey Davy, a rising superstar of British science who gleefully inhaled shedloads of the gas – and I mean that literally: he built a complex breathing chamber so as to wallow in the stuff – and hosted laughing gas parties for his bohemian friends, such as the drug-addled Samuel Taylor Coleridge, and the more sober Robert Southey who subsequently wrote 'I am sure the air in heaven must be this wonder-working gas of delight'.

Clearly, Priestley and Davy had discovered a potent anaesthetic that should have gone straight into the hands of dentists every-where, but both utterly failed to market it for such purposes, even though Davy had even experimented with nitrous gas as a cure for toothache. Instead, the young gas-guzzler took up a prestigious post as a chemistry lecturer, while Priestley made the less prestigious career move of keeling over dead. So, despite its obvious medical potential, nitrous gas instead became a crowd-pleasing novelty for travelling stage shows and science lectures, where audiences gleefully whooped as hapless volunteers flailed joyfully around auditoria, stumbling into things and narrating their mind-warping trips.

Understandably, the authorities weren't best pleased by all the kerfuffle, and laughing gas – the potential vanquisher of sur-gical agony – instead acquired a dodgy reputation as a source of public titillation. In fact, even when someone finally noticed the anaesthetic properties, things still didn't go as planned. The American dentist Horace Wells had watched one such public performance in 1844, and was fascinated by the prospect of operating on patients without causing them pain. But, despite a successful private trial, his inaugural public demonstration was an unmitigated disaster. The gas was incorrectly administered and the patient sprinted from the chair, screaming bloody murder. The potential miracle cure therefore acquired such a poor reputation (again), that it wasn't used in dentistry for another 20 years. Thankfully, in 1846 a new surgical anaesthetic called ether was introduced – followed soon after by cocaine and chloroform – to the tremendous relief of patients everywhere.

DIY DENTAL

Looking around our bathroom, we see it's stocked with various dental products – toothbrush, toothpaste, floss, mouthwash – and though these things aren't all necessarily modern in their inception, their popularity is a relatively recent trend. The toothbrush in our hands might be a medieval Chinese technology, but it wasn't available to Queen Elizabeth or the stink-breathed Louis XIV. Why? It seems the Chinese technology just simply didn't catch on, and there are only a few recorded examples of Europeans using such devices between the sixteenth and eighteenth centuries. The modern toothbrush probably owes more to a certain William Addis who rediscovered the idea in 1780 while serving time in a London jail for inciting a riot. The story goes that, after becoming understandably disappointed with the cleaning power of tooth rags, Addis drilled holes in a pig bone left over from his dinner and affixed bristles from a handy sweeping brush into the recesses. A mere thousand years after the Chinese had invented the toothbrush, Addis had invented the toothbrush. Of course, he was much better at marketing it, and the company he founded is still making hygienic products today.

Okay, it's probably time to stop brushing now, mostly because there's toothpaste all down our front. It suddenly dawns on us that we probably should have flossed beforehand, but it can't hurt to give it a go now instead, so we pick up the reel of dental floss and unspool it between our fingers. This, of course, begs another question: if Addis is the vaguely deserving hero of the toothbrush, then who gets the credit for flossing? Well, again, our ancestors had probably picked away at their gums for thousands of years – we now know toothpicks were being used by *Homo habilis* 1.6 million years ago – but if we're going to be specific about who popularised it, then the kudos should go to the American dentist Dr Levi Spear Parmly who, in 1815, waxed lyrical about the benefits of silk dental floss in preventative tooth-care.

Dr Parmly had travelled far and wide, practising in Britain, Canada and France, and was progressive in viewing oral hygiene as an issue of regular maintenance, rather than dramatic intervention. He also wins historical brownie points for doing pro bono dentistry work on kids – what a guy! His brother Dr Eleazer Parmly had the honour of being personal dentist to President John Quincy Adams, but the sibling connection didn't end there. In fact, there were five Parmly brothers in total, of whom four were dentists (presumably the other one must have dreaded family reunions and the never-ending conveyor belt of tartar anecdotes), and those 80 per cent of Parmlys who cared about oral hygiene would have been pleased to witness the burgeoning availability of tooth-care products as the nineteenth century trundled onwards.

Not only were dentists now practising from specially equipped offices, with reclining chairs having been first invented in 1790, but by the 1850s patients had access to better teeth-cleaning gadgets in their homes too. Toothbrushes were now widely available across Europe, North America and the Far East, and by the 1870s the traditional scrubbers of charcoal soot, powdered cuttlefish, salt and chalk were being replaced in bathroom cabinets by mass-produced jars of dentifrice, featuring the novel ingredient of soap, meaning you could actually wash your mouth out. But despite the anti-bacterial improvements in toothpaste, talk of bad breath was soon to escalate, not decrease, thanks to a cunning marketing campaign that launched a global super-brand from fairly obscure origins.

GET FRESH

Having brushed and flossed, it's time we gargle that weirdly tingly concoction we call mouthwash, so as to freshen our breath and nuke any bacteria lurking in hidden recesses. While the Romans were happy to quaff Portuguese piss, and scented herbs were common in the medieval era, it was in the nineteenth century that anti-bacterial mouthwash appeared in our ancestors' bathroom cabinets. Listerine, named in honour of Joseph Lister, the Scottish surgeon who'd discovered its germ-swatting properties, was the commercial name for the chemical compound phenol, and initially its uses were limited to treating oral infection, or for cleaning floorboards.

But an advertising masterstroke in the 1920s saw the phenol phenomenon explode almost overnight, with the deployment of social anxiety marketing similar to that which had propelled Odorono into the public consciousness. While Louis XIV's mouth had reeked like something had died in there, it had been his mistress who'd been forced to react with sweet-smelling musks. But no longer would the perpetrator get away with it, and the victim be forced to suffer. Listerine was there to crush the newly labelled crisis of halitosis, and ensure that nobody had an excuse for putrid breath. Sales were astonishing, company profits rose 7,000 per cent in just seven years, and the rest, as ever, is history.

Brushing our Teeth

Despite the astonishing increase in the popularity of hygienic mouthwash, it was probably the 1940s that had the greatest impact on modern tooth-care. This was when plastics replaced the silk in dental floss and the animal-derived parts of the toothbrush – not only was nylon stronger, cheaper and more hygienic, it was also much easier to mass produce. Another widespread revolution was the addition of fluoride to the water supply, a discovery born of dogged investigation begun in 1909 by the young American dentist Dr Frederick McKay and the more senior Dr G.V. Black. They had acquired data that showed 90 per cent of the children in Colorado Springs suffered brown staining to the teeth, but – curiously – this mottling, or 'Colorado Brown Stain' as they named it, inexplicably prevented the onset of tooth decay. McKay was puzzled but suggested the residents switch water source, an idea with considerable success.

McKay then travelled to Bauxite, Arkansas, to investigate whether the local aluminium mine was causing similar staining to local children's teeth. Here, he made contact with the chief chemist of the aluminium company, who was astonished to discover high levels of fluoride in the water. The case had been solved! Except, by 1931, McKay and Black's initial mystery of fluorosis preventing tooth decay was still playing on the mind of Dr H. Trendley Dean, a dental researcher at the National Institute for Health. It was Dean who made the connection that tiny doses of fluoride inhibited dental caries without also staining the teeth, and in 1945 the city of Grand Rapids, Michigan became the first in the world to add fluoride to the water supply. Within 11 years, the city's 30,000 school kids were showing a 60 per cent reduction in caries.

Yet, it wasn't just technological improvements that boosted oral hygiene; there was also a cultural shift in daily habits. It had long been known that healthy soldiers needed healthy teeth, and during the Second World War the US Army had instituted a new policy requiring its troops to brush every day, with hugely encouraging results. Within years of the war ending, dentists across the world were espousing the benefits of twice-daily brushing and regular flossing. Whereas Lord Chesterfield had followed this advice and destroyed his teeth, the softer plastic brushes now meant there was minimal danger of scrubbing one's mouth into a yawning chasm of toothless horror.

Now, with sophisticated dentistry available, and cheap oral hygiene products crammed in our bathroom cabinets, we have few excuses for letting our teeth rot away. And it's clear we've discharged our bathroom duties for this evening, so we gargle a swig of cool water, wipe our mouth on the towel and shuffle drunkenly towards the bedroom.

11.53 p.m.

GETTING INTO BED

Our teeth are cleansed, our tummy is full and our bloodstream pulses with excess wine. Despite the inevitable desire to make a midnight snack, it's probably best we hit the hay. After all, while our species may be brilliant technological innovators, we're still lumbered with the biological imperative to snooze for one third of our existence. And so we swap our party clothes for comfy PJs, and head for the bed.

The bed is a dominant character in our life and, if we reach old age, we'll spend around 250,000 hours snoring into our pillows. Many people are born in hospital beds; then as naughty kids we resist being sent to bed for as long as we can; then as grumpy teens we refuse to leave it until midday; then we expend great effort trying to get people we fancy into bed with us, until we find 'the one' and it becomes the honeymoon bed of matrimonial über-bonking; but eventually we end up back in the hospital bed, surrounded by gently beeping machines, where some of us will peacefully pass away in our sleep. Beds, then, come in many forms and convey all manner of sociological meanings about their owners. There are the plush four-posters in elegant hotels; sleeping bags in rain-soaked tents; battered old sofas in friends'

298

living rooms; high-sided cots in freshly painted nurseries; space-saving bunks in cramped submarines; sagging double mattresses in master bedrooms; and even folded-up cardboard boxes in grimy alleyways.

Yet, despite their variety, they are an almost universal presence in human life. Virtually all of us begin and end our day supine, and it's been the case for tens of thousands of years.

STONE AGE BED(ROCK)

Seventy-seven thousand years ago, in what is now the KwaZulu-Natal province of South Africa, humans like you and me sheltered in the Sibudu caves, squirrelled inside the sandstone cliffs. These *Homo sapiens* were sophisticated sorts – it was their descendants who exited Africa to colonise Europe, drove Neanderthals to extinction and conquered our planet – and among their innovative technologies were glue and the sewing needle, cunning aids to the creation of useful stuff. When we make our bed each morning all we do is straighten the covers, but for these people, making the bed was more likely a case of stitching it together by hand, from a gathered pile of leaves and rushes.

Having excavated the caves, archaeologists have found the remains of inch-thick mattresses of flora, in among which are bits of stone tools, charred bone and animal fat, suggesting our ancient ancestors enjoyed snacking on freshly barbecued meat while tucked up at night. Many of us know that there's nothing more thrilling than naughtily scoffing an illicit snack in bed, but it's also a dangerous game – mattress crumbs are the bane of any sound sleeper, inevitably waiting until 3 a.m. before they launch their prickly assault against exposed skin. But, compared with biscuit remnants, our prehistoric ancestors had a much greater enemy to contend with: dank caves are also home to legions of creepy crawlies, which would undoubtedly have been lured by the rotting flesh left on the discarded animal bones. So how did cave dwellers deal with the incessant scuttling of flies, beetles and mosquitoes?

It seems there were two complimentary systems of prevention: firstly, choice of materials. Such ancient mattresses were lined with leaves from River Wild-Quince, a tree that naturally produces an insect-repelling chemical, and this may have minimised the lethal scourge of malaria. Secondly, when the mattress got a bit gross – either with fly droppings or too much animal grease – it was burned to cinders and a new one was simply plonked onto the ashes. Combining these two techniques apparently worked as a long-term solution, as archaeologists have discovered at least 15 separate layers of burned organic ash in the same cave system, dating between 77,000 and 38,000 years ago. So, for tens of thousands of years, it seems beds were constantly in use, but – as with our own bedframes, mattresses and sheets – they had a temporary lifespan.

But the remains at Skara Brae, Orkney's picturesque Neolithic village, reveal that the absence of metal tools didn't stop the occupants from filling their homes with permanent furniture such as shelves, cupboards, dressers, seats and, of course, beds. This was still the Stone Age, but in Germany – for example, at the Neolithic site of Württenburg – wood was starting to be carved into these sorts of household objects; but the people of Skara Brae lived in a treeless land. So, in a charming validation of the Flintstones, all of their stuff was basically made out of rock, though there were definitely no pet dinosaurs running amok in the lounge.

In the earliest incarnations, the beds seem to have been built into the walls themselves, but later designs instead set them into the floor, with cot-like elevated sides. They also came in two distinct sizes, possibly in 'his and her' sets. They seem pretty uninviting, and it's easy to imagine the torture of trying to get forty winks while curled up on a cold slab, but people would surely have lain on straw mattresses and soft animal hides to cushion their bodies. There has even been a suggestion that some beds had a mounted curtain for maintaining privacy, though that may say more about the social mores of the Edwardian archaeologist who excavated the site than the people who lived there.

SNOOZING WITH THE PHARAOHS

Tonight, however, we are not sleeping on lumps of rock. No, we shall shortly be snoozing in a bedframe supported on four legs, the kind that monsters and/or adulterers can hide under when children/unexpected spouses walk into the room. From this, we might conclude that legs are the more modern bit of the bed's design . . . but they're not *that* modern. Perhaps inevitably, the first mention of the four-legged bedframe comes from the Egyptians again – you're probably sick of hearing about them, but hang on in there, the book's nearly over!

Unlike the socially egalitarian people of Skara Brae, Egypt's empire was built upon strict hierarchical divisions between the classes, and a person's place in society influenced how they slept. The elite slumbered in a single bed, his or her weight being supported by a lattice woven from strips of leather or reed strung tautly across the frame. The four legs suspended the occupant off the ground, literally and symbolically elevating them above the lowly cushion-slumpers of the peasant classes, and so these legs became worthy of elegant ornamentation to emphasise this distinction. After all, if you could afford it, wouldn't you have lion paws carved into the feet of your bed?

Egyptians weren't just snobbish, though. They were also extraordinarily superstitious and, much like children lying alone in the dark, worked themselves into a terrified tizz at the thought of what might lurk in the shadows. The accepted ghost-busting deterrent was to inscribe drawings of protective gods into the wooden frame to deter visitation from the sinister undead, imbuing the bed with magical properties, though sadly not with the ability to teleport like in Disney's *Bedknobs and Broomsticks*. A secondary form of protection, one with a more earthly pragmatism, was against the nocturnal vampirism of malaria-spreading mosquitoes. The Egyptians were unaware of how the disease was transmitted, but weren't fans of being nibbled in their sleep, so the wealthy erected netted curtains around the bedframe to protect themselves, while Herodotus tells us that the poor slept under their fishing nets, no doubt giving bedtime a somewhat pungent aroma.

Of course, our bed has soft covers to ensure warmth, and while animal hides and reeds may have sufficed for the Stone Age, the Egyptians were just like us. The rich could afford excellent quality linen, and these sheets may have been suitable all year around, as lavish master bedrooms sometimes had thicker walls to stabilise the temperature extremes in the cooler winters and baking Saharan summers. But while this sounds perfectly familiar, there were also curious deviations from our norm.

We're used to sleeping horizontally, but Egyptian bedframes seem to have deliberately bowed in the middle, or even sloped gently downwards, thereby necessitating a footrest at the bottom of the bed to stop the occupant sliding out. However, oddest of all, wealthy snoozers opted not for the comfy pillows and cushions enjoyed by the peasant classes, but for curved headrests made of ivory, alabaster or wood, often mounted on an ornamental column. These firmly held the head in place – possibly to protect elaborately coiffeured hairdos from the horror of morning bed-head – and one can only imagine that any tossing and turning at night resulted in a broken nose or a squashed ear. Of course, they may have padded their neck with cushions, but we simply have no way to prove it. As far as the surviving evidence goes, elite Egyptians preferred to have perennially sore heads.

LYING LOW

Egyptian peasants, by contrast, resided in a small mud-brick house which boasted only four rooms, and featured very little in the way of furniture. Of these rooms, one would likely have been the sleeping quarters for women, while males would have shared an earthen or reed platform covered in padded fabric, which also served as a couch and eating area during the day. This sounds pretty cosy, like the sort of fort you made as a kid with sofa cushions, but it doubtlessly required some tolerance of the bedfellows' nocturnal habits, and it's easy to imagine anyone suffering from sinusitis being banished to the flat roof with a mattress of papyrus rushes, where their irritating snuffling and snoring would only bother the birds.

It's tempting to apply a universal rule that sleeping nearer to the floor was always a sign of slumming it, or of servile status. In China, this may have been true. The wealthier classes adopted raised beds around 3,000 years ago, while the poor were very much relegated to the floor, eating, relaxing and sleeping upon a clay platform called a *kang*, which was warmed during the day by a liberal scattering of burning embers from the fire. This brings to mind the fairy tale of the neglected Cinderella, cruelly forced to sleep in front of the kitchen fire while her bitchy step-sisters lay in clean beds and planned their glamorous outfits for the ball. Sadly, one suspects very few of these Chinese peasants ended up snaring themselves a handsome prince, but things did improve with the later development of a sophisticated under-floor heating system called *huodi*, which kept the floors permanently warm and free from filthy cinders.

Getting into Bed

The Japanese, however, were different. In their culture everyone was a floor snoozer, regardless of rank. That's not to say there weren't differences in bedding for the lowly and the lofty, though – the poor slumped on coarse straw mattresses, while the rich chose the springy, foldable *tatami* mat woven from sedge. The latter gained popularity around 800 years ago when they became fitted to the dimensions of an individual human, making them very much the medieval precursor to the modern camping roll mat. The old *tatami* (about 180 x 90 cm) is still a standard unit of measurement in Japan today, despite the fact these mats expanded to the size of carpets in the fifteenth century.

Tatami mats weren't all that comfy by the sounds of it and, while the wealthy aristocracy could drape themselves in expensive silken covers to keep warm, one imagines there were quite a lot of important people hobbling around, complaining about their backs – something disappointingly absent from most samurai movies. Equally odd to western eyes were the traditional Japanese pillows (*makura*), as they were often a cylinder filled with buckwheat, wrapped in paper and placed on top of a lacquered wooden box. As with the Egyptians, the pillow supported the neck, rather than cushioning the head, and so protected elaborate hairstyles. Other versions were also available, such as a latticed bamboo model or the porcelain pillows which could be heated or cooled by filling them with boiling or icy water.

But the mercantile boom of the 1600s brought the wider availability of cotton, and this led to the development of the much more famous *futon*. Now, I must admit that I used to think a futon was a low wooden couch that could be turned into a bed, but this is a horrible Westernised mangling of the word. In fact, the Japanese *futon* required the felling of zero trees. Instead, at its simplest, it's a bedding set comprising two elements: a thin mattress called a *shikibuton* (laid atop the *tatami* mat), and a duvet called a *kakebuton,* although various other coverings gradually emerged over time, including the slanket-esque *yogi* – a wearable duvet with sleeves that could even be stuffed in winter for added warmth.

SLEEPING ON THE MOVE

Tomorrow morning, we'll hopefully get around to making the bed, depending on the severity of our hangover, but imagine that instead of fluffing up the pillows and straightening out the ruffled covers our duties consisted of grabbing the pillows, folding the blankets, lifting the wool mats and cramming the lot into the corner of a fabric tent, so that the bed vanished entirely from the floor. This is how some Kyrgyz people live today. Though they possess meagre furniture, and dress in recognisably modern clothing, these traditional nomads often sleep in beds that are little more than quilted blankets (*tushuks*), stuffed with animal fur plonked over woven mats of reeds, felt or wool. Given that the bed really has to be made every day, I'd be curious to know whether Kyrgyz teenagers are still as lazy as I was at that age, but I'm guessing probably not. For these nomads, everything in their lives, even their tent homes, can be folded up and carried upon the backs of horses, donkeys and camels, as it has been since the age of the famous Scythian tribes of the eighth century BCE.

In the medieval era, the great Turkic nomads – including the Huns, Magyars, Seljuk Turks and the Mongols – swept through Eurasia with devastating speed, swatting mighty empires out of the way like they were annoying children clinging to their ankles. Some of these marauders, such as the Seljuks, settled and assimilated Persian influences, but they kept core elements of their identity. Even when they were then toppled from power by the Ottoman Turks, the illustrious Ottoman Sultan Mehmed II still continued the nomadic tradition when decorating his lavish

Topkapi Palace. He may not have been able to fold his palace up at night, and throw it over his horse's back, but he wasn't going to fill its rooms with furniture. There would be no tables, chairs or beds; he insisted on sleeping in the traditional arrangement of pillows and cushions sprawled across the floor, or piled onto a wide, low wooden platform. This item of furniture was introduced to Europe and America in the eighteenth century, where its name – ottoman – remains synonymous with these ancient nomadic peoples, even though it has shrunk to become a padded storage box, or footstool.

As the modern age dawned, the Japanese, much like the Koreans, remained floor sleepers well into the late twentieth century, and only recently have western beds snuck into ordinary society, having first conquered business hotels. Yet there's no sign of the old ways vanishing entirely, and people may continue to prefer *futons* and *tushuks* over bedsteads and headboards for many decades to come. But, tonight we'll be snoozing in a raised bed, so, how did this custom come to dominate in the West?

THE ANCIENT SOFA BED

Egyptian peasants had slept on floor cushions, while their masters had lain rigidly still like a patient in an MRI machine in raised beds. For the Greeks, then, the perfect solution was to combine the best of both. Perhaps it was because they didn't give a damn about their hairstyles, but the solidly carved headrest was chucked out – as was the footboard at the bottom of the bed – to be replaced by a comfy pillow (*proskefaleion*) and a flexible headboard (*anaklintron*) to stop it tumbling off the back. This resulted in the couch-like *kline*, from where we get the word 'recline'.

Such novel emphasis on comfort allowed Greeks to toss and turn as much as they wished at night, but it also enabled the use of the *kline* as daytime furniture, especially for eating meals and socialising with male-only company. The bedframe was thereby co-opted from a formal sleeping device, with its own specific room, into imitating the dual functionality of the Egyptian peasants' communal floor platform. But instead of many blokes huddled together, as if clinging to a padded life raft, now the combination of dining and slumbering was available to the individual, though *klines* could also be shared during feasts if needed. Even those living on a modest budget may have been able to stuff a mattress with weeds, straw or wool, plonk it on a simply hewn wooden bedframe, and wrap it in sheets of coarse linen or leather. And when night fell, and the temperature dropped, tired Athenians could wrap themselves up in a thick woollen duvet called a *stromata*, and drift off to sleep, no doubt to dream of Pythagorean equations and Olympic glory.

This arrangement sounds perfectly pleasant, but the sophisticated Persians, who were the bed-making experts of the ancient world, scoffed at such ugly pragmatism. Only those with huge cash reserves could come close to matching Persian opulence by snapping up the fabrics of the celebrated Cyprian weaver Helicon of Salamis but most people, even the comparatively wealthy, made do with coarse bedclothes. While stoic Spartan soldiers camped out with their mates, lying on thistles to toughen them up, even the servants and slaves in Athens were afforded a better level of basic comfort, getting to lie on reed mats or straw bales, or even sometimes being permitted cheap bedframes that squatted at ankle height, elevating them incrementally above the status of dogs ... or just about.

Yet, despite the relative similarities between rich and poor, moderation wasn't long-lived in the Mediterranean. The Romans borrowed heavily from the Greeks – mostly by crushing them in battle and enslaving all the clever ones – and they adapted the reclining couch to their own ends, renaming it the *lectus discubitorious.* While the early days of the stoic Roman republic prompted little evolution from the Greek *kline*, by the time of the glorious empire in the first century CE, all that Persian splendour was pouring into the Mediterranean via Roman-controlled Egypt. Chinese silks, in purple and gold, were the ultimate bed linen for the aristocracy, but it wasn't just the fabric that symbolised luxury. They also splurged on elegantly crafted wooden bedframes, embellished with ivory, silver, gold or other precious metals, taking pride of place in sleeping chambers and dining rooms.

The richer a person was, the gaudier their sofa-bed. The debauched teenage emperor Elagabalus – also the inventor of the whoopee cushion – had both his dining couches and private beds sculpted from solid silver, which, while a lovely talking point over dinner, wasn't sufficiently distracting to stop his bodyguards murdering him when he was just 18. The irony here was that, with real dramatic flair, Elagabalus had apparently already built himself a jewel-encrusted suicide tower in which he had planned to hang himself with a silken rope, or stab himself with golden blades, if things went wrong. Ah, the best laid plans, eh?

IN BED WITH THE ROMANS

We can assume that the doomed emperor's sleeping bed, known as the *lectus cubicularis*, followed the novel Roman fashion of being raised even higher up off the ground, necessitating a footstool to clamber into it, and it may possibly have been draped in a fabric canopy to protect its august occupant from dust, errant birds, mosquitoes or whatever else went bump in the night. Such private beds came in single and double sizes and were supremely comfortable for both sleeping and shagging in, although there's some debate as to whether a newly married couple would consummate their matrimonial union in this bed, or in a ceremonial one known as the *lectus genialis*.

This was also known as the *lectus adversus* because it was placed very publicly in the unroofed atrium of a large house, opposite a sacred statue of the god Janus that guarded the front door. Most scholars have suggested this was merely a symbolic couch, from which the bride and groom could receive guests into their new home, but a few imaginative classicists have wondered if it was the location of newlyweds' inaugural bonking session, in full view of the invited guests. As uncomfortably awkward as that sounds, at least it would have been comfier than losing your virginity on the backseat of a rusty Toyota.

The main problem for classicists is that Roman bedrooms are hard to identify, and not many beds survive, so we're unsure how ordinary Romans slept. But we might assume those lowly straw mattresses that had borne the bodies of Greek underlings were also common in the Roman world too. For all its glorious pomp, there was as much grinding poverty in the ancient empire's capital as there was in Dickensian London.

THE GREAT BED

As we clamber into our raised bed, taking care not to drunkenly stub our toes or smash our knees on the frame, it's easy to forget that owning something like this was rare for most people in the past. If we look at Saxon sleeping arrangements, it doesn't seem like people slept alone, or in pairs, much at all. The famous poem *Beowulf* suggests the great wooden mead-halls of chieftains and kings housed multi-purpose benches, pushed up against the interior walls, upon which drunken warriors could snooze overnight. But the poem also describes a monstrous creature bursting into the mead-hall and tearing these warriors limb from limb, so its factual accuracy might be a teensy bit dubious.

During the Middle Ages, communal sleeping was the norm. Servants in castles and aristocratic houses bedded down on straw-stuffed sacks, their heads resting awkwardly on logs, as they huddled together in the cavernous great halls for warmth. Indeed, such was the common occurrence of sharing a bed with random people that even medieval guidebooks for foreign tourists translated handy phrases for chastising snorers, duvet hoarders and energetic dreamers who thrashed about in their sleep. That said, a phrasebook can't have been all that useful in the dark, when you could neither find it, read it, nor work out which of your many bedfellows to berate in your broken English.

Of course, not everyone was forced to endure other people's unwashed feet kicking them in the face. Trusted servants might have earned the honour of sleeping in the lord and lady's bed-chamber (*solar*), curled up in a little truckle bed like a human guard dog. And, indeed the owners of the house would enjoy far superior comfort to everyone else, for they – and perhaps they alone – would own a handcrafted wooden bed. Intriguingly, the medieval 'great bed' is well known from manuscript illustrations and paintings, often depicting monarchs and saints in exultant repose, but such images often show them in an upright position, as if the bed sloped downwards. This may simply be an artistic tradi-tion – painting someone in supine pose makes them look dead – but actually there may be a more physical explanation. While some medieval beds had adopted wooden planking by this time, many still stretched ropes across the frame to support the mattress. These inevitably sagged, bowing in the middle like a hammock, and inadvertently forcing the occupant's body to contort into a hunched-over position. Consequently, regular tightening of these ropes was needed, and this possibly instigated the lovely bedtime phrase 'sleep tight', which we still utter to children today.

Yet, even with wooden planking, high-status medieval beds also came complete with bolsters, slotted under the pillows, to prop up the sleeper, so perhaps that was just the expected posture of posh slumber? In any case, this inability to lie totally flat required the development of chunky headboards, to ensure those bolsters and pillows – some of which were scented with aromatic herbs and spices – didn't slide down the back. While simple rope-strung beds boasted a straw mattress called a *paillasse,* overlain with a linen *matelas* and a hand-stitched quilt called a *courtpointe,* big spenders could enjoy the feather-down *coquette* which required servants to plump and smooth the bedclothes with a specially designed stick called a *baton de lit.* If you're a bit of a neatfreak you might now be thinking 'ooh, what a good idea', but be wary not to ask for one when staying in a Parisian hotel, as *baton de lit* is now a French euphemism for male naughty bits.

Making the bed may sound like hard work, but servicing an aristocratic bedchamber was a big honour, and might have been one of the duties of the great English writer Geoffrey Chaucer when he was King Edward III's *valet de chambre* in 1367. Thankfully for the author of *The Canterbury Tales,* he wasn't the unlucky bloke tasked with plucking the mattress feathers from the enraged geese, and he doubly profited from that guy's bravery by using any spare quills as pens. In fact, King Edward would not have settled for mere goose down. Top-of-the-range bedding necessitated the stealing of feathers from the much more regal, but equally scary, swan.

While beds may have seemed permanent fixtures in bed-chambers, medieval lords spent many months of the year away from their main residences, which meant all of their best-loved possessions – including beds and tapestries – often went on tour with them. High-status beds were designed to be disassembled, carried around and put back together with chains, like flat-pack furniture, though one imagines no king ever had to endure the maddening frustration of a missing screw. Eventually, medieval great beds swelled in size, becoming symbolic of status, so were less likely to be dismantled.

By the thirteenth century the elegant woodwork included chunky headboards that evolved into partially projecting, and then fully covering, wooden roofs called testers. These were supported by four posts projecting from the corners of the bed, and from them silken drapes and furs could be hung, creating a private cocoon to shield the occupants from the prying eyes of servants, or to trap heat. In Renaissance Italy, testers and four-posters were commonly replaced with free-standing beds that lay beneath suspended fabric canopies which elegantly dangled from the ceiling via an arrangement of cables and pulleys. If that sounds like a theatre set, then that was probably what they were going for, as getting in and out of bed each day probably involved a choreographed dance between servants and expectant slumberers to ensure no one became accidentally ensnared in the expensive drapery.

BEDS OF STATE FOR HEADS OF STATE

Such majestic beds didn't just have to be private snooze venues, they could also be a locus of royal power. In medieval France, up until the violent lopping-off of King Louis XVI's head in the 1790s, the monarch would even sit before parliament on his so-called *lit de justice* (bed of justice), which was essentially a comfy throne formed from five carefully placed cushions, and covered with an elaborate canopy known as a *baldaquin*. This whole get-up was intended to heighten the ceremonial magnificence of the monarch, but was presumably wonderfully pleasant on the royal backside too... and why not?

Away from the assembled throng, the Sun King Louis XIV

turned his sumptuous palace at Versailles into a shrine dedicated to his own glory, and a key focal point was his bedroom. Having witnessed terrible political infighting among the aristocracy during his youth, Louis found a way of managing these troublesome egos by giving them meaningless, yet prestigious, ritual duties. Each morning Louis would awaken to find extraordinarily powerful men in his room, but they weren't there to assassinate him. Instead, one would open his bed curtains, while the next would lean in to rub away the beads of sweat on his body; a third might proffer the king a pre-warmed shirt.

This first ritual (called the *petit lever*) was a fairly intimate experience between the monarch, his doctors, and the most prestigious courtiers who had paid for right of access. Next, however, the king decamped to a second chamber for the *grand lever*, where one hundred lesser nobles watched him begin his day with a shave and then pick out an outfit. What's more, the reverse process of going to bed – called the *coucher* – also applied at night. While this sounds maddening (and indeed Louis and his descendants sometimes enjoyed a couple of hours' hunting before they felt ready to face the voyeuristic weirdness of the morning ceremony), the *levée* was remarkably effective. The nobles spent all their energy squabbling among themselves over who got to wield the king's socks, and neglected their old thoughts of insurrection. A slightly more modest version of the ritual called the *toilette* was soon adopted in the British royal court.

One didn't even need to be royal to inject some theatre into the bedroom. These days, most of us are only comfortable having friends at our bedside if we're recovering in hospital, or need flu medicine delivered from a pharmacy, but at Versailles ladies held court from under the covers to commemorate major moments in life, whether the tragic death of a husband, or the wonderful birth of a child. A bed was more than just a place of sleep and sex.

TEN IN THE BED, AND THE LITTLE ONE SAID . . .

The young man can't believe his luck. He has travelled many miles to court his young love, and has been welcomed into her family's home as a worthy suitor. But now it's dark and bedtime beckons. Things suddenly become awkward as he realises he has nowhere to sleep, but the riposte from his future father-in-law is not one he's expecting: 'You may sleep in her bed.' Excited at the prospect of some intimate contact with his betrothed, the young man strips off to his underclothes and is about to get into the bed when the father walks in holding a sack – 'put this on', he says. The suitor does as he is told, only to realise that he has effectively donned a straightjacket. Then the young woman shuffles into the bedroom wearing exactly the same thing, and as they clamber into bed, they laugh at the ridiculousness of their predicament. They can't do anything naughty, but at least they are face to face. Then suddenly a wooden board slides down between them, and all hope of romance is extinguished – they may be sharing a bed, but that's all they are doing.

Bundling was a custom in seventeenth-century Britain and America in which courting couples could be prised apart during the nocturnal hours, despite sharing the same mattress. A recent study suggests that 40 per cent of eighteenth-century English brides were already pregnant when it came to their wedding day, and bundling was presumably designed to combat such scandal. Overcoming the bundling sack and vaulting the bundling board was an exhausting conundrum that would have frustrated even Harry Houdini, so we can assume many couples probably admitted defeat.

Bed sharing was a common solution to a lack of space and less affluent rural families in Ireland often crammed into a single bed – a practice charmingly called pigging – right up until the twentieth century. With so many people stuffed into a small space, etiquette inevitably developed, with boys and girls at opposite ends and the smallest kids nearest their parents in the centre, creating a sort of gendered Russian doll effect, and possibly inspiring the nursery rhyme, 'There were ten in the bed, and the little one said: "Roll over"'. Bizarrely, though, it wasn't just family members who were snuggled up under the covers. We would be horrified if, when checking into a hotel, we found another family asleep in our room, but this renting of the family bed was especially common in colonial America during the 1600s, having begun as a Dutch tradition called *queesting*. Visiting guests, or even paying strangers, sometimes crawled under the sheets alongside mother, father and the kids, hoping to share the communal warmth.

WARM AND TOASTY

King David of Israel, the unexpected slayer of Goliath, was old and infirm. Despite his many covers, he just couldn't stay warm at night. So his advisors sought out a novel twist on the hot water bottle, delivering to the aged patriarch an exceedingly beautiful virgin to share his bed. The biblical author in Kings 4:1 goes to great lengths to point out that David didn't seduce this nubile girl, but that's a bit of a shame for comedic reasons given that her name was Abishag. Just imagine the tabloid headlines.

As we climb under the covers, we might decide to switch on the electric blanket – depending on whether we have an accompanying bedfellow or not – but, as King David showed, this isn't such a modern idea and various attempts to warm the night bed have been tried, with some more dangerous than others. Spare a thought for King Charles II of Navarre whose exit from this mortal world was the result of a gruesome accident: it seems that hot coals from his mechanical bed-warmer ignited the sheets, causing the disabled monarch to burst into flames like a flambéed Christmas pudding.

King Charles was widely disliked, and had even managed to acquire the epithet Charles the Bad, so some moralists declared this was God's cruel justice being played out. Still, I'd be surprised if the crowned heads of Europe, upon hearing the news, didn't go to bed a tad anxious that night, for fear of being turned into human kindling. After all, most of them used the same technology: a copper or silver warming pan, filled with hot coals. A less effective, but safer, option was to wrap hot stones in blankets, and, later on, those on modest budgets preferred a water-filled belly-warmer made of stoneware which remained popular well into the 1900s. Of course, water wasn't the only liquid one could use – the Victorian prime minister of Britain William Gladstone turned his into a bedtime thermos of tea. Honestly, we Brits really do fan our own stereotypical flames, don't we?

SLEEPING ALONE

While sharing a bed was commonly a problem of necessity, by the seventeenth century a burgeoning middle class was starting to enjoy the comforts of a marital bed designed just for two, though in the case of the famed diarist Samuel Pepys this intimacy led to some awkward scenes. At one point, his wife screamed at him for three nights in a row after she'd caught him fondling the maid, and then later interrupted his sleep to threaten him with scorching tongs drawn from the fire. It perhaps hadn't occurred to Pepys that betraying his wife might come back to haunt him; but he'd made his bed, and now he very much had to lie in it.

The move towards lower bed occupancy wasn't just linked to greater affluence. Particularly in Britain and America, newly built eighteenth-century houses employed a novel architecture of circulation in which rooms were separate from one another, being set off from a central atrium or staircase, so accessing the master bedroom no longer required traipsing through all the other rooms first. This increased amount of personal space had a knock-on effect for social mores, with a sudden obsession for privacy exploding into the public consciousness, causing Victorian artists to censor depictions of bedroom scenes in their work, for fear of public outrage.

But the other interesting development was the return, after two millennia, of the single-occupancy bed. In an era of prevalent tuberculosis and cholera, there emerged a hygienic justification for enjoying one's own clean sheets and it was also commonly believed, by those of a more fanciful mind, that young children would be enfeebled by sharing a bed with adults, as the aged crones would steal their youthful vitality like some sort of wrinkled soul-parasite. Not everyone agreed with this slightly paranoid notion, and John Harvey Kellogg – the famed dietician – derided it in his book *The Ladies' Guide in Health and Disease*. That said, Kellogg worried about young brothers and sisters sharing beds, due to what he saw as the inevitable problem of 'promiscuous sleeping', or what we might call incest, which is definitely enough to put you off your cornflakes. In fairness to him, he also advised against babies sleeping in the parental bed, for fear of accidental suffocation, which we know from coroner reports and donations to medieval saintly shrines had been a cause of common tragedy in the preceding centuries.

Yet, it wasn't just the children who were thought to be in dire peril. There was even heated debate about whether married partners should co-sleep. Some thought it killed the romance to have to lie next to your snoring, farting partner; others thought two people would inevitably disturb each other, by one being too hot, cold, stressed or alert; moralists – as ever – worried that such proximity induced improper sexual temptation; and physicians thought it wasn't very hygienic to wallow in someone else's bodily excretions. As the German scholar, Bernhard Christoph Faust, summed it up in his *Catechism of Health*, 'it is therefore advisable for every child, and every adult, to lie alone, in order to enjoy sound sleep.' Consequently, husbands and wives often found themselves occupying twin beds, or separate rooms, for the good of their health.

UP ALL NIGHT?

Pepys might have been up all night, trying to argue himself out of the doghouse, but the notion of nocturnal activity wasn't necessarily alien to him. According to an intriguing theory, for almost all of medieval history up until the eighteenth century, people did not sleep through the night, but instead had 'first sleep' for around four hours, before getting up and pottering around for a bit; perhaps to do some cooking, or cleaning, or praying, or saucy romping with the spouse – or even to embark on a midnight crime spree – before returning to bed for a sequel snooze named 'morning sleep'. The French named this interim period *dorveille*, a portmanteau word combining elements from *dormir* (to sleep) and *reveiller* (to wake up), which makes it sound like the entire French nation sleep-walked around en masse, like a Gallic-themed zombie apocalypse, but people were very much awake. Though this sounds decidedly weird to us, it is actually in better keeping with our biological body-clock, which does apparently split eight hours of snooze into two phases of four hours. Perhaps scientists will one day be recommending it to us all.

DON'T LET THE BEDBUGS BITE...

As we snuggle up under the covers, our sheets are crisp and clean, but even if they were a bit grimy we could just bung them in the washing machine and all the nasty stuff would be sluiced off in a whirlpool of soap suds. But how did our ancestors cope without such modern luxury? Well, in truth, not that well. Mosquitoes, lice and other parasites were an unwelcome co-habitant of many a historical bed, as we've seen from the Stone Age and ancient Egypt. Indeed, bio-archaeologists discovered in 2015 that even the Romans – despite their public toilets, sewers and bath houses – were plagued by fleas, mites and dangerous intestinal worms.

During the Middle Ages things were no different, though it was said that some particularly ascetic monks deliberately introduced fleas into their sheets so that they might suffer like Christ. These were rather extreme efforts towards slumbering self-sabotage, and much more common were attempts to get rid of the little blighters instead. While Carthusian monks claimed to have solved the infestation issue by pursuing a vegetarian diet – presumably assuming that the blood of a cabbage-muncher might be off-putting – the average medieval person enjoyed a range of options when defending their bed from attack. These included decorating the bedroom with sprigs of fern or alder, rough cloths, lit candles, loaves of bread doused in turpentine, bowls of milk containing hare's gall bladder, rags dipped in honey or onion juice, or even wolf-skin cloaks laid on the bed.

While it's fun to imagine each night was a medieval assault course, where all manner of booby-traps were set, it's doubtful that all of these tactics were combined in unison and, in any case, one may rightly question their effectiveness. That said, another common custom of trying to suffocate fleas in a locked chest might sound cartoonishly idiotic, but was, in theory, not a bad idea, as even fleas need to breathe. So common was it to find bugs in the bed that people became blasé about it, with Samuel Pepys writing, 'Up; finding our beds good, but lousy; which made us merry' – a strange contradiction by our standards.

The Italians began to circumnavigate the problem by adopting iron-framed bedsteads which provided a far less inviting home for lice, but the stubbornly stoic British clung onto their wooden bedframes, and in 1819 a publication called *The Young Woman's Guide to Virtue, Economy and Happiness* rather bafflingly suggested that all infested objects of wooden furniture be boiled in a metal cauldron filled with vitriol solution, so as to kill off the bugs. This conjures up some extraordinary mental images of a young woman wrestling her bedroom furniture into a bubbling pot, but in practice we can presume the smarter ladies opted instead to apply the liquid vitriol to the furniture, rather than try to dunk an entire bed like it was a massive biscuit in a cup of tea.

Alas, even this didn't always work; the stately bed in London's Mansion House, draped exotically in golden-embroidered damask, had to be burned in 1824 after close inspection revealed 'it is the receptacle of all sorts of vermin'. Even the stubborn British had to admit that the writing was on the wall for wooden bedframes. By the mid-nineteenth century the dual combo of metal bedsteads, and mass-produced cotton sheets which could be cleaned in boiling water, finally ended the long reign of the bed bugs.

DON'T FORGET TO FLIP THE MATTRESS

With so many individual beds to make in an upmarket nineteenth-century home, one would have imagined that the process might have been simplified, but that's failing to appreciate the heroic obstinacy of Victorian Britain. Instead, making the bed became an arduous endurance event for housemaids, who might daily be demanded by their overzealous mistresses to strip off every bed in the house, so as to ensure everything was well aired. It's worth noting that a single, well appointed bed was a lot more complex than our own today, and comprised an eiderdown, several pillow cases, four blankets, three sheets, an under-blanket, the feather mattress and the horsehair mattress that lay over the springs.

Consequently, a decent-sized home might have had only five or six such beds, but enough linen to stock a modern hotel for a week. As for the cumbersome mattresses, which the maids were expected to lift up to the windows and flip over, most expensive ones were sprung with metal coils by the arrival of the late nineteenth century, though they could still be stuffed with a boggling array of materials from swan feathers at the top end, to straw at the bottom, via options including horsehair, seaweed, wood shavings and leaves. Oddly enough, despite the peerless comfort, feather beds were the subject of tremendous suspicion from such medical luminaries as Kellogg and Bernhard Christoph Faust who advised that children should never sleep on them.

Given the huge physical effort it took to make a Victorian bed, it's a wonder people had to wait until the 1970s for the far simpler slumberdown (now known as the duvet) to arrive from Sweden and transform the daily chore into something that lasted only a minute, rather than half an hour. But, then again, there are millions of teenagers for whom straightening out a duvet is an exhausting burden that definitely contravenes their human rights.

Of course, our own bed-making can wait for the morning, for now is the time to get some shut-eye. Oh, but hang on! Have we remembered to set the alarm? Dammit, where's that clock when you need it?

11.59 p.m.

SETTING THE ALARM CLOCK

Before we allow ourselves to drift off into a fitful slumber, we must set the alarm for the following morning, or else we'll inevitably snooze until noon.

Having reached this final part of the book, let's go full circle and return to where we began. Back then we asked how societies measured time, but let's turn our attention to how the individual divided up their day, beginning, of course, with the early morning wake-up call. Artificial lights, thick curtains and technological gadgets have allowed us to shift the boundaries of day and night, so we no longer have to go to bed at dusk nor rise at dawn. Yet, the alarm clock is not nearly as modern as we might think, and people have been struggling with early starts for millennia. So, just how old is this morning ritual?

CAUSE FOR ALARM

The Academia was a secluded retreat set away from the centre of ancient Athens – its olive trees and curtained wall turning the former public gardens into a private cocoon. Here was an excellent place for quiet introspection, or impassioned debate, far from the noisy burble of urban life. Formerly it had been a gymnasium, full of sweaty youths with pendulous genitals, but now it was the home to one of the greatest educational institutions in history, the famous school established by the philosopher Plato. You'd think that a guy with that sort of esteemed reputation would have aspiring students queuing at his door, like devoted fans camped outside a boy band's hotel window, yet it seems Plato might have suffered with a bit of an attendance problem – apparently, his students struggled to get out of bed in time for his lectures.

I say 'apparently' because the sources for this particular anecdote are highly unreliable, but it's possible that the illustrious thinker, perhaps aggrieved by his lazy pupils, may have constructed an ingenious antidote to their extended lie-ins, what we might now call the world's earliest alarm clock. The mechanism is completely unknown to us, and the whole story is based on only five words reported by Athenaeus: 'Plato built an alarm clock'. Subsequently, various scholars and engineers have imagined what it might have looked like, and one suggestion is that it was formed from three vessels stacked up on top of each other, with the top container filled with water that drained very slowly through a narrow funnel into the one beneath it. After a set number of hours, the gradual drip drip of water might finally have filled this secondary container to the brim, thereby forcing out any trapped air through a narrow side vent, and this may have produced a whistling noise. Once this had happened, perhaps, the water might then have drained into a third storage container, ready to be manually poured back into the top one again.

It may sound like a rudimentary bodged job, but, whatever the actual design, the concept was seemingly a fully automated timekeeper with a programmable alarm function. So, as we reach over and start poking the buttons on our alarm clock, we're merely repeating what might have been a nightly ritual for Plato.

And if he wanted to get up earlier, all he possibly had to do was reduce the amount of water in the clock so the whistle screeched sooner. Easy! Apparently Plato's pupil Aristotle modified the design to replace the whistle with even noisier copper balls that, at the correct hour, were dropped onto a metal dish to make a deafening clang.

Of course, relying on a machine is one thing, but having another person rouse us isn't a bad idea either. These days it's routine for a hotel receptionist to ask if we'd like a wake-up call in the morning. Sometimes this results in an automated service telephonically greeting us with an eerie robotic cadence, but in my experience it has more often been a polite member of staff who has picked up the phone, called my room number and then patiently tried to snap me awake as I incoherently mumble: 'Who is this? What do you want? Oh God, is the hotel on fire? Wait! Am *I* on fire? No, it's okay. I'm not on fire... Who is this?' This diligent hospitality may sound modern, but the principle was equally common in the busy cities of nineteenth-century Britain where knocker-uppers were paid to walk up and down the streets, banging on windows with a long, slender pole until those inside confirmed that they were awake.

These human alarm clocks were sometimes freelance and knew the individual preferences of their customers, who could leave the requested wake-up time chalked on the door or window. But in the rows of industrial tenement houses, erected close to capacious mills and factories, the knocker-uppers were company employees charged with awakening the workforce en masse at 3 a.m., so there was no way of fooling them, and ignoring the knock merely resulted in a fine from one's boss. Pleasingly, even knocker-uppers needed to be woken up in time to do their shift, so they were dragged from their beds by the brilliantly titled knocker-uppers' knocker-uppers – proof, if ever you needed it, that even the bountiful English language has occasional moments of dubious quality control.

However, in the 1870s, wind-up mechanical clocks with settable alarm functions first became available to the masses, putting the snoozer in charge of their own rousing responsibility. How did this cunning gadget come about? Well, to make sense of it, we need to go all the way back to the ancient era, and have a gander at the evolution of the automated time-keeping gadget.

DRIP, DRIP, DRIP

Plato's whistling contraption was (if it existed) a *clepsydra*, or water clock, and though he possibly added the noisy functionality to make it a novel invention, the idea of measuring time with water had probably originated in ancient Egypt. During the reign of Pharaoh Amenhotep I, in around the year 1500 BCE, an enterprising priest decided to compare the length of the day and night using a water clock, over the course of 24 hours. Somehow, on the summer solstice, he deduced that there were 18 hours of daylight and just six of darkness, but on the winter solstice he found the exact reverse. I'm no scientist, but 18 hours of winter darkness seems positively Arctic in its extremity and he was, of course, living in balmy Egypt at the time. Presumably, he had fudged his calculations by using winter seasonal hours of just 40 or so minutes. Either that or he was very drunk.

Perhaps the most famous water clock in ancient Greece can still be seen today in the Roman *agora* of Athens, where you might stumble past an eight-sided building known as The Tower of Winds, possibly built in the second century BCE. This elegant construction, bestrewn with ornate meteorological sculptures, was the Swiss Army knife of classical science and boasted the dazzling techno-trio of sundial, weather vane and water clock. The water clock was a favourite toy of the ancient Greeks, who cheekily employed it to limit the length of speeches in legal trials, deploying it as a stopwatch that counted down from a set number. However, it could also measure out equal hours of 60 minutes, yet the Greeks didn't necessarily want that.

An accurate clock was of little use if it was out of step with available sunlight – smug pedantry only gets you so far when you're crashing around in the dark and end up accidentally tumbling down well shafts – so ancient engineers had to come up with methods to make the water clock mirror the variability of solar time. As strange as it sounds, their challenge was to make it less accurate. The simplest way to do this was to alter the speed at which liquid exited the outflow pipe of the top tank, thereby filling the clock-tank quicker/slower to create shorter/longer hours, respectively. One likely method was to dangle a cone-shaped plug (imagine a modern bath plug) from a see-saw. In the summer, the see-saw tipped downwards so the plug slowed the water's escape to a trickle, and in the winter it was tipped upwards so the plug was dragged out of the hole and the water rushed through more quickly.

Perhaps due to water's tendency to evaporate in glorious Aegean sunshine, clocks using liquids were not the only option. Hourglasses containing sand grains could also be equally handy speech-timers, though they had to be inverted after every hour, which meant that, just like naughty toddlers intent on playing with the knife drawer, you couldn't take your eye off them for long. But when the Roman Empire collapsed in 476, Europe had a bit of a slovenly spell – often unfairly dubbed the Dark Ages – and some of this sophisticated technology got lost down the back of the proverbial sofa. This meant that as the former powers of Europe tried to re-find their feet, other cultures were leaping ahead in the sophistication stakes.

A RIGHT ROYAL CLOCK-UP...

It was the beginning of the ninth century and, sat on his throne in Aachen, the illustrious Charlemagne believed himself to be the unrivalled political heavyweight of his era. As the Holy Roman Emperor – the ruler over much of France and Germany – he had exerted great effort in establishing diplomatic links far and wide, with a glitzy PR campaign that emphasised his all-conquering majesty. Four years before he had sent gifts to who he thought was the 'King of Persia', perhaps hoping to forge an alliance with the Abbasids against the Umayyad dynasty in southern Spain, and when Charlemagne gave a gift he expected a respectfully submissive reply, even from the Pope. So when emissaries arrived with a hoard of gifts carried all the way from 'Persia' he must have been thrilled to find out what treasures had been bestowed upon him by a new member of his fan club. His joy probably wasn't long-lived...

The Sultan Harun al-Rashid, fifth caliph of the Abbasid Arabs, had sent eye-popping gifts – silks, candelabras, perfumes and even a live elephant. He had spent a fortune and it was one hell of a show, but the greatest pressie was a sumptuous water clock, elegantly fashioned from brass. The Islamic craftsmen had seem-ingly taken Aristotle's chiming alarm clock and gone to town with it; upon each passing hour, little balls tumbled down to strike a cymbal and a skilfully carved horseman would pop out of one of 12 doors, like a gorgeously hewn whack-a-mole game. This wasn't just a functional clock for timing speeches, this was technology as art.

For the hubristic Charlemagne, receiving it must have been like buying your partner a book token for Christmas, and receiving a gift-wrapped jet ski in return. The Frankish histories tried to

327

spin it back in their favour, with the monk Notger the Stammerer writing:

> **At this sight Haroun, the bravest inheritor of that name, understood the superior might of Charles ... and thus broke out in his praise: '... How can I make worthy recompense for the honours which he has bestowed upon me?'**

But, despite the propaganda, the Sultan's dazzling gifts had crushed the Holy Roman Emperor's pretensions to greatness. Charlemagne had tried to impress the founding patron of Baghdad's much-celebrated House of Wisdom library by doing the medieval equivalent of driving past his house in a second-hand Honda Civic, only to see a brand new Lamborghini parked in the driveway.

Based on this intricately dazzling water clock, the Islamic world was miles ahead in technological sophistication. As if to prove the point, around 70 years after Charlemagne's embarrassment, another heroic ruler of medieval yore, England's Alfred the Great, pioneered his own alternative to the hourglass. It was called the candle clock, and it burned down with reliable constancy so that one could see the hour of day advancing as the wax melted. This was by no means a bad idea – adding candles to the temporal arsenal of water, sand and sunlight showed pragmatic ingenuity – but it was just a bit ... well, drab. Am I being harsh? Well, maybe, but consider what the Chinese were doing at the same time.

EASTERN TIME

These days, how do we tell the time? The options are fairly limited: we can ask someone to tell us, we can look at a clock or we can squint at the sun like Crocodile Dundee. Basically, when trying to fathom the hour, we either use our sense of sight or our sense of hearing. But what about smelling the time? Two centuries after King Alfred's death – during the Song Dynasty of medieval China – the candle clock got a rather aromatic upgrade with the invention of the incense clock in which incense sticks, or powders, were carefully calibrated to burn for standardised periods of time inside beautifully ornate censers. Once they'd melted through, weighted bells would drop down from the censer onto a metal dish, producing a pleasing chime – a similar mechanic to Aristotle's alleged alarm clock. This, in itself, was clever but the truly ingenious bit was that different incenses were used for each hour of the day, so a person could walk into a room and know the time just by sniffing the air. Incense clocks were popular in homes and temples, and spread into Japan, but they never caught on outside of Asia; this is odd because medieval China was significantly further advanced, and the West really should have been nicking their ideas.

After all, not only had Chinese inventors improved the reliability of water clocks by using mercury, which doesn't evaporate or freeze, but they had also blended mechanical intricacy with massive-scale engineering feats. The perfect example of this fusion was the huge water clock, or cosmic engine, built by the polymath Su Song in 1088. It was about ten metres in height, and featured three storeys stuffed to the rafters with time charts, astronomical devices for tracking the movement of the stars, and automated mannequins that announced the time by smashing loud bells. Extraordinarily, the whole gamut of gadgets was autonomously powered by a self-perpetuating waterwheel erected inside the base of the tower, making it the first clock in history to function unaided.

It took years to build, but tragically only stood for less than half a century before it was destroyed by marauding invaders who captured it, dismantled it, moved it, tried to put it back together and then realised they had no idea what they were doing. Sadly, Su Song had unhelpfully hidden parts of his schematic drawings, eager to preserve the secrecy of the project, and so when he snuffed it no one else could rebuild the tower. And I don't just mean no one in the Middle Ages. Such was the standard of Chinese medieval ingenuity, even a team of modern researchers struggled to solve Su Song's puzzling conundrum when charged with reconstructing a scaled-down replica for the National Museum of Natural Science in Taichung.

TICK TOCK

The cosmic engine was a true 'clock'. Technically speaking, any temporal device is a horologe, which admittedly sounds like something out of the Harry Potter books, but originally the word 'clock' was only used for a timepiece which chimed, taking its name from the Latin word for bell (*clocca*). It was during the fourteenth century that this linguistic evolution occurred, and that's no coincidence as this was when mechanical clocks became widely established in Europe, shifting the onus of timekeeping away from the mere orchestration of religious routine. So, how do modern horologes compare with their innovative medieval precursors, and at what stage did they start to migrate from civic belltowers into our front rooms?

The earliest clock designs weren't terribly accurate, and that's putting it kindly. Though relatively simple, their mechanics are fiendishly hard to describe, so, here goes . . . Medieval clocks were powered by gravity, but don't start imagining any sexy sci-fi imagery. When I say gravity propulsion, I mean it in a massive-weight-dangling-on-the-end-of-a-rope kind of way. The device utilised something called a verge escapement, which was a long, thin, upright rod with two small blocks (pallets) attached to it to function as catches – one on the left of the rod and one on the right. The verge rod also acted as a pivot for a horizontal crossbar (foliot) with a heavy weight dangling on both ends.

Pushed up against the rod was a saw-toothed escape wheel – imagine a king's crown with loads of jagged triangular peaks – and this was on the end of a crankshaft around which a tightly coiled rope was wrapped, attached to a whopping great stone. So, thanks to gravity, this massive deadweight would drag the rope down, making it unwind and thereby rotating the horizontal crankshaft. This made the escape wheel turn a brief distance, until one of its jagged saw-teeth was caught by the catch (pallet) on the verge rod, stopping it in its tracks. The energy of this collision made the verge rod rotate on its axis, swinging the weighted crossbar (foliot) like a clothes line in the wind (incidentally, 'foliot' derives from the French word *follet,* meaning someone who dances like a lunatic, which sums me up pretty well).

This swinging movement would briefly release the catch again, and allow the escape wheel to turn once more, but – thanks to the weights on either end of the crossbar – the swing would correct itself back the other way, thereby closing the catch again. The whole process would repeat itself over and over, creating the tick-tock sound of saw-tooth upon catch, until the rope had totally uncoiled itself from the crankshaft and some unfortunate engineer had to clamber up all those stairs to rewind it again. Phew! Okay, let's have a brief moment of recovery ... after all, it's midnight and our brain is gently pickled in alcohol. Feeling better? Right, onwards we go.

Though exceptional technological achievements, and a symbol of a city's cultural prowess, these clocks were an enormous faff to install. The bells could weigh something like four tonnes each, while the clockwork was cast in chunky iron, and required crossbar weights nearly as heavy as a modern car. Understandably, getting one of these monster contraptions into a tower 50ft off the ground was an arduous undertaking that took years of careful co-operation between blacksmiths, rope-makers, carpenters, bricklayers, stonemasons, bell-founders and the horologists themselves; and, even then, once installed, the infernal things would often break down and have to be repaired or replaced. Still, by the fourteenth century, improvements to mechanical clockwork permitted the numerical hour to be chimed too, so 4 p.m. would warrant four bongs, thereby alerting people to the actual time, rather than just the single bong of a passing anonymous hour.

But the clock as we know it was still a work in progress and medieval clock faces were totally unrecognisable to our eyes. Prior to the fourteenth century, the hour hand remained rigid, and it was the hours which rotated past on a dial; verge clocks were simply too inaccurate to bother with a minute hand. What was needed was a more naturally stable system for ensuring a regular beat that ticked like... well, clockwork. The initial advance came from coiled springs, which aided miniaturisation and allowed Elizabeth I of England to receive a decorated wristwatch for Christmas. But, coiled springs were not the silver bullet for this problem – instead, the great game-changer in the history of horology was to be the pendulum.

THE PENDULUM SWINGS

The story goes that sometime around 1581 a young medical student was attending Mass in the vaulted Romanesque cathedral of Pisa when his attention began to wander. The cathedral is a gorgeous building in which one's eyes can't help but trace the journey of the tapered granite columns that sprout from the floor, morph into rounded arches of white and black marble, and climb upwards to lift one's gaze heavenwards to the gilded, frescoed ceiling of the interior dome. Perhaps it was this skyward beauty that stole his attention from the service, or maybe he was just bored of priestly droning, but the young man looked up and found himself transfixed on something utterly captivating. Hanging from the ceiling of the nave was an incense lamp, gently swaying back and forth to sprinkle the congregation in godly deodorant (as recommended by Thomas Aquinas). The young man became enchanted by its metronomic rhythm and found himself timing the lamp's trajectory against his own pulse.

But what was so enthralling about this mere censer, repetitiously swinging over oblivious heads? Well, it was its eerily unnatural energy which carried it one way, and then back the other, when all logic demanded that it should settle, dragged down by its weight. He was right to have paid such close attention, as he'd just stumbled upon nature's fascinating pendulum effect. So who was this curious, easily distracted youth? To most of the people in that cathedral, he was just another student daydreaming through Mass, but while history doesn't remember those other pew-dwellers, it's been a little kinder to the young prodigy named Galileo Galilei.

From this simple beginning, Galileo's pendulum research continued for many years, and it was he who first discovered the counter-intuitive law stating that two pendulums of the same length will swing at the same rate, even if one is pushed with much greater speed through a wider arc. Of course, this was just one of many important intellectual feats achieved by the celebrated Italian, who also turned out to be fairly good at astronomy, but we shouldn't heap all the praise on Galileo alone. After all, the seventeenth century was an era of great scientific enquiry and his peers in mainland Europe – many of whom bounced ideas back and forth between themselves like intellectual volleyballs – included the polymath geniuses Rene Descartes, Blaise Pascal and Marin Mersenne.

But the talent didn't end there, either. Just 25 years after Galileo's

death, England's Royal Society gathered a roster of brilliant luminaries, including The Beatles of experimental philosophy: Isaac
Newton, Christopher Wren, Robert Hooke and Robert Boyle.
With all these boffins on the scene, it was inevitable that horology
would be due for an upgrade, but though Galileo had fiddled
about with clocks in later age, he never actually completed one
of his own – he was far too busy calling the Pope an idiot, and
preparing for 'Bohemian Rhapsody' fame – so it was the Dutch
scientist Christiaan Huygens who first added a pendulum to a
clock in 1657, using it to replace the crossbar (foliot) of medieval
timepieces. But despite the improvement, Huygens' design still
lost about 60 seconds over the course of a day. Surely the titans
of seventeenth-century science could do better than that?

Well, yes they could. In fact, the breakthrough had already
come in 1644, when the French polymath Marin Mersenne
had noticed that a pendulum of 39.1 inches swings for an exact
second. Yet, despite this discovery, the Seconds Pendulum still
wasn't incorporated into Huygens' clock of 1657, as it needed to
be allied up with another new bit of kit. Remember the rod-based
verge escapement in the medieval clock? Well, put a pendulum
in that mechanism and it has to swing through an arc of about
80 degrees to function, and cramming a 39.1-inch pendulum in
a clock big enough to allow that wide sweep was as impractical
as trying to dance the can-can in a locked wardrobe.

Instead, the English scientist Robert Hooke – who was the
George Harrison of the Royal Society, being the really talented
one everyone forgets about – invented the anchor escapement.
This was essentially a metal claw suspended over the jagged-tooth
escape wheel which reduced the arc of a 39.1-inch pendulum
down to just 4 degrees. So, instead of swinging wildly through
80 degrees, now it just gently shuffled left to right like a self-
conscious dancer in a busy disco. With this handy double act
now working in tandem, the clock face that we see on our wall

today – the scurrying minute hand chasing the dawdling hour hand – could finally emerge on the scene. These timepieces might be accurate to within a second per day, and, more importantly, people could actually fit one into their house, rather than having to drag it up the staircase of a massive belltower.

The first to make these domestic clocks was the English craftsman William Clement in the 1670s. He crammed his long pendulum, and the two-handed face, into a tall box of wood and brass construction, kick-starting a craze for this design that is still fashionable today among antique dealers. In fact, you might have inherited one of these grandfather clocks from your relatives, or picked one up at auction. But while we see them as beautiful, slightly outdated relics of yesteryear, 350 years ago such mechanical timepieces were sexy technology. Though they were expensive objects, people could saunter confidently around town, showing off their hand-crafted pocket watch designed to fit into their snazzy new waistcoat, which was standard hipster attire in King Charles II's fashion-crazed reign. And, once a person tired of the city, they could return to find an elegant grandfather clock in the salon of their well appointed home, quietly counting the seconds with the unrelenting patience of a world-class hide-and-seek player.

Time was no longer regulated by the Church, or powerful medieval guilds; it had eluded the restrictive grasp of the daily call to prayer, or grand proclamation from lofty clock towers. After thousands of years, time finally belonged to the people to use and squander as they wished. All they had to do was wind their clocks regularly, and even this chore would eventually vanish. After all, our alarm clock requires electricity, but while we might feel this is a twenty-first-century luxury, are electrical timepieces really so modern? Never mind our grandfather clock, would our great-great-grandfather have been able to recognise an electric clock? Surprisingly, the answer is probably yes.

THE 'CURRENT' TIME?

We're in our bed, clumsily fumbling with the alarm clock in the darkness. It is a little mains-powered plastic box with a digital face, perched on a bedside table, and if we were to smash it open – let's be honest, plenty of us angrily thump the thing hard enough in the mornings – then we wouldn't find a tiny pendulum inside, instead we'd be more likely to see crystal. It was the discovery in 1929 of quartz's high-frequency resonance in an electronic circuit – a natural oscillation that emits incredibly consistent rhythmic pulses – that led it to conquer the world as the go-to technology for mass-market timekeepers. But, it took nearly 40 years for quartz crystals to be used in consumer products, meaning that for 150 years prior to the 1970s, there were several other contenders in the electrical clock category.

The first forays into electrical timepieces dated back to when Napoleon and Wellington were scrapping it out on the fields of Waterloo in 1815. The electrostatic clock, as built by the Italian physics professor Giuseppe Zamboni, used two oppositely charged dry pile batteries stationed either side of a pendulum, and relied upon electrostatic charge to send it swinging back and forth. While this sounds like the sort of elementary experiment we did in our physics class at school, in fact the batteries were so highly charged that the clock could have allegedly ticked for 50 years before it ran out of juice, so that was an impressive start.

But despite the efficiency of this prototype, electrostatic clocks weren't mass marketed and instead the big public success in the nineteenth century was electromagnetic clocks which, as the name suggests, used electrified magnets to repel and attract the pendulum back and forth. Between the 1840s and the First World War, it's possible our ancestors might have owned such a timekeeping gadget if they were rich enough, though mechanical clocks were much more common. In the 1930s, when many homes were being connected up to the power grid, electromagnetic clocks were superseded by the synchronous electric clock which relied upon the natural oscillations of 50–60 hertz occurring in the Alternating Current delivered to people's plug sockets.

This did away with the pendulum altogether, waving goodbye to nearly 300 years of its crucial constancy, and waving hello to children cramming metal objects into electrified wall sockets (my brother did this in France as a kid, and literally flew across the room!). Today, it's possible that our bedside alarm clock still runs off the AC current, but since the 1970s it's been much more common for clocks and wristwatches to harness the oscillations of quartz crystals instead. Initially these timekeepers were state of the art, and acquiring an LED watch was brain-meltingly exciting, but now we can pick up a basic quartz watch for less than the price of a decent sandwich. I've even seen them being given away as gifts in packets of breakfast cereal.

Regardless of how clocks were powered, most continued the tradition of having minute and hour hands revolve around the face, with William Clement's 1670s aesthetic remaining just as common in the 1970s. But, since then, digital displays have become more commonplace. Thankfully, we are spared the confusion of having the internal calculations being projected onto the screen and, instead of rapidly evolving squiggles of digital noise, some clever mathematical conversion turns the frequencies into binary numbers, and these become hours, minutes and seconds on the display for us to notice, ignore and then later shout at when we're late for work.

But tonight, the alarm clock is our ally, not our enemy, and as we finally manage to hit the right button, and exhale with relief as the correct time is set for tomorrow's wake-up call, we feel the room growing hazy and our muscles surrender to fatigue. It's been a long, enjoyable Saturday in our twenty-first-century home.

Setting the Alarm Clock

Some of the things we did today were simply unachievable in the lifetime of our great-grandparents, and the reassuring quality of modern clothes, food, plumbing facilities and hygienic gadgets means ours is a comfortable existence of minimal peril.

And yet, had we been joined today by our Stone Age ancestors Ug and Nug – teleported here in some ingenious time machine – they would have recognised almost every one of our daily rituals. They too washed in water, ate crops and animals, wiped their bums, donned clothes, played with their pets, communicated with friends, got drunk, dined together, picked food out of their teeth, told the time and slept in beds.

Since the emergence of our species, 107 billion people have struggled with the everyday problems of existence, and with the arrival of each new generation came an evaluation process, as the old ways were either maintained or replaced. But at the centre of the constant cultural churn were humans like you and me, doing their best to improve their lot and muddle through the daily struggles of being alive. History doesn't repeat itself – people do.

And, tomorrow we'll repeat ourselves once more. But for now, it's time to say 'Goodnight, sleep tight and don't let the bedbugs bite...'.

ACKNOWLEDGEMENTS

Thanking all the people who helped shape this book would require a whole other chapter, so forgive me if I keep it simple.

I would be nothing without my loving family. In particular, my brilliant brother never rubs his superior intellect in my face, which is nice of him, and my mother and father are the kindest, most supportive parents I could have possibly hoped for. It's undoubtedly from them that I get my passion and curiosity for what makes other people tick.

I am also blessed to have a bunch of friends who manage to be steadfast, generous, clever, and funny. Some I have known since I was five years old, some I only met in the past couple of years, but all of them have made my life immeasurably better. I probably owe them a lot of drinks, if only to apologise for all the times I started a conversation with 'did you know ... ?'

I must also thank Richard Bradley and Bill Locke of Lion Television for having given me a TV career, even though I turned up at their office for my day at work sporting blue hair and a heavy metal T-shirt emblazoned with satanic skulls. Similarly, I am hugely grateful to the comedy geniuses of *Horrible Histories*: Caroline Norris, Giles Pilbrow and Dominic Brigstocke, who not only trusted in my historical judgment when I ruined their jokes with my precious facts, but who were so generous with their time as I clumsily experimented with the mysterious art of comedy writing.

As for this book, it would never have happened without my wonderful agent Donald Winchester. Before he agreed to sign me, I met him in a café and spent 90 minutes pitching an idea at him which, he knew after only five minutes, was basically unpublishable. Any other agent might have told me to get lost. Charitably, Donald waited until I had stopped droning on, and instead asked if I had any other ideas. Fortunately, I did. It's been a pleasure working with him ever since.

My editor at Orion, Bea Hemming, is prodigiously clever and it was her idea to set this book during a modern day. I am doubly indebted to her for first having offered me a chance to become an author – something I had always thought about, but never knew how to achieve – and then for patiently teaching me that the key to good writing is editing. Apparently, you don't have to cram your entire vocabulary into a single sentence. Who knew?! Hers was the gentlest of red pens.

Of course, it takes an army to publish a book, and Orion has quite the taskforce. Though I'd like to thank everyone involved, big props must go to the eternally cheerful Holly Harley, the marketing gurus Claire Brett, Marissa Hussey, and Hannah Atkinson, and the queen of publicity, Kate Wright-Morris. My copy editor, Kay Macmullan, did a magnificent job of rendering my punctuation suitable for human eyes, and spotted plenty of unfinished sentences that made zero sense. Once my words had been corrected, it was a thrill to see them being made to look all fancy by Helen Ewing, and I was utterly blown away by the brilliant cover jacket created by Steve Marking and Harry Haysom. I must also salute Paul Hussey, the brigadier-general who kept the whole operation running smoothly.

ACKNOWLEDGEMENTS

Because I wrote this book without a research assistant, my heartfelt thanks also go to the expert #twitterstorians who so graciously read my manuscript and suggested improvements/pointed out glaring errors. Not only are they esteemed scholars but they are also friendly, witty, and engaging. If you are on Twitter, go follow: Dr Peter Frankopan, Dr John Gallagher, Amber Butchart, Dr Fern Riddell, Dr Kate Wiles, Dr Sophie Hay, Dr Sara Owen, Dr Matthew Pope, Dr Rebekah Higgitt, Dr Vanessa Heggie, Dr Chris Naunton, Dr Gillian Kenny and Dr Sara Perry.

Twitter didn't just introduce me to these fine historians, it also kept me sane while I sat alone in my office for up to 16 hours a day. If you ever tweeted me, or played along with one of my pun-tastic word games, then feel proud in the knowledge you probably stopped me from taking my many books and erecting them into a temporary shelter in which to hibernate. Seriously, the idea crossed my mind at least once a month. Thanks, Twitter!

Finally, I must honour my beautiful wife. Though we've been together for ten years, it was only during this writing process that we got engaged, bought a house, and got married. I am not the easiest person to live with at the best of times, and I've had my ups and downs. Yet, despite my flaws – and the fact she had to share me for two years with an overheating laptop and a massive library – her patience, support and love has been immeasurable. I am so grateful to have her by my side. Thank you, Kate.

SELECT BIBLIOGRAPHY

Before you put this book down, I just want to pay tribute to the hundreds of brilliant historians whose research I have read in preparation to write this. History is a collaborative discipline – a vast edifice of constantly changing knowledge – and it's constructed by countless squadrons of tireless scholars who beaver away in their own fields and then unselfishly share their findings with the rest of us. It's only thanks to their superhuman curiosity, diligence and talent that I was even remotely capable of scribbling this book. Well, that, and a massive quantity of chocolate biscuits.

Isaac Newton famously said he was 'standing on the shoulders of giants', an image that suggests a confident genius imperiously surveying the world from his lofty perch. I'm actually quite bad with heights, so instead I clumsily scrambled up the shins of giants, and eavesdropped on their conversation to try to scoop up as much of their vast knowledge as I could. This book, then, was not intended as a definitive history of daily life, but as a tasting menu of lovely historical morsels that I've gleaned over a decade of professional curiosity. But, if you want to go deeper into the detail, I've included a reading list of other fantastic books worthy of your perusal. For a full biography please see my website: www.gregjenner.com.

SELECT BIBLIOGRAPHY

TIME

Empires of Time: Calendars, Clocks, and Cultures, Anthony F. Aveni (Basic Books, 1989)

Time's Pendulum: The Quest to Capture Time – From Sundials to Atomic Clocks, Jo Ellen Barnett (Perseus Books, 1998)

The History of Clocks and Watches, Eric Bruton (Black Cat, 1989)

At Night's Close: Time in Times Past, A. Roger Ekrich (Phoenix, 2006)

The History of Time: A Very Short Introduction, Leofranc Holford-Strevens (Oxford University Press, 2005)

Seize the Daylight: The Curious and Contentious Story of Daylight Saving Time, David S. Prerau (Thunder's Mouth Press, 2005)

TOILETS

Privies and Water Closets, David J. Everleigh (Shire Publications, 2008)

Flushed: How The Plumber Saved Civilization, W. Hodding Carter (Atria, 2007)

Sitting Pretty: An Uninhibited History of the Toilet, Julie L. Horan (Robson, 1998)

Bum Fodder: An Absorbing History of Toilet Paper, Richard Smyth (Souvenir Press, 2012)

Clean and Decent: The Fascinating History of the Bathroom and the Water Closet, Lawrence Wright (Penguin, 2000)

FOOD

Food in the Ancient World, Joan P. Alcock (Greenwood Press, 2006)

Oxford Companion to Food, Alan Davidson (Oxford University Press, 1999)

Food: A Culinary History, Jean-Louis Flandrin & Massimo Montanari (eds.), Albert Sonnenfeld (trans.) (Columbia University Press, 2013)

Feast: Why Humans Share Food, Martin Jones (Oxford University Press, 2008)

The Cambridge World History of Food (2 vols.), Kenneth F. Kiple & Kriemhild Conee Ornelas (eds.) (Cambridge University Press, 2000)

Bread: A Global History, William Rubel (Reaktion, 2011)

An Edible History of Humanity, Tom Standage (Atlantic, 2008)

SELECT BIBLIOGRAPHY

WASHING

Clean: An Unsanitized History of Washing, Katherine Ashenburg (Profile, 2011)

The Book of the Bath, Francoise de Bonneville (Rizzoli International, 1998)

Bogs, Baths & Basins, David J. Everleigh (Sutton, 2002)

Clean: A History of Personal Hygiene and Purity, Virginia Smith (Oxford University Press, 2008)

PETS

Amazing Dogs: A Cabinet of Canine Curiosities, Jan Bondeson *(Amberley, 2013)*

A Perfect Harmony: The Intertwining Lives of Animals Throughout History, Roger A. Caras (Purdue University Press, 2001)

Some We Love, Some We Hate, Some We Eat: Why It's So Hard to Think Straight About Animals, Hal Herzog (Harper Perennial, 2011)

Looking at Animals in Human History, Linda Kalof (Reaktion, 2007)

Reigning Cats and Dogs: A History of Pets At Court Since the Renaissance, Katherine MacDonogh (Fourth Estate, 1999)

In the Company of Animals: A Study of Human–Animal Relationships, James Serpell (Cambridge University Press, 1996)

Medieval Pets, Kathleen Walker-Meikle (Boydell, 2014)

COMMUNICATION

Masters of the Post: The Authorized History of the Royal Mail, Duncan Campbell-Smith, (Penguin, 2012)

America Calling: A Social History of the Telephone to 1940, Claude S. Fischer (University of California Press, 1994)

Revolutions in Communication: Media History from Gutenberg to the Digital Age, Bill Kovarik (Continuum, 2011)

The Invention of News: How the World Came to Know About Itself, Andrew Pettegree (Yale University Press, 2014)

The Victorian Internet: The Remarkable Story of the Telegraph and the Nineteenth Century's On-Line Pioneers, Tom Standage (Bloomsbury, 2014)

SELECT BIBLIOGRAPHY

Writing on the Wall: Social Media – the First 2000 Years, Tom Standage (Bloomsbury, 2013)

CLOTHES

The Devil's Cloth: A History of Stripes, Michel Pastoureau (Columbia University Press, 2001)

Cotton: The Fabric that Made the Modern World, Georgio Riello (Cambridge University Press, 2013)

Japanese Fashion: A Cultural History, Toby Slade (Berg, 2009)

The Berg Companion to Fashion, Valerie Steele (ed.) (Berg, 2010)

DINNER ETIQUETTE

Food in Chinese Culture: Anthropological and Historical Perspectives, K.C. Chang (ed.) (Yale University Press, 1977)

Around the Roman Table: Food and Feasting in Ancient Rome, Patrick Faas (Chicago University Press, 2009)

The Art of Dining: A History of Cooking & Eating, Sara Paston-Williams (National Trust Books, 2012)

The Invention of the Restaurant: Paris and Modern Gastronomic Culture, Rebecca L. Spang (Harvard University Press, 2001)

The Rituals of Dinner: The Origins, Evolution, Eccentricities and Meaning of Table Manners, Margaret Visser (Penguin, 1992)

Consider The Fork: A History of How We Cook and Eat, Bee Wilson (Penguin, 2013)

ALCOHOL

Man Walks into a Pub: A Sociable History of Beer, Peter Brown (Pan, 2011)

The Spirits of America: A Social History of Alcohol, Eric Burns (Temple University Press, 2004)

And a Bottle of Rum: A History of the New World in Ten Cocktails, Wayne Curtis (Three Rivers, 2007)

Drink: A Cultural History of Alcohol, Iain Gately (Gotham Books, 2009)

An Inebriated History of Britain, Peter Haydon (The History Press, 2005)

SELECT BIBLIOGRAPHY

The Story of Wine, Hugh Johnson (Mitchell Beazley, 2004)

Uncorking the Past: The Quest for Wine, Beer, and Other Alcoholic Beverages, Patrick E. McGovern (University of California Press, 2011)

Champagne – Classic Wine Collection, Maggie McNie (Faber and Faber, 2000)

A History of the World in Six Glasses, Tom Standage (Atlantic Books, 2007)

DENTAL HYGIENE

Medicine in the Days of the Pharaohs, Bruno Halioua & Bernard Ziskind (Harvard University Press, 2005)

The Making of the Dentiste, c. 1650–1760, Roger King (Ashgate, 1998)

The Greatest Benefit to Mankind: A Medical History of Humanity from Antiquity to the Present, Roy Porter (Fontana, 1999)

The Excruciating History of Dentistry, James Wynbrandt (St Martin's Press, 2000)

BEDS

At Home: A Short History of Private Life, Bill Bryson (Black Swan, 2011)

Sleeping Around: The Bed from Antiquity to Now, Annie Carlano & Bobbie Sumburg (University of Washington Press, 2006)

The Time Traveller's Guide To Medieval England, Ian Mortimer (Vintage, 2009)

If Walls Could Talk, Lucy Worsley (Faber and Faber, 2012)

GENERAL

The Horse, The Wheel, and Language: How Bronze Age Eurasian Riders Shaped the Modern World, David W. Anthony (Princeton University Press, 2010)

Pompeii: The Life of a Roman Town, Mary Beard (Profile, 2009)

China's Golden Age: Everyday Life in the Tang Dynasty, Charles D. Benn (Oxford University Press, 2004)

Handbook to Life in Ancient Mesopotamia, Stephen Bertman (Facts On File, 2003)

SELECT BIBLIOGRAPHY

Daily Life in Ancient Rome: the People and the City at the Height of Empire, Jerome Carcopino (Penguin, 1991)

The Oxford Illustrated History of Prehistoric Europe, Barry Cunliffe (Oxford Paperbacks, 2001)

Cro-Magnon: How the Ice Age Gave Birth to the First Modern Humans, Brian Fagan (Bloomsbury, 2010)

Science: A 4000 Year History, Patricia Fara (Oxford University Press, 2010)

Daily Life of the Ancient Greeks, Robert Garland (Hackett, 2008)

The Leopard's Tale: Revealing the Mysteries of Catalhoyuk, Ian Hodder (Thames and Hudson, 2011)

Furniture: A Concise History, Edward Lucie-Smith (Thames and Hudson, 1979)

A Cabinet of Roman Curiosities, J.C. McKeown (OUP USA, 2010)

Ancient Worlds, Richard Miles (Cambridge University Press, 2008)

The Prehistory of the Mind: A Search for the Origins of Art, Religion and Science, Steven Mithen (Phoenix, 1998)

The Indus Civilisation: A Contemporary Perspective, Gregory L. Possehl (AltaMira, 2010)

The Lost Civilisations of the Stone Age: A Journey Back to Our Cultural Origins, Richard Rudgley (Century, 1998)

The Cambridge Companion to the Aegean Bronze Age, Cynthia W. Shelmerdine (Cambridge University Press 2008)

Life of the Ancient Egyptians, Eugen Strouhal, Deryck Viney, Werner Forman & Geoffrey T. Martin (Liverpool University Press, 1997)

INDEX

INDEX

'beerstone', 246
Bell, Alexander Graham,
132–5
Belyaev, Dmitri, 117–18
Beni Hasan, tomb illustrations, 120
Bentham, Jeremy, 185
Beowulf, 309–10
Bernardo de Treviso, 254
Berosus of Chaldea, 13
bicycles, 156, 192
binary code, 139
Black Death, 104, 255
Black, Dr G.V., 296
Blondel, Jean-François, 51
Bloomer, Amelia, 192
Boleyn, Ann, 121
Bonvesin da la Riva, 239
Borda, Jean-Charles de, 7
Bouchaud, Émilie Marie
('Polaire'), 186
Boyle, Robert, 334
braccae (trousers), 188
braies (breeches), 180
Bramah, Joseph, 52
Brando, Marlon, 205
brandy, 256, 260
bread, 80–4; and riots,
riots, 81; sliced, 84; and
dental erosion, 273–4
breakfast cereals, 62–4
breastfeeding, of baby
mammals, 116
Briseux, Charles-Etienne,
51
British Standard Time, 26
Brummell, George 'Beau',
204
'bundling', 314
burqas, 195
Byzantine Empire, 164,
178, 229

Cadet de Vaux, Antoine
Alexis-François, 18
Caius, John, 121
calendar, oldest known, 6

Caligula, Emperor, 228
Cambyses II, King of
Persia, 123
canned food, 70–2
canonical hours, 15–16
can-opener, invention
of, 72
Capone, Al, 268
Caracalla's Baths, 96–7
Carolus, Johann, 147
Carter, Howard, 179
Çatalhöyük, 30–1
Cathars, 123
cats, 122–4, 126
Censorinus, 2
chamber pots, 36, 38, 40,
230
champagne, 206–10
Champnes, Rev. E.T., 154
champu head massage, 109
Chanel, Coco, 192
Chappe, Claude, 153
Charlemagne, 327–8
Charles I, King, 148
Charles II, King, 48, 129,
149–50, 185, 208, 335
Charles VI, King of France,
128
Charles II ('the Bad'), King
of Navarre, 315–16
chasqui relays, 161–2
Château Gaillard, toilet
chutes at, 44
Chaucer, Geoffrey, 123, 311
Chesterfield, Lord, 51, 58,
237, 288, 297
Chetham's Library, 123
chiens-goûteurs, 129, 227
chimpanzees, 86–7, 114
chintz, 176
chiton, 194–5
Chivalric Code, 103
cholera, 54, 56, 317
chopsticks, 232–3, 238–9
chugi sticks, 42, 58
Churchill, Winston, 22
Cilgerran Castle, 44

Claudius, Emperor, 239,
279
Clement of Alexandria, 98
Clement, William, 335, 337
Cleopatra's Needles, 12
Cloaca Maxima, 40
clocks, 16–17, 322–38;
water, 325–30; candle,
328–9; medieval, 330–2;
pendulum, 333–5; electric
and electromagnetic,
335–7
close-stools, 47–8, 51, 57
clothing, 87, 171–205; Neolithic, 172–4; Egyptian,
174–5, 179, 193; Chinese,
178, 181; Roman, 180, 196;
medieval, 182–3; Indian,
193, 196; Minoan, 193–4;
Greek, 194–5; Islamic,
195; Japanese, 197–9
cocktails, 258
codpieces, 184
coffee houses, 149–50, 218
Coleridge, Samuel Taylor,
292
collops, 69
Columbus, Christopher,
73–5, 101
Columella, Junius
Moderatus, 119
common cold, 67
communications, 131–70;
Greek, 158–9; Persian,
159; Roman, 159–61;
Incan, 161
Cooke, William Fothergill,
155–6
cooking, beginnings of, 66,
211–12
Coors Brewing Company,
267
corsetry, 185–7
Coryat, Thomas, 230
cotton, 175–6
courier networks, 159–60
Crapper, Thomas, 55

INDEX

Crimean War, 155
crinolines, 201–2
Cromwell, Oliver, 148
crucifixion, 40
Crusades, 102–3, 162
Cumming, Alexander, 52
cuneiform, 139–41
Cursus Publicus, 160–1, 164
cutlery, 228–32

Damascus, Umayyad
   Mosque, 16
David, King of Israel, 315
Davis, Jacob, 190
Davy, Humphrey, 292
daylight saving, 20–6
De Vries, David, 101
Dean, Dr H. Trendley, 296
Delaware River, 102
Demosthenes, 253–4
denim, 189–90
dental floss, 294–5
dentistry and dental
   hygiene, 271–97; Neo-
   lithic, 273–6; Egyptian,
   275–7; Chinese, 281–2;
   Islamic, 283; medieval,
   283–6; and anaesthetics,
   291–3;and fluoridation,
   296
deodorants, 113–14
Descartes, René, 126, 333
dhoti (loincloth), 193
Diagonal Star Table, 10
Dickens, Charles, 109–11,
   230
dining chairs, 223
Diodorus Siculus, 123
dishdasha (tunic-dress), 195
Djoser, Pharaoh, 275–6
Dockwra, William, 167–8
dogs, 118–21; weddings
   of, 126–7; as royal pets,
   128–30
Dolní Věstonice, burnt
   hearths at, 211
Domesday Book, 144

Donkin, Bryan, 72
Donne, John, 230
Duc de Sully, 107
Duc de Vendôme, 47
Duc d'Orleans, 208–9
Duchamp, Marcel, 55
Duchesse de Bourgogne, 47
Duke of York, *see* James
   II, King
Durand, Peter, 72
duvets, introduction of, 321

earth closets, 57
Edgar the Peaceful, King,
   262–3
Edison, Thomas, 134–7
Edward, Duke of York, 121
Edward III, King, 177,
   197, 311
eggs, 78–80
Elagabalus, Emperor, 308
Elizabeth I, Queen, 45, 105,
   166, 183–4, 199, 204, 287,
   293, 332
Elizabeth of Bohemia, 128
Ely Cathedral, cat roasted
   at, 124
Encyclopaedia Talmudica,
   35
Epicrates of Ambracia, 38
Erasmus, Desiderius,
   234–5, 239–40
etiquette, telephone, 136–7;
   traditional Chinese, 219;
   handbooks, 237
Etruscans, 142, 196, 278–9
Eubulus, 253, 259
Eupolis, 38
Evans, Sir Arthur, 90
Exeter Cathedral, cat-flap
   at, 123

famine, 60–1, 77–8
farthingales, 199–201
Fauchard, Pierre, 289
Faust, Bernhard Christoph,
   317, 321

Fawkes, Guy, 105
feather beds, suspicion
   of, 321
Feetham, William, 110
flapper girls, 202
Fleming, Stanford, 23
Florentine Reckoning, 4
Floyer, Sir John, 108
fluoridation, 296
Fontainebleau Palace, 48
food and eating habits,
   59–84; Roman, 59, 68,
   73–4, 78–80, 214–16,
   221–2, 226, 228, 234–6,
   239–40; Egyptian, 68,
   78–9, 221, 226; Jewish
   and Islamic, 69–70, 226;
   communal eating and
   feasting, 211–41; medieval, 216–17, 223, 234;
   conversation at table,
   235–7; table manners,
   238–41
food-tasters, 227
Ford Mandible, 278
forica (public latrines),
   38–9
forks, 229–31
Fowler, Captain William,
   220
foxes, taming of, 117–18
Franklin, Benjamin, 17–18,
   77, 150
French Revolution, 6–8,
   200
futons, 304–5

Galen, 54
Galileo Galilei, 333–4
Gayetty, Joseph, 58
Genghis Khan, 178, 262
George IV, King, 109, 185–6
George V, King, 22
Gerald of Wales, 44
Germ Theory, 54–5, 71
Germany, adopts daylight
   saving, 22

INDEX

geysers, 111
Gilgamesh, 81
gin, 256, 260–2; bathtub, 267–8
Girard, Philippe de, 71–2
Gladstone, William, 316
Godin Tepe, 245, 252
gongfermers, 44
gorillas, 87
Gospel of St John, 222
Goyet Cave, 117
grace, before meals, 226
Gray, Elisha, 132–4
Great Exhibition (1851), 53, 112–13
Great Plague, 48
Great Stink (1858), 56–7
Greenwich Mean Time, 21, 23
grog, 258
Groom of the Stool, 44
grooming, 86–7
Guiche, Comte de, 48
Gully, Dr James, 110
Gutenberg, Johannes, 145–6, 157

Hadrian's Wall, 144, 160, 180
Hajji Firuz Tepe, 252
halitosis, 295
Hall, Joseph, 177
Halley, Edmund, 150
Hambledon Hill, hill-fort at, 212
hammams (Turkish baths), 100–1, 103, 109
Hammurabi, King of Babylon, 152
Hampton Court Palace, 83
Harappan civilisation, 33–4, 73, 88–9, 175, 193
Harington, Sir John, 45, 50, 52
Hart, Sarah, 155
Hartington, Lord, 240–1

Harun al-Rashid, Sultan, 327–8
Helicon of Salamis, 307
Heliopolis, 4, 12
hemerodrome, 159
Henry VIII, King, 44–5, 83, 166, 185
Henry III, King of France, 129
Henry IV, King of France, 47, 107
Herculaneum, 119, 143
Herodotus, 12, 34, 159, 175, 302
Hesiod, 37, 239
Hesi-Re (dentist), 276
hieroglyphs, 139
Hildegard of Bingen, 123
Hill, Rowland, 168–9
Hippocrates, 54, 277
Hitler, Adolf, 120
Hogarth, William, 261–2
Holyrood Palace, bath-house at, 105
Homer, doubtful existence of, 92
Homo heidelbergensis, 231
Hooke, Robert, 334
Horace, 51
Horemheb, Pharaoh, 276
horses, 161–2
hot air balloons, 163
hot springs, 87, 102
hour glasses, 326
hours, of 60 minutes' duration, 16, 326
House of Lords, 177
House of Wisdom, 328
Houses of Parliament, 56
Huang Ti, Emperor, 282
Hubbard, Gardiner Greene, 133
Hudson, George Vernon, 19
Huguenots, 178
Hunter, John, 290
huodi (under-floor heating), 303

Huygens, Christiaan, 334
hygiene, personal, 85–114; Harappan, 88–9; Egyptian, 89–90; Minoan, 90–1; Greek, 91–4; Roman, 95–7; ritual washing, 97–100; Christianity and, 98–9; Islam and, 99–100; medieval, 102–4
'Hymn to Ninkasi', 247
hypocaust (under-floor heating), 95

Ibn al-Shāṭir, 16
Ibn Fadlan, 101
Ibn Sina, 283
Ichcahuipilli (cotton armour), 176
Iliad, 92, 213–14
Incas, 76, 140, 161, 176
incense, 103, 329, 333
incest, 317
India, spice trade, 73–4; caste system, 97; cotton trade, 175–6; dental hygiene, 279–80
Indian Mutiny, 156
influenza, 67
Instruction of Ankh-sheshonq, 277
Intercolonial Railway of Canada, 23
Inuit, 172
Irezumi (tattoos), 198
Irish Potato Famine, 61, 78
Isabeau of Bavaria, 128

Jackson, Andrew, 240, 263–4
Jackson, Dr James Caleb, 63
James I, King, 105, 128–9
James II, King (Duke of York), 150, 167–8, 185
James, William, 157
jeans, 189–91

INDEX

INDEX

Reuters News Agency, 156
Revere, Paul, 290–1
rhymma (soap), 93
Richard the Raker, 44
Richelieu, Cardinal, 231
Richmond Palace, flushing toilet at, 45
river swimming, 108
River Wild-Quince, 300
rock 'n' roll, 190
Rodrigues, Father João, 235
Roederer, Louis, 209
Rohwedder, Otto Frederick, 84
Roosevelt, Franklin D., 269
Rousseau, Jean Jacques, 108
Royal Mail, 166–8
Royal Muslin, 176
Royal Society, 72, 334
Royal Tunbridge Wells, 109
ruffs, 203–4, 235
Ruinart, Nicolas, 209
Ruins of Yin, 232
rum, 256–8, 264
Rupert of the Rhine, Prince, 129
Rus, 101
Russell, W.H., 155

Sabinian, Pope, 15
St Apollonia, 283
St Augustine of Hippo, 125
St Benedict, 99, 231, 249
St Brigit of Kildare, 248
St Cyril, 142
St Francis of Assissi, 125
St Jerome, 98–100, 103
St Luke's Day, 124
St Methodius, 142
St Paul, 143, 160
St Paula of Bethlehem, 99
St Simeon Stylites the Elder, 99
St Thomas Aquinas, 103, 126, 333

St Veronica Giuliana, 116
sake, 244
Salah (periods of prayer), 16
sanitation, 28–58; Egyptian, 34–5; Greek, 36–8; Roman, 38–41; Islamic, 41–2; medieval, 41, 43–4; Japanese, 42–3, 58; Chinese, 42, 58; French, 46–8, 50–1
Saqqara funerary complex, 275
saris, 196–7
saunas, 101–2
sausages, 68–9
Saxons, 101, 180, 189, 247–8, 260, 281, 309
scurvy, 258
Selassie, Haile, 130
semaphore, 152–4
Semmelweiss, Ignatz, 54
Seneca, 39, 74
sewers, 32–3, 38–40, 56, 88
sewing needles, 172, 299
Shakespeare, William, 140
Shen-Nung, Emperor, 282
showers, 110–11
Shujing, 262
Sibudu caves, 299
Sicily, Roman invasion of, 13–14, 94–5
silk, 177–9, 183–4
Silk Road, 178
sirwaal (trousers), 189
Skara Brae, 31–2, 300–1
slave trade, 75
smallpox, 67, 75, 108
smock races, 183
Smollett, Tobias, 51
Snow, Dr John, 54, 56
soap, commercialisation of, 112–14
soap operas, 114
Socrates, 69
Southey, Robert, 292

Spanish Armada, 152
Spartans, 94, 158, 307
speech, origin of, 86
spices, 73–5
spitting, 239–40
spoons, 228–9
stockings, 183–4
Strabo, 74
Strasburg, newspaper printed at, 147
Strauss, Levi, 190
strophium (breast-band), 180
Su Song, 329–30
sumptuary laws, 197–8
Sun Tzu, 140
sundials, 9, 12–14, 17
Suśruta, 281
swan feathers, 311, 321
symposia, 254
synthetic fibres, 179
syphilis, 290

tabellarius, 159
tablecloths, 234
Tarquinius Superbus, King, 40
tatami mats, 304
Tawell, John, 155
Teach, Edward 'Blackbeard', 258
telegraphy, 151, 153–7, 162
telephone, invention of, 132–7
temperance movements, 264–5
Thames, River, 43, 56
thawb (tunic-dress), 195–6
Theophano, Princess, 229
Theophrastus, 36
thermae (Roman baths), 95–7, 104
Thirteen Club, 220
Thirty Years War, 147
Timaeus of Tauromenium, 259

INDEX